THE SANTA FE TRAIL

THE
SANTA FE TRAIL

BY
R. L. DUFFUS

UNIVERSITY OF NEW MEXICO PRESS
ALBUQUERQUE

To
Nairne Louise and Marjorie Rose

"Danger, privation, heat and cold are equally ineffectual in checking their career of enterprise and adventure."
— AUGUSTUS STORRS, 1824

AUTHOR'S NOTE

THIS volume does not pretend to exhaust the historical possibilities of the Santa Fe Trail. To do so would require a lifetime and many volumes. The fact that this is a second edition suggests that the original book was at least mildly interesting to a few persons. It indicates to me, too, that the change in our lives since the first edition appeared in 1930 has been almost as great as those between the original Santa Fe Trail and our present bewildering system of transportation. In 1930 the Trail was a story that is told. In 1971 we can almost say the same thing of the railroads that replaced it. The miracle of our national development, especially in the Southwest, has never stood still.

R. L. DUFFUS

July, 1971

CONTENTS

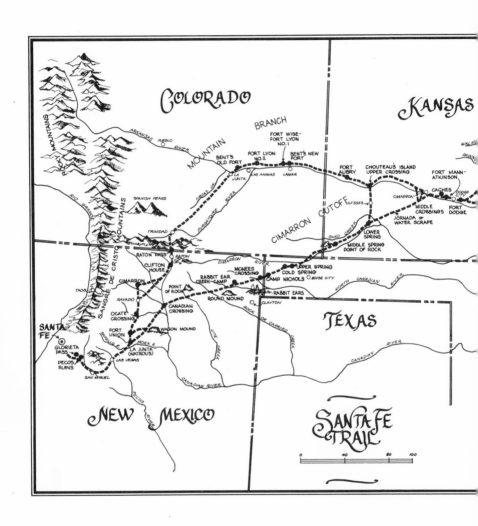

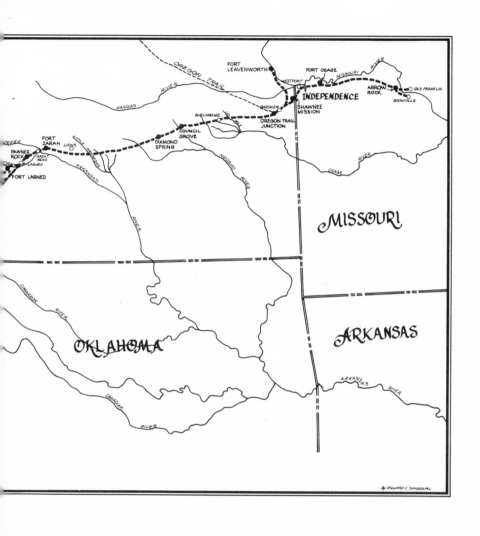

By Richard C. Sandoval

The SANTA FE TRAIL

CHAPTER I

" CATCH UP! CATCH UP! "

IF YOU travelled to the Missouri River in the golden days of the Santa Fe Trail you found yourself at last on the far brink of civilization. Behind you were settlements still raw from the hands of the builders; prairies still steaming from the first spring touch of the plow; then lines of rails, leaping westward, bearing wood-burning locomotives with great smoke-stacks shaped like inverted cones; then villages where bells swung to and fro on quiet Sunday mornings and people plodded to church along streets lined with ancient elms; then factories and mills, rising with the muddy torrents of the industrial era; then cities where traffic jammed in the streets and theatres dazzled the eye at night.

Behind you could be heard the voices of reformers denouncing human bondage, inveighing against property and the use of meat, demanding, of all things, equal suffrage; behind you were communities in which women wore pounds and pounds of wool, exposure of the ankles was considered indecent and exposure to the night air dangerous; behind you were soft living, indigestion, politics, intolerant religions, slums, and a growing national boredom which it took the vast blood-sucking leech of the Civil War to cure.

But in front of you, you knew, were opportunity and romance. When you jumped off from the west bank of the Missouri into the plains country you said good-bye to the best and worst of civilization and entered a region in which the life lived and the people who lived it did not belong at all in the nineteenth century or the Occidental world. You went back through the lost ages — back through the ages of exploration and discovery, back through mediæval times, back into a manner of existence that antedated King Arthur, the Roman Empire, and the great days of Greece. You went forth into a bright fabulous morning, like that which shone upon the human race in the dawn of time, cruel and beautiful, treacherous and alluring. You travelled as men did when Homer sang, into lands as mysterious as any of those into which Odysseus wandered. To the northwest lay Oregon. To the west lay California, not known in the Trail's early days as the land of gold. To the south lay the wild plateaus and steaming jungles of Mexico.

The wilderness was laid out on a scale that dazed and delighted eyes used to the pocket landscapes of New England. You passed from the lush prairies to the short-grass country, from that to burning deserts. You came upon milky rivers half sunken in their shining sands. You saw mountains glistening like polished silver in the remote distances, or hanging like faint clouds above the horizon. Day after day, as you travelled your fifteen or twenty miles between sunrise and sunset, the horizon slowly altered. You slept under the bright stars, or huddled in your tent, or under the shelter of your wagons, while thunder-storms beat down with dreadful violence. You shot elk and deer. The wild fowl rose in clouds from the water courses. The buffalo crossed your path in uncounted hordes, swathed in moving clouds of dust. Indians hovered on all sides, some friendly, some hostile, some only bold enough to steal your horses in the dead of night, some ready to pour your heart's blood out if your vigilance for an instant relaxed. You met Mexicans riding beside the caravans, packers and trappers coming in with furs, French-Canadians, New Englanders, Missourians, some tinctured with Indian blood, all deeply affected by Indian ways of living, often dirty, roistering, and rum-swilling, but going down with laughter, splendid and self-reliant, into the valley of the shadow of death.

You suffered from heat, thirst, mosquitos, gnats; you ate rigorously plain food and slept on the hardest of beds; but if you were young and in health you attained at last to an inexpressible hardihood and buoyancy. You passed, one by one, landmarks that would be graven for ever on your memory — Council Grove and Cottonwood Creek; Pawnee Fork; Sand Creek; the desert between the Arkansas and the Cimarron, where for sixty miles there was no water; Round Point; Point of Rocks; Rio Gallinas and San Miguel. Your stock died, or stampeded, or were run off or shot down with arrows by the Indians. Your wagon wheels broke and you had no wood with which to mend them. Your blackened tongue hung out between your teeth as you neared the Middle Spring and crazy mirages danced all around the sky. Or you took the mountain route and struggled over the Raton, sometimes in snow-storms or hail-storms, at the rate of two miles a day.

But finally you saw the cultivated plains below and the little Spanish towns and the low roofs and cathedral tower of your long-hoped-for goal. Cold-blooded observers compared Santa Fe to a huddle of brick-kilns. But after six weeks in the wilderness you saw in it a city of desire. You gave a wild whoop, waved your hat like a crazy man, and tore down the last slope. The old capital waited, with its buyers for your goods, with its spiced Mexican food, with its liquors from Taos and its wines and brandy from El Paso, with its gambling, with its lounging, brown-skinned men, with its women walking proudly and seeking unabashed the eager eyes of strangers.

That was how you went to Santa Fe when the Trail was in its glory. And because no one will ever go to Santa Fe in that way again, let us go in the fashion that is left us, through the pages of old diaries, forgotten memoirs, and dusty records, across corn-fields, through busy city squares, over deserts where the wagon ruts have for ever disappeared or have deepened into irrigation ditches. Let us sit around the old campfires, before the ashes quite grow cold, and throw on such leaves — no, let us be frank, such buffalo chips, such *bois de vache* — as we still can find. Perhaps, as our eyes strain into the mist and dark, the fierce and glowing memories of the old Trail will again flame into vivid reality. Again we shall sleep under the naked sky and again in the bright morning hear the stamping of many hoofs, the shouting and swearing, the cry that begins the day's march, " Catch up! Catch up! "

CHAPTER II

DAWN ON THE TRAIL

THE TRAIL was rich with human memories before the first white man set foot in North America. Long and long ago the buffalo and those who hunted them followed the course later to be taken by rolling wagons and marching men. At its western terminus, in the valley of the Rio Grande, lived from time beyond history the Cliff Dwellers and their successors, the Pueblo Indians. Over great portions of it there must have swept more than one ancient migration, perhaps descending from the north, perhaps coming up out of the crowded old civilizations of the south. Had red men kept their history, as white men so quaintly do, there would have been little for the white explorers, from Coronado, shining in armor, down to Lieutenant Pike in his ragged regimentals, to discover. When the white man finally came he merely gave new names to landmarks which had guided wayfarers for uncounted generations.

But it is with the white man that we are mostly concerned, for it was his wars, his struggle for trade, his itch for land and gold, his insatiable curiosity to learn what lay behind the beyond, his love of danger and adventure for their own sake, that made the Trail a continuous and living thing. Even so we begin in a kind of golden mist, through which explorers drifted heroically, yet vaguely, looking for a region where nuggets and precious minerals strewed the ground, and where people lived in shining cities and made their commonest utensils out of the metal for which Europeans were ready to shed rivers of blood — their own as well as other people's. It was thus that the Spaniards came, splendid, terrible, and sometimes pathetic. It was they who rang up the curtain on the great epic of the Trail. The golden legend had solidified into fact in Mexico and Peru. Yearly the galleons, rich with loot, went back to Spain. Why not more riches in the no less mysterious countries of the north? And side by side with the soldiers, who peered with burning eyes at every new horizon to catch sight of gilded domes, went the patient, implacable priests, hungering and thirsting after what they thought was righteousness. The clash of swords and lances, the shine of armor. Sweating men in tucked-up cassocks, with dangling crosses. So, in the Trail's dawn, the white race first traversed its prairies, endured its deserts, and penetrated its mountain passes.

The curtain rises upon a prelude far from the main scene of our drama. It is April 1528. Don Panfilo Narváez has landed at Tampa Bay, Florida, in the lordly manner customary at the time, to conquer and hold a new kingdom. The wishes of the existing inhabitants and rulers of the region are not to be considered, since it is assumed that they are infidels and therefore entitled to no mercy in this world or the next. With the adventures of Narváez himself on this edifying quest we are not concerned. He passes out of our story at about the time that the expedition which he has sent inland to explore his new possessions has dwindled down to four men. The most important of these four unfortunates, as they had every right to consider themselves, is Alvar Nuñez Cabeza de Vaca — or, translated literally, Alvar

Nuñez Cow's Head. This name is said to have been handed down to him by an ancestor who had been useful to his monarch by placing such an object for his highness's guidance at a fork in a critical trail. It has thus a symbolism of which something might be made. At any rate De Vaca has a bull-headed obstinacy all his own which is to stand him in good stead. One of his companions is a Moroccan negro named Esteban or Estabanico and possessed of a temperament. The others are Andrés Dorantes and Alonzo del Castillo Maldonado, who would give anything to be back in Spain and out of the fix in which they now find themselves.

It is to be eight years from the time they said good-bye to their commander before De Vaca and his companions will see any white faces other than their own, and these faces will belong to some troopers commanded by Captain Diego de Alcaraz, whom they are to encounter on the frontier of Mexico. Those eight years are to witness the first crossing of the North American continent by white men. The devoted four are to concoct one of the first descriptions of "the humpbacked cow" and they are to be the first Europeans to come in contact with the plains Indians. De Vaca is to set all this down in very readable Spanish and his narrative is to focus the restlessness in many a fierce and ambitious heart.

Our next scene reveals Francisco Vasquez Mendoza, governor of Northern Mexico, a man hot for riches and honors. De Vaca has related his amazing experiences to Don Antonio de Mendoza, viceroy of New Spain, and Mendoza has relayed it, together with the negro Estebanico, to Coronado. Estebanico is unlettered but eloquent. He tells tall stories of golden cities and fabulous kingdoms. Very well, says Coronado, let him go forth again and bring in more detailed information as to where those cities and kingdoms lie and just how golden and fabulous they are. Estebanico can do nothing but obey. He goes, apparently, as far as the Zuñi pueblos of the lower Rio Grande, and thence sends back a messenger to say that he has found " the greatest thing in the world." This, thinks Coronado, can be no other than the seven golden cities of Cibola, of which rumors have been current for some years.

Meanwhile a Franciscan missionary friar, Marcos de Niza — that is to say, Marcos of Nice — has been ordered to continue north in case there are heathen souls to be saved. Eager for converts as other Spaniards are eager for gold he now tucks up his skirts and hurries on toward present Arizona. On the way he meets news that Estebanico's dabbling at a pueblo in the new-found world has cost him his life. He has been butchered by his Indian hosts. Startled but not dismayed the friar continues his journey until he hears tales of a nearby town which he subsequently describes as larger than the City of Mexico. Doubtless this is the ancient pueblo of Hawikúh, which the Zuñi occupied until 1670. It was, as Friar Marcos says, " made of stone, with divers stories and flat roofs." Marcos does not court martyrdom at the moment, perhaps because if he perished no one could carry back to Mexico news of what he has seen. He pauses only long enough to take possession of the country and its unsuspecting inhabitants in the name of the Spanish Crown. Then he hustles south, arouses the credulous Coronado, and in company with the now-excited governor goes to Mexico City to report to the Viceroy.

Coronado's imagination is aflame. There is no doubt in his mind that the fabled Cibola has been at last discovered, nor much doubt that its riches will exceed those which Cortez found in Mexico itself. His enthusiasm stirs Mendoza to action. Coronado is ordered to proceed overland to Cibola. Hernando de Alarcón is dispatched by sea to the Gulf of Lower California, from which he is to effect a junction with Coronado — an objective never realized, though Alarcón does indeed go far up the Colorado, perhaps as far as Yuma. Coronado is getting together what the veracious Pedro de Castañeda de Naçera describes as "the most brilliant company ever collected in the Indies to go in search of new lands." There are three hundred Spaniards, the pick of the adventurous youth of the capital. There are eight hundred Indians. The tailors, armorers, and bannermakers do their best. There is a great flutter of silks and velvets, a dazzling glitter of polished metal as the expedition sets forth. Never will Coronado know a greater day than this.

Disillusionment begins all too soon. The march to "Cibola," or Hawikúh, is difficult. Their fancy clothes are ragged and dusty, the banners droop in the broiling sun, and the pueblo turns out to be a mean village instead of a great and wealthy city. Coronado thinks bitter thoughts of the departed Estebanico, perhaps hardly less bitter ones of the holy Friar Marcos. However, there may be gold farther on. He pushes forward into the Indian country and winters at a place which he calls Cicuyé, which is probably the modern Pecos, southeast of Santa Fe. Here he has the misfortune to encounter another gifted liar, an Indian from an eastern tribe whom the Spaniards call El Turco. El Turco declares that the golden lands of the old legend do indeed exist but that they are farther on. He says, according to Castañeda, "that the lord of that country took his afternoon nap under a great tree on which were hung a great number of little golden bells which put him to sleep as they swung in the air. He said also that everyone had their ordinary dishes made of wrought plate, and the jugs, plates, and bowls were of gold." This land, says El Turco, is called Quivira.

Coronado, still preserving his touching faith in humanity, believes this story, and in the spring sets forth for Quivira. We might view him and his followers with more whole-hearted admiration if it were not for the treachery and cruelty with which they have already treated the Indians. El Turco witnesses this misconduct but keeps his opinion of it to himself. He rides beside Coronado, and the Spaniards go jingling cheerfully across country, into a land as strange to them as the mountains of the moon. They burn with thirst, tighten their belts to quiet the gnawing pains of hunger, are wet with torrential rains, lie awake marvelling at the splendor of the stars at night. Thus they march in a generally eastern direction across the Pecos and the Rio Colorado, as far as the 100th meridian. They encounter vast herds of bison, which the Spaniards were later to call *cibolos*, probably after the name first given to the not-so-golden cities of the Rio Grande. Coronado keeps a diary, but not in such terms as to make his exact route certain. It is possible that he may not even have crossed the present northern boundary of Texas. But his journal says that, after reaching a point some two hundred and fifty leagues from the Rio Grande, he left all but thirty horsemen and with this handful turned directly north.

" I travelled," he reports to his king, " forty-two days after I left the force, living all this while solely on the flesh of the bulls and cows which we killed, at the cost of several of our horses which they killed, because, as I wrote your Majesty, they are very brave and fierce animals; and going many days without water, and cooking the food with cow-dung, because there is not any kind of wood in all these plains, away from the gullies and rivers, which are very few. It was the Lord's pleasure that, after having journeyed across these deserts seventy-seven days, I arrived at the province they call Quivira." It is reasonable to believe that the expedition crossed the Arkansas River somewhere around Dodge City, unless one clings to the theory that the horses and men of 1541 were feebler creatures than those of 1821. If Coronado did cross the Arkansas he then and there intersected the future line of the Santa Fe Trail, and the thin smoke of his burning buffalo chips rose in air which was to be perfumed with many fires of that sort in years still in the womb of time. But he saw no wraiths of strange, long-haired men on horseback, coming from the East, no shadows of white-topped wagons rolling sunward in the late afternoon. He felt no premonition of the doom that was to overtake this splendid new empire, fresh from the hands of the gods, that he was finding for his king.

At the crossing of the river he turned downstream, that is to say in a northeasterly direction. For twenty days he plowed along the sand-hills, almost certainly along that great road which three centuries later was to be churned to mud and ground to dust by the wagon wheels of the caravans going up from the Missouri to Santa Fe. He may have gone as far as Wichita, where less than four centuries later were to be heard the banging and clanging of factories making airplanes. Surely the devout Spaniard would have crossed himself and murmured prayers if that vision had risen like a mirage above the prairie. But there were no visions, no glorious realities. The golden cities of Quivira turned out to be no more than the miserable and temporary shelters of Indians far lower in the human scale than those in the Rio Grande valley. Their chiefs were lulled to sleep, not by golden bells, but by the buzzing of flies, and they drank their broth from bowls of bark or earthenware.

And now the perfidy of El Turco dawned upon the explorers in all its completeness. We shall never know what passionate and long-cherished yearning for revenge had led the Indian on. Perhaps a Spanish knife had found the heart of someone he loved. For days he had ridden, silent, sombre, with this cavalcade of armored men, always luring them on, always promising riches beyond the next horizon. Coronado put him to the question in the worse than savage Spanish manner, and racked a confession out of him. He had planned to lose the Spaniards in the desert and leave them to die of hunger and thirst. Coronado ordered him strangled and set out again for the south, a disgruntled and disappointed man. But instead of retracing his steps he seems to have cut straight across from the bend of the Arkansas to the settlement which he called Tiguex and which was probably near the present site of Bernalillo, New Mexico. It took him forty days to come back, and for a great part of the way, even after leaving the Arkansas, he was probably not far away from the main line of the future Trail. So we may, without stretching the possibilities too far, put Coronado down as the first man to make a round trip between the vicinity of Santa Fe and central Kansas.

We see him coming back empty-handed, ragged, battered, without having found any riches or " any settled country out of which estates could be formed for all the army." He does not know that any significance attaches to this journey of his — the first to be made by white men between the Missouri valley and the Rio Grande. He will die more ignorant of the portent of his great adventure than Columbus was of the real meaning of the New World. He dallies with the idea of going back to Quivira. But his horse falls with him and he is injured. His men lose faith in him and begin to murmur. In the end he gives it up and goes back to Mexico, and so bows himself in melancholy fashion off our stage.

Two devoted missionaries are left behind. One of them, Fray Luis de Padilla, a former soldier, described as an "*hombre belicoso*," goes back across the plains to Quivira. We may let our imaginations play upon that lonesome journey if we like. He reaches Quivira alive, still bellicose, still resolute to save these hordes of pagan souls. At first he is successful. He pushes farther toward the north and east. Andrés del Campo, a soldier of Portuguese birth who had been his sole white companion, appears in Mexico many months later with the tragic news that the friar has found martyrdom at the hands of a war party of northern Indians. We do not know exactly how Del Campo got back from Quivira, but he would naturally have followed Coronado's route over the Santa Fe Trail. If he did, he was the first white man to travel it alone. The other missionary, Fray Luis de Escalona, remained, apparently in safety, at Pecos. Three others of Coronado's veterans are said to have been found, forty years later, when Fray Agustín Rodriguez went to New Mexico. But they were Mexican Indians, not Spaniards.

For more than a generation there were no further explorations of Quivira, nor any attempts at settlement in the region later to be known as New Mexico. One reason was that the tribes in New Mexico and in the northern part of Old Mexico had been rendered bitterly hostile by Coronado's avarice and cruelty. For another reason, no amount of avarice and cruelty seemed likely to squeeze much gold out of the Indians of either Cibola or Quivira. A few Franciscans, it is true, did go into the Pueblo country, and others are said to have ventured as far as Quivira. But none came back from that far region to tell the tale. Several, including Fray Agustín Rodriguez, were killed by the unregenerate Pueblo Indians.

But the line of Spanish settlement could no more be held back than could the line of English settlement along the Atlantic a few generations later. It advanced slowly, but it advanced. In 1582 Don Antonio de Espejo and Fray Bernadino Beltrán made a trip up the Rio Grande to rescue some imperiled friars. Nine years later Gaspar Castaño de Sosa went as far north as the pueblo of Picurís. He intended settlement, for he brought wagons and a small company of settlers. This was certainly the first time that anything on wheels had rolled past the site of Santa Fe. But de Sosa had neglected to take out a license, and he was overtaken by a force sent out from Mexico and dragged ignominiously home. Spanish policy never sanctioned the highly individualistic Yankee way of settling new territory. A few years later, indeed, we hear of Captain Leyva de Bonilla and Antonio Gutiérrez de Humaña on an unauthorized trip to New Mexico and from there to Quivira. They, too, may have added footsteps to the Trail. Leyva de Bonilla was killed by Gutiérrez de Humaña, who then had an unknown end, and only an Indian from Mexico returned to tell the story.

A Trail, to be important, must lead between two markets. If these markets are also two opposing civilizations the Trail becomes significant and glamorous, like Marco Polo's trail to China. The time was coming when a civilization was to be planted in New Mexico — and planted several years earlier than the seeds of that great Anglo-Saxon civilization which was finally to come streaming across the Missouri River, down over the mountains, through the passes into Santa Fe, and over the dust and sand of the still more westerly plains and mountains to the Pacific Coast.

THE conquest of New Mexico was the work of Don Juan de Oñate, an ambitious citizen of Zacatécas. It was nominally a private enterprise, but it was carried out under contract between Oñate and the Viceroy of Mexico, Don Luis de Valesco, and was later sanctioned by a decree of King Philip. After some years of preparation the expedition set out early in 1598 — four hundred men, eighty-three wagons, and seven thousand head of cattle. It is interesting to observe that wagons were used in these early expeditions, whereas for the next two centuries much trade between New and Old Mexico was being carried on by means of pack mules. Oñate moved, in a caravan which rivalled those which were to travel the Santa Fe Trail in its palmiest days, down the Conchos and up the Rio Grande. It was obviously necessary that, with so much stock, he should always keep within reach of a plentiful supply of water. He passed near the present site of El Paso, reached the Pueblo country, and was remarkably successful in inducing the Indians to submit to the Spanish Crown. Later he sent soldiers to subdue the people of Ácoma. The lesson he taught them was taken to heart

by the other Indians, who saw that they must choose
between being Spanish and being dead. Nevertheless,
the heathen rituals lingered. They linger to this day,
though the Indians have been Christians for eight or
nine generations.

But Oñate longed for more worlds to conquer. From
the Indian, known only as José, who had survived the
ill-fated expedition of Bonilla and Humaña, he learned
of the great buffalo plains to the east and north — that
is, of Coronado's lost and almost forgotten country of
Quivira — and set out thither with a force of eighty
men. As to his route, like most of the routes followed
in those dim and inaccurate years, we must guess a
little. He may, as some suppose, have gone down the
Canadian River, crossed the present state of Oklahoma,
and followed Coronado's footsteps to Wichita. The
enterprise was not fruitful, unless the reported killing
of a thousand unfriendly Indians can be regarded in
that light. Having marched out, Oñate and his little
army marched back again. They had dissipated some
of the mystery of the great plains. If the Spaniards in
the immediate future did not travel them very often it
was only because they did not expect to find there the
silver and gold and precious stones of which they had
once dreamed. The old fables were losing their power
to lure men on.

Oñate did not, as was once supposed, found the city
of Santa Fe. He had his capital on the Rio Grande,
probably on the west bank opposite the pueblo called
since his time San Juan de los Caballeros — that is to
say, as some translate it, St. John of the Gentlemen.
This quaint title was bestowed because the Indians vol-
untarily moved out of their houses in order to afford
shelter for their Spanish guests. The city was ordered

established at Santa Fe in 1609, two years after the settlement of Jamestown, under the governorship of Pedro de Peralta. But for a long time afterwards, so far as any records tell, the future Trail to the Missouri remained untroubled by the feet of white men. Friar Benavides, writing about 1630, mentioned Quivira as though he were familiar with it, but omitted to explain how and why. Captain Alonso Baca is said to have gone as far as a great river which was probably the Arkansas, about 1634. Governor Peñalosa, who ruled the little colony at Santa Fe from 1661 to about 1665, asserted that he had visited Quivira. This statement is doubted; nevertheless, it shows that the region had not been entirely forgotten. As a matter of fact it was as easy for the New Mexicans to cross the plains of Kansas as it was for them to go to Old Mexico — it was even easier, for the deserts were less forbidding. All they needed was an errand.

If we had the documents which were destroyed during the great Pueblo revolt of 1680 we might learn a few additional facts about the early days of the Trail. We must, however, rest content with the belief that even in the seventeenth century it was travelled by occasional missionaries, prospectors, and Indian traders. After the beginning of the eighteenth century it was certainly never a mystery to the Spaniards. When they wished to travel it they did. Or if they refrained it was because they valued their scalps more than anything the valley of the Arkansas could be expected to yield. In due season they came to look on the plains and deserts to the eastward as a buffer placed there by the Almighty to protect them from their enemies, the French. But they knew well enough how easily those plains and deserts could be crossed by eager and resolute men.

Long before the Santa Fe Trail came into active being as a factor in the destinies of nations they foresaw its possibilities.

So did the French. There was something in the very whirling of the earth, in the glow of setting suns, that drew men westward. The eastern peoples came like moths to the flame, first a few, then many. The Trail had to be, and was, rediscovered from the east.

CHAPTER III

FRANCE FINDS THE WAY

THREE NATIONS — Spain, England, and France — were now trying seriously to introduce into North America the blessings of European civilization. The English held the Atlantic seaboard from Massachusetts to the borders of the Spanish province of Florida. The French held the mouth of the St. Lawrence, and by 1718, the year of the founding of New Orleans, the mouth of the Mississippi also. How far west their holdings extended was a matter which at the end of the seventeenth century remained uncertain. Their search for furs, at least, ended at no theoretical boundaries. They went as far as they could and took all the profit they could, a method of proceeding which was not so much French as human.

Behold them, then, in the late 1690's, beginning to trouble the calm of New Mexico. The tendency toward trade between the Spanish settlements on the Rio Grande and the French settlements in the Illinois country was a natural one. Only the insistence of the Spanish on keeping to themselves prevented the future Santa Fe Trail from buzzing with activity. Even so it must have seen many little caravans going forth with beads, iron pots, guns, powder, lead, fire-water, and other articles craved by the Indians, and returning laden with furs. It is tantalizing not to be able to visualize these caravans more clearly. But the evidence is fragmentary. Only occasionally do we catch the silhouettes of these marching men against the sky. In 1693 three deserters from La Salle's expedition are marched with De Vargas to New Mexico and settled. Then and later any not too obnoxious outlander with a trade at his finger's ends was likely to be welcomed. In 1698 one of the padres ransomed two little French girls from the Navajos. Where did they come from? From somewhere in the Illinois country, no doubt. Perhaps their blood still runs in the other stream of Latin blood which still makes up a good fraction of Santa Fe's racial inheritance. About 1700 a French force wiped out a town of the Jumano Indians, somewhere in western Texas, or perhaps Kansas. The headwaters of the Rio Grande were rich in beaver. The Red, the Missouri and the Arkansas were the predestined approaches to the wild, wild West of that robust day. The French inevitably used them whenever they could evade or placate the Apaches and Comanches, who straddled militantly across their upper reaches.

The songs of the voyageurs were heard in 1717 at San Juan Bautista, on the Rio Grande, where a French trading expedition did a brisk business with the Indians. In 1719 Frenchmen were on the Arkansas, making a treaty with the evasive and light-fingered Pawnees. That same year Governor Valverde of New Mexico, setting forth to chastise all and sundry hostile Indians upon whom he might come, crossed a high corner of Colorado, just as the transcontinental freighters were to do later on, and ventured into Kansas. According to his own story he went farther than Coronado, though how he knew this is a mystery. He could not have gone much farther or he would have run into the oncoming French. The next year Pedro de Villasur Valverde's second in command, was dispatched to the eastern plains to stir up such trouble as he could. With him rode fifty or sixty Spanish troopers and about one hundred and forty Indians. He found even more trouble than he had contracted for. Somewhere in western Nebraska his men were attacked by the Pawnee, whom the French, following their treaty of two years before had thoughtfully equipped with the latest styles of firelocks and ammunition, and massacred almost to the last man. Not more than six, perhaps not so many, ever got back to Santa Fe. This was one of those grim defeats, comparable with those suffered by Braddock, St. Clair, and Custer, by which the Indian has occasionally revenged himself for the white man's arrogance.

The share the French had in the disaster did not endear them to the Spaniards. Yet the volatile Gauls were not to be rebuffed. When actual hostilities were not in progress they continued to drift across the plains and knock at the very doors of the Spanish capital. In 1727 they were around El Cuartelejo, out on the plains of southwestern Kansas. In 1739 the two Mallet brothers led a party of nine from the Illinois country to Santa Fe. Precisely who the Mallet brothers were we do not know. They seem to have come down from the Sioux country, starting, perhaps, near the present Sioux City, and crossing portions of Nebraska, Kansas, and Colorado. Arrived in Santa Fe they settled down quite amicably and stayed nine months. Whether they were detained by the Spaniards or really liked Santa Fe is not remembered. They may have remained from preference. The little, isolated city, dreaming in the sunlight, sitting around its piñon fires when there was

rain or snow, had, as we shall see, its charms; it could
enchant men's souls like the island of Circe. But the
Mallets, like most frontiersmen, had itching heels. They
returned, dividing forces. Four men of the party went
down the Canadian and Arkansas Rivers to the Mississippi, and then down the Mississippi to New Orleans.
Two stayed in Santa Fe; the others went overland
along the Santa Fe Trail to the Illinois. But, unhappily,
they did not write down their adventures; it was enough
to have lived through them.

The very next year, that is to say in 1740, another
party of Frenchmen came to Santa Fe by way of Taos,
unless, which is barely possible, the reference here is
to the Mallet party. At any rate two of this batch of
visitors ate the lotus leaf and stayed, and we find their
names in the New Mexican annals. One of them, Jean
de Alarí (later Alarid), married and settled down as
a respected barber. The other man, Louis Moreau
(Morín, Moran, Mora?), turned out badly—so badly
that in the end the authorities could think of nothing
better to do with him than to end his thieving and un-
moral career by taking him out into the middle of the
plaza on a fine morning and shooting him.

But the Frenchmen were not downhearted as a result
of occasional casualties. On the great western trails
death was never far away; one faced it as gaily as possible; if one of these happy-go-lucky voyageurs escaped
it once he came back singing to try his luck again. The
four members of the Mallet party who reached New
Orleans told their story to Governor Bienville, just as
De Vaca long before had told his to Mendoza. They
had no golden cities to describe; still, they convinced
Bienville that there was a profitable trade to be done
in New Mexico. Bienville therefore delegated Fabry

de la Bruyere, with several of the Mallet veterans as guides, to go and investigate. Bruyère accordingly went up the Canadian River, failed to reach Santa Fe, but succeeded in making a peace with the Comanches and in settling disputes between the Comanches and other Indians along the route. If these treaties had been kept the road to Santa Fe would have been open so far as the Indians were concerned. As long as the Indians were at war among themselves any party which got through one tribe was sure to be stopped by the next, and perhaps murdered as punishment for getting into bad company. But the Comanches, in their simple, childish way, believed that the Great Spirit had sent them peace in the East in order that they might make war upon the Spaniards in the West. They descended upon the pueblos in the valley of the Rio Grande, plundering, burning, and killing.

Not being able to trade with Santa Fe the Frenchmen traded with the Indians. In 1748 a party of thirty-three visited the Jicarilla Apaches, northwest of the little Spanish capital, and sold them muskets, which were more than likely to be used against the Spaniards or the Pueblo Indians. The Spaniards were by this time seriously worried over the possibility of an attack by the combined forces of the French and their Indian allies. Such an attack might easily have succeeded, for the garrison at Santa Fe was weak and the line of communication with Old Mexico was long and tenuous. But peaceful French traders kept drifting in as though nothing were the matter. In 1749 Pierre Satren and two others who had been trading at Taos were picked up and brought down to Santa Fe. They seemed harmless and after being cross-examined before the governor in the old Palace they were allowed to remain and work at their respective occupations. A year later seven more were brought in. This time the governor, fearing that if they were allowed to return to French territory they would sooner or later serve as guides for a hostile army, sent them down to Sonora. Two years after this four Frenchmen, all from New Orleans, wandered in. The year after that there were two from New Orleans and two more from Illinois. There was more than chance in all this. The Trail was trying hard to be born. The westering sun lured these Frenchmen onward, in constant peril from Indians, wild animals, and inhospitable deserts, just as it was later to lure the Americans.

The two Frenchmen who came from the Illinois country in 1752 were apparently Luis Feuilli and Jean Chapuis, to give the names as the Spaniards spelled them. With them they brought a French license to explore a route to New Mexico and open up a trade. But French licenses were not at the moment in high favor in Santa Fe. The viceroy at Mexico City had already decreed that no more French traders should be allowed to return to their own country, either with goods or without them. Governor Capuchin of New Mexico accordingly ordered the goods carried by Feuilli and Chapuis to be sold and the proceeds used to defray the expense of sending the two unfortunates to Mexico. The purchaser was Tomas Ortiz, who paid the tidy little sum of four hundred and four pesos.

How long it would have taken the French to discover that they were not wanted in New Mexico it is impossible to guess. Certainly they had the enterprise and audacity to cross any plains and any deserts, to climb any mountains, however high, to swim any rivers, however broad and deep, to endure any hardships, to fight

or outwit any tribe of savages, if only something of
value were to be had at the end of the journey. But in
1755 an event took place in Europe which had its shat-
tering echoes in America. Maria Theresa of Austria
declared war on Frederick the Great of Prussia. Rus-
sia, Sweden, and France joined with her in the hope of
wiping the upstart Frederick off the map. In 1757
England, to keep the scales balanced, came to Frederick's aid. In America the French, the English, and
their respective redskin allies and associates fought to
a finish. When the smoke cleared away, in 1763, the
American possessions of France had vanished into history. Canada went to England, together with the eastern portion of the Mississippi valley. The western part
of the valley went to Spain, and with it the key city of
New Orleans.

Thus at a stroke the French menace to New Mexico
was for ever removed. That is, the political menace
vanished. The change of flag did not, of course, turn
the 60,000 French inhabitants of Canada and the
Mississippi valley into Englishmen or Spaniards, nor
did it change their habits over night. The French of
Canada, as everyone knows, speak their ancestral language to this day, and so do those of Louisiana. The
French of St. Louis, Vincennes, and Kaskaskia did the
same thing until they were swallowed up by the rush of
Anglo-Saxon settlement. Under whatever government
they could not resist the pull of the West. Their feet
were restless, they loved the winds which had swept
across a thousand miles of prairie. So, as late as 1795,
we find the governor of New Mexico moved to order
the arrest of all French traders found in his province
and the confiscation of their goods. Sporadic efforts
were indeed made by the Spaniards themselves during

the latter part of the eighteenth century to open up
trading routes, from St. Louis by way of the Arkansas
River, from New Orleans by way of Natchez, the Red
River, and San Antonio. Pedro Vial, a Frenchman in
the employ of Spain, was sent to find a trail from
Santa Fe to St. Louis in 1792-93.

Two obstacles defeated these efforts. One was the
Indians, who never stopped fighting among themselves,
and who held up trade for much the same reasons that
make civilized governments blockade the ports of other
governments with which they are at war. The other
obstacle was the opposition of what we may call the
vested interests who controlled the trade with Old
Mexico. These interests were human enough not to
relish competition. If the trade of New Mexico were
to be expanded they preferred to do it themselves, in
their own way, and to their own profit. They were at
one with the provincial officials in desiring to keep the
mountains and plains on the northeast a barrier, rather
than permit them to be used as a road. There is no
doubt, to be sure, that Spanish trappers and traders
swarmed in the Rocky Mountains north of Santa Fe as
far as the Gunnison River and as far west as the Colorado, long after the treaty of 1763. But their presence
there was illegal, and though they must have come to
know the region like a book they kept no incriminating
records. When they died their heroically acquired
wealth of information died with them, and the explor-
ing had later to be done all over again by the Americans. But it is doubtful that the later explorers found
one single prominent feature of this wilderness landscape that had not already been long familiar to the
Spanish and the French. The Trail was known. It
was venerable. It was sprinkled with blood and sweat

and bones, long before the dawn of the nineteenth century.

So trade across the plains continued. But, despite the continued smuggling by the French, it drained westward instead of eastward. It centred, in the latter half of the eighteenth century, at Taos, with Pecos a secondary point. Taos was the more important because it was readily accessible from the Rocky Mountains and the great plains. The white population of the trading village of San Fernandez de Taos, which is distinct from both the Pueblo de Taos and the later Rancho de Taos, grew from 160 in 1760 to 1351 in 1799. The temporary population, at the time of the great annual fairs in July and August, was much greater. To Taos came the Comanches, Arapahoes, Pawnees, Utes, and other Indians of plain and mountain, making a truce even in the midst of the bitterest wars, and bringing buffalo hides, deer-skins, and sometimes captives to be exchanged or sold for slaves. They bought whatever an Indian needed most — horses, knives, guns, ammunition, blankets, strong drink, and the trinkets which were the staple of the Indian trade everywhere.

To Taos the beautiful, high under the chilly peaks of the Sangre de Cristo, amid its green meadows, watered by icy streams, came also the mountain trappers with their rich stores of beaver. Up from Chihuahua rode the crafty merchants of Mexico with imported goods from Spain and with great silver dollars which were prized as ornaments among the Navajos. They were not legally permitted to sell fire-arms to the Indians, but if they did not human nature in New Mexico was different from what it was at other points along the long Indian frontier. From El Paso came a wine which was described as quite as good as any of the Spanish imported vintages, and there was also the "brandy of the Pass," and little Taos had its own famous brand of "lightning," highly esteemed for potency if not for flavor. We may imagine the glowing spectacle when half a dozen varieties of Indians in multi-colored blankets and head-dresses, a scattering of Frenchmen and later on of Americans, and all the possible gradations of Mexicans and Spanish, assembled in this lovely valley at the foot of the great range. This was the golden age of Taos, when here were concentrated the money and the merriment, the drinking and the singing, the wooing and the fighting, of twelve months of lonely and dangerous life and an empire of wilderness. The crown was soon to pass to Santa Fe. Had it not done so we should now be talking, not of the Santa Fe Trail but of the Taos Trail. And men did cling tenaciously for a long time to the habit of going to Santa Fe by way of Taos.

After the Taos fair was over the merchants took their accumulations of goods and went south in a great caravan, hundreds of burros moving in a cloud of dust, muleteers shouting, bells on the leaders jingling, to attend the annual January fair at Chihuahua. They could ride contentedly, too, to the jingling of money bags, for their profits, owing partly to an ingenious system of accounting, by which a " dollar " might mean eight, six, four or only two reales, were large. They bought with the cheaper variety of dollars and sold for the dearer. By this ingenious method they every year drained New Mexico and its satellite regions of the greater portion of their wealth. Attempts were made to limit their takings by fixing legal equivalents in barter, but these regulations, like similar ones everywhere and always, failed. The valley of the Rio Grande was rich.

It could stand much plundering, even though it was
sometimes hard to tell which were worse, the traders or
the Apaches and Navajo. It produced maize, wheat, a
little cotton, garden truck, cattle, sheep, goats, mules,
burros, and some fruit, in addition to what was had by
dickering with the Indians.

But the traders from Old Mexico were not so wise
but what they fouled their own nest. They made the
mistake of keeping the country poor and in debt. In
1788, a typical year of that period, they carried $30,000
worth of money and goods to Chihuahua — a large sum
as money went in that time, but not impressive from a
population of more than 22,000 souls. The fact was
that life in New Mexico was kept to the bare essentials,
and remained in that condition until the American
traders began pouring goods into the country. We may
readily see why the New Mexican consumer welcomed
the Yankee merchants, when finally they came. We
may also see why the native traders, who had what
amounted to a monopoly, did not care to see the
French, the Spanish of Louisiana, or, least of all, the
energetic and ambitious Americans, coming in to spoil
it. It is also perfectly clear that the Spanish authorities
in New Mexico, who it is to be suspected made the traders pay dearly for every privilege, hoped that things
would continue for ever and ever exactly as they
were.

But it does not seem likely that the population
longed for change. Because it was unrealized the poverty of New Mexico was not a grinding poverty. There
was nothing with which to compare it except the excessively simple life of the red man. The Chihuahua Trail
was almost the only direct means of communication
with the greater outer world, and that was travelled

ordinarily only twice a year, as the caravans came and went. The clangor of the busy human life of other regions, in Mexico, on the Atlantic seaboard, across the water, was heard but faintly. New Mexico was a world of its own, dreaming its own quaint and sometimes charming dreams. Its people spoke a language that to this day has kept some of its seventeenth-century Castillian inflections. They lived, as we see them across the desert of the years, romantically. But beyond the mountains and the plains the lapping of waters which had been barely audible when Santa Fe was settled had risen to a great westward-sweeping tide. Then there had been wilderness clear to Cape Cod and the Virginia Capes. Now a new nation was being created east of the Mississippi, a lusty nation, a nation whose people had an itch for travel and a hunger for land.

Spain ceded Louisiana to France, or rather to the Corsican, Napoleon Bonaparte. Napoleon wasted in San Domingo the armies which were to have occupied the newly regained territory. Three American commissioners appeared opportunely on the scene. They wanted a few square miles. Napoleon sold them an empire. Lewis and Clark went to Oregon. Over the eastern horizon, preceded by two or three other forerunners of the American Idea, looked a young man rejoicing in the name of Zebulon Montgomery Pike — an ambitious army officer embroiled in the imperial conspiracies of Wilkinson and Burr and forecasting the war of conquest which was to come more than a generation after his death. Individuals figured vividly in the rush of events. But there was no holding those events back. They did not depend upon individuals. They were cosmic. The declining colonial civilization of Spain, the rising pioneer civilization of the United

States, strong and valiant and remorseless, stood face to face and measured strength.

The bells of the cathedral at Santa Fe rang out, people crossed themselves at sundown as they rode or walked or worked; Taos swarmed with a dozen babbling races; Spanish governors fat and thin, kindly and brutal, rotten with corruption or comparatively honest, sat in the venerable *Palacio* overlooking the plaza; the handful of troopers drilled, lounged, made love, got drunk, pursued but rarely caught the predatory Navajo and Apache; iron was sold at a dollar a pound, which was more than any but the rich could afford to pay, and imported tobacco was valued at four dollars a pound. Small replicas of this life went on in little mountain villages, dirty, wretched, and idyllic.

But in a world which does not permit permanency in anything, not even in the heart of a desert, all this was doomed to change — not at once, not without condign punishment for many who constituted themselves the instruments of change, but none the less inevitably. If there had been a prophet in Santa Fe at the turn of the eighteenth century he would have heard in his trances the cracking of whips, the creaking of iron-bound wagon wheels, seen clouds of dust on the eastern horizon, heard, too, perhaps, the roar of cannon, and even, provided he had been the seventh son of a seventh son, the snorting of that strange metallic beast which was to imprison the once free Indian and make Santa Fe a neighbor of New York. But there seems not to have been such a prophet. Santa Fe dreamed on, in a remoteness of which we in this day of radios and airplanes cannot even conceive. It dreamed, and some of its dreams were beautiful — so beautiful that they softened the hearts of those who came to shatter them.

CHAPTER IV

" EL VIAGERO PIAKE "

WE CANNOT be sure that we know the name of the first American citizen who visited Santa Fe. Trappers, some of them of Yankee origin, had been wandering over the West for many years before the opening of the nineteenth century. They came and went among the wild tribes, going with sure feet where there were no maps to guide them except those they carried in their own heads. Often they left their bones in the wilderness. Seldom did they leave behind them any written records. Of the heroic achievements of these men we can only speculate, and wonder, for a thousand epics are lost in their forgotten lives. Only one name emerges from the mists of the lost decades — that of John Peyton, bearer of a good old Virginia name, who seems to have been in Santa Fe in 1773 and 1774. Unlike the Frenchmen Peyton did not go to Santa Fe of his own volition. He belonged to a party captured by the Spanish in the Gulf of Mexico. Suspected of being a spy he was sent to New Mexico, imprisoned in the dungeons near the Palace and subjected to cruel mistreatment. In February 1774 he escaped, and with two companions, one of them a girl, managed to reach St. Louis. He must have told his story but it was not of a kind to induce others to follow in his footsteps. Thirty years went by before there was a deliberate attempt by Americans to open up trade with Santa Fe.

In 1804, the year after the Louisiana Purchase, William Morrison, a merchant of Kaskaskia, entrusted a French Creole named Baptiste La Lande with a stock of goods such as might be supposed to be in demand in New Mexico, and sent him forth into the wilderness. This was the last that Morrison ever saw of La Lande, though he certainly received news from some source that the faithless Baptiste had arrived safely in Santa Fe. He had, in fact, done so, though with what adventures on the way we unfortunately do not know. He went through the Pawnee country, sent in word when he reached the Spanish frontier, and rode grandly into the little capital under escort of a troop of horsemen dispatched by the governor.

There is no doubt that La Lande was a lamentable rogue. "Finding," as Pike says, "that he sold the goods high, had land offered him, and that the women were kind, he concluded to expatriate himself and convert the property of Morrison to his own benefit." The temptation was great, for there was no effective American law west of the Missouri River. And, like many other rogues, Baptiste seems to have possessed a charm that won him friends and enabled him to fit comfortably into the easy-going life of his new home. We shall never know whether he had wickedness in his heart when he bade farewell to Morrison or whether he fell from grace after he had tasted the pleasures of Santa Fe. It is pleasantest to think that some dark-eyed Mexican girl, walking proudly, speaking softly, set his pulses to throbbing and made Santa Fe appear to him the central garden of the earth. Certainly he did not set out to be a historic figure. He thought of himself, if

he gave the matter any consideration at all, as merely
one more Frenchman in Santa Fe, and no more and
no less important than the others — except, possibly,
in being rather more of a devil with the women.   But
because the American flag had been fluttering for some
twenty-six years over Kaskaskia, Baptiste, unworthy
though he may have been, became the symbol of a great
nation's destinies.   Retribution, if deserved, never
overtook him.   He flourished like a green bay tree, and
died, as the chronicler Pino says, leaving " *una gran
familia y grandes riquezas.*"

Next, apparently, came James Purcell, or, as his
name was spelled by Pike, Pursley.   We have to put
in the qualifying adverb, for we cannot be quite sure
that other and nameless Yankees did not precede him.
Pike speaks of meeting in Mexico several American deserters and runaways from justice, and some of these
may have visited Santa Fe.   In fact, Pike actually did
meet in Santa Fe a certain Solomon Colly, " formerly a
sergeant in our army and one of the unfortunate company of Nolan."   The reference is to a raiding party
which Philip Nolan led into Mexican territory in 1801.
Nolan may have been hunting wild horses, as his
friends said, or he may have been on a filibustering
expedition.   The Spaniards, to be on the safe side,
treated him as an invader, attacked, and killed him,
hanged one of his men and imprisoned the rest, Colly
among them.   So it may be that Colly preceded both
La Lande and Purcell in Santa Fe.   But this fact would
have no great significance, since he went there against
his will and played no remembered part in the events
that followed.

Purcell was a bird of quite a different feather from
La Lande.   Pike, who gives us most of what we know

about him, admired him as much as he detested La
Lande. He was, in the famous explorer's words, "the
first American who ever penetrated the immense wilds
of Louisiana and showed the Spaniards that neither
the savages who surround the desert which divides
them from the habitable world, nor the jealous tyranny
of their rulers, was sufficient to prevent the enterprising
spirit of the Americans from penetrating the arcanum
of their rich establishment in the New World." The
language was high-flung but Purcell richly deserved it.
He was a native of Bardstown, Kentucky. In 1799,
finding his home town dull, he left it, and four years
later was in St. Louis. From St. Louis he embarked
with two companions on a trading expedition to the
great plains. What followed was a matter of luck, most
of it bad luck. The intrepid trio had planned to strike
the headwaters of the White River, follow it down to its
junction with the Arkansas, go down the Arkansas to
the Mississippi, and descend the Mississippi to New
Orleans — a long and arduous but not impossible
jaunt. Then they changed their minds and were about
to start back for St. Louis overland when the Indians
stole their horses and left them afoot. This was much
like being left in the middle of the Atlantic in a small
boat. They were resourceful and built themselves a
canoe. The canoe spilled in the rapids and they lost
almost their entire equipment. Such were the hazards
of Far Western life in those days.

At this low ebb in their fortunes they were lucky
enough to meet a party going up the Missouri River,
and Purcell, not yet tired of the wilderness, decided
to go with them. We must be patient in following his
wanderings — they reflected the way in which things
happened in those days. A vagrant, dangerous, happy-

go-lucky life went on along the rivers and the trails, and Purcell had fallen into the habit of it. A little later he was trading with the Paducahs (later and more properly called the Comanches) and the Kiowas, who had been driven into the Colorado mountains by the warlike Sioux. The Indians were on Spanish territory and wished to have permission to remain there. So they asked Purcell to go into Santa Fe and present their case to the governor. He went, something about the little city brought peace to his wild heart, and he remained. He arrived, wrote Pike, in June 1805, " and has been following his trade as a carpenter ever since; at this he made a great deal of money, except when working for the officers, who paid him little or nothing." Pike adds, and after learning his story one is not inclined to disagree, that he was " a man of strong natural sense and dauntless intrepidity." According to Pike, Purcell had found gold at " the head of La Platte," had carried it around for months, and then threw it away because it was too much bother. In the wilderness salt, powder, or tobacco was worth a good deal more than gold. But when Purcell related his experience to the Spaniards something of the old lust for yellow metal flared up in them and they demanded that he lead them to the scene of his discovery. He refused because, as he told Pike, he feared that the journey would take them into American territory and give them wealth that properly belonged to his own countrymen.

Whether the women of Santa Fe were as " kind " to Purcell as they were to La Lande is nowhere stated. Probably they were, for except officially and in moments of excitement the little city was a place of kindness. Its hospitality was proverbial. Nor, to tell the truth, were its standards of morality more than human nature could bear.

We come now to the courageous, patriotic, and almost boyishly ingenuous figure of Lieutenant Pike. One cannot think of Pike as very Machiavellian, although he may have been considered a tool by the two arch-conspirators, General James Wilkinson and Aaron Burr. Certainly he did not know the depth of these gentlemen's infamy. He lied, it is true, but not much or very successfully. He was but twenty-seven when he set out for the Southwest — old enough to know his trade of soldier, not old enough to see through the onion-like wrappings of deception with which his wily patron, Wilkinson, had surrounded himself. We are not concerned with either Wilkinson or Burr, beyond making note of the probability that they plotted to set up in the Mississippi valley a government independent of the United States, and perhaps, by way of full measure, to annex some or all of Mexico. But some internal evidence on this latter point does appear in Pike's narrative and consequently has a bearing on our story. The objectives which Burr and Wilkinson sought clumsily and treacherously were to be brought about, in part, by forces which the Pike expedition helped to set in motion. The Trail over which Pike and his ragged and starving handful struggled was later to be traversed by armies carrying his own flag and by endless dusty caravans.

Although the Louisiana Purchase was perhaps the best real estate bargain, for the purchasers, in the history of the world, there was much uncertainty as to precisely what it was that the United States had bought. Particularly was it uncertain just where the boundaries ran between the United States and the Spanish provinces.

Both governments claimed more than they expected to get. Some Americans maintained that Louisiana extended to the Rio Grande and some Spaniards that New Mexico extended to the Missouri — though this may have been merely in a spirit of good, clean fun. The boundary line of the Arkansas was not actually fixed until the treaty of 1819. In 1806, when Pike set out, there was actual danger of war between the two countries. Three expeditions took the field that year. One of them was a force of one hundred cavalry and five hundred New Mexican militia under the command of the genial Don Facundo Melgares. In May Melgares met and turned back Captain Sparks, who had been sent by the Washington government to ascend the Red River and reach the continental divide. Then Melgares made a bold sweep northward, as Coronado had done more than a century and a half earlier, to the " great buffalo plains," crossing the Arkansas River and negotiating with the Pawnee chiefs in the name of Spain in what was certainly American territory. Finally came Pike, whose force was insignificant compared with that of Melgares, but who was destined to march with it to everlasting fame. Besides being brave and hardy he had the logic of history on his side. He represented an advancing civilization, Melgares a declining one.

Pike's orders came, not from Washington but from his friend Wilkinson, then commander-in-chief of the United States army as well as governor of the new territory of Louisiana. His tiny command included two lieutenants, one of whom was Wilkinson's son, a surgeon, a sergeant, and sixteen privates. He also had with him at the start fifty-one Indian chiefs who had been on a visit to the Great White Father in Washington and who were now carrying their impressions of Yankee civilization back to their tribes. His narrative, written first as a soldier's report, ranks next to those of the Lewis and Clark expedition in its description of western travel in the early years of the last century. After more than a hundred years it retains the freshness of those marvellous times.

Pike left Belle Fontaine, outside old St. Louis, at three o'clock in the afternoon of July 15, 1806. He went up the Missouri River to the Osage villages, probably crossed into Kansas near what is now Hoover, Bourbon County, and proceeded to the Pawnee towns. Dr. Elliott Coues locates these towns on the Republican River, near Red Cloud, Webster County, Nebraska. On the way Pike had his first unpleasant surprise. He came upon the traces of Melgares' cavalcade and surmised that his plans had been betrayed — as indeed they had been — and that the Spaniards were looking for him. Had the two unequal forces met upon the prairies Pike would undoubtedly have been turned back, as Sparks had been, or taken prisoner almost at the outset of his journey, and Pike's Peak would now be known by another name. But the meeting of Pike and Melgares, though it did take place, was to be delayed a little.

On September 25th Pike wrote in his journal: " We marched at a good hour and in about eight miles struck a very large road on which the Spanish troops had returned and on which we could yet discover the grass beaten down in the direction which they went." He was still near the eastern end of the Kansas-Nebraska boundary — farther east, probably, than any armed Spanish troop had ventured for many decades. From this point he followed Melgares' hoof-prints almost all the way to the New Mexican boundary. Since Melgares probably travelled a good part of the way over the route long known to the Spaniards, and since this route was over much of its extent the real Santa Fe Trail, he was now on the historic highway. But since both he and Melgares had made a swing northward in order to reach the Pawnees, and since he went far afield in the Colorado mountains, Pike did not follow the entire Trail.

Melgares, with some fantastic idea of extending the Spanish influence into these remote regions, had left Spanish flags with the Indians. Pike, very diplomatically, allowed the red men to keep these flags but presented them with American flags to keep the others company. The idea seems to have been that if the Spaniards came back the Spanish colors would be produced, and if the Americans came the American flag would be flown. Perhaps nothing could be more amazingly indicative of the uncertainty in men's minds at that time than this clash of Spanish and Yankee sovereignty in Webster County, Nebraska.

Parting amicably with the Pawnees, whose sons and grandsons were to be an unholy nuisance on the Santa Fe Trail, Pike continued southward and westward and struck the Arkansas River at Great Bend. Then he went on for a considerable distance along the line of the future Trail, past Pawnee Fork, Pawnee Rock, Ash Creek, and the present towns of Garfield and Kinsley. Now he was in the buffalo country. At one time he estimated that there were three thousand in sight, though that was not a great number as buffalo went. Then he crossed to the south bank of the Arkansas and presently saw, surely not without a quickening of his pulses, " a mountain to our right, which appeared like a small blue cloud." Probably this was the Peak to which his own name was later given.

Before he left the Arkansas Pike sent young Wilkinson and part of his command down the river. They had their troubles, as most wilderness travellers did, but eventually got safely home. The diminished company went resolutely forward, and on November 15th were on the river which the Spanish called Las Animas and the French La Purgatoire, and which the cowboys of later days were to corrupt to Picketwire or Picketiwire. Observe that he had now been almost four months on the road and that winter was coming on — the terrible winter of the high Rockies. He might have been justified in turning back, but the thought seems not to have occurred to him. He had not yet fulfilled his instructions — nor his destiny. He had been in what was later acknowledged as Spanish territory from the moment that he crossed the Arkansas. If he had continued to the southwest he might have made his way over the Raton Pass and reached the Spanish settlements without much difficulty. He must have known their general direction. But instead he turned west and north to explore the mountains. He did not climb the "Grand Peak" which was to be named after him, though he did scramble up a neighboring mountain. On Christmas Eve he was probably near the present site of Salida, Colorado. Then he looped back on his trail and camped near Canyon City.

His situation had gradually grown desperate. The cold was intense, the snow deep, and no game could be found. There was naturally no shelter, except such as could be improvised. When the morning of January 19th dawned several men were crippled by weakness and exposure and all had been without food for four days. Pike made up his mind to make one more forlorn effort to find food, and not to return to camp if he were unsuccessful. But luck was coming his way at last, luck that was both to save his life and to make him famous.

" We were inclining our course to a point of woods," he writes, " determined to remain absent and die by ourselves rather than return to our camp and behold the misery of our lads, when we discovered a gang of buffalo coming along at some distance." They went back to camp with enough meat for several days. On January 23rd this, too, was gone and Pike " strove to dissipate the ideas of hunger and misery by thoughts of distant homes and relatives."

Finally the young commander decided to leave behind those of his men who could not travel and make a last effort to break out of the mountains. His exact route cannot be traced on modern maps, but after terrible hardships he emerged on Sand Creek on January 28th, and two days later was on the Rio Grande near its junction with the Conejos. Here the more tragic phase of his adventures comes to an end, and a serio-comic, at times even idyllic phase begins. Then, and afterwards, he declared that he believed himself to be, not on the Rio Grande but on the Red River, and " of course in territory claimed by the United States." That he should really have thought this seems more than a little improbable, but it was his story and he stuck to it. Reacting with the buoyancy of youth from the hardships he had undergone he again began to think in imperial terms.

His surgeon, Dr. John Robinson, a civilian, had come down with him to the Rio Grande, and now was assigned to play a new rôle. Before leaving Illinois Robinson had received from the outraged William Morrison, who, it will be remembered, had sent Baptiste La Lande to Santa Fe two years earlier, a bill for the misappropriated goods. Pike now sent Dr. Robinson into Santa Fe — a fact which seems to prove that he knew where Santa Fe was, and consequently where he himself was — to confront the embezzling Creole with the evidences of his guilt. The errand was pure subterfuge. Robinson was a spy. As Pike himself phrases it, " Our views were to gain a knowledge of the country, the prospect of trade, force, etc., while at the same time our treaties with Spain guaranteed to him, as a citizen of the United States, the right of seeking the recovery of just debts." Robinson was instructed not to reveal his connection with Pike's expedition. He was to seem a mere bill-collector, who had, as it were, dropped in by chance.

Pike sat in his little fort and waited. On February 16th a Spanish dragoon and a Pueblo Indian drew rein in front of the little fort. Robinson, it appeared, had made his way safely to Santa Fe. To these visitors Pike explained that he was preparing to go down the river to Natchitoches, in the present state of Louisiana — a difficult feat, since Natchitoches is not on the particular Red River of which Pike was speaking, and he himself was not on any Red River but on the Rio Grande.

Ten days after this two French trappers — it seems to have been the most natural thing in the world that the mountains should be full of French trappers — dropped by to report the advance of a Spanish force. On the instant Pike's nine ragged men started putting their weapons in order, being eager, as Pike said, to " have a little dust with the Spaniards." But this was no part of Pike's plan. He left his gate open and stood there as Don Bartolomé Fernandez rode up with a troop of fifty dragoons and fifty mounted militia. Then, and not till then, if we are to believe his story, he learned that the Rio Grande was actually the Rio Grande and not the Red. The meeting was amicable. Pike surrendered to an obviously overwhelming force and allowed himself to be taken exactly where he wanted to go, to Santa Fe. Fifty

Spanish troopers were detailed to guard the fort, repulse any American armies which might be wandering about the neighborhood and rescue the members of Pike's party who had been left in the mountains. All of these men eventually got back to civilization, though two of them, Dougherty and Sparks, froze their feet and were crippled for life.

Pike in his report had to pretend indignation at being taken as a prisoner through the Spanish provinces. Yet his pilgrimage seems to have been one which any young officer, fresh from the wilderness, might have welcomed. There was no lack of that feminine society which soldiers crave, though we are not given to understand that any of the Americans overstepped the bounds of pre-Victorian propriety. At Ojo Caliente the captives first witnessed the " dance which is called the fandango." " We were frequently stopped by the women," says Pike, " who invited us into their houses to eat; and in every place where we halted a moment there was a contest who should be our hosts. My poor fellows who had their feet frozen were conducted home by old men, who would cause their daughters to dress their feet, provide their victuals and drink, and at night give them the best bed in the house. In short, all their conduct brought to my recollection the hospitality of the patriarchs and caused me to sigh with regret at the corruption of that noble principle by the polish of modern ages." This kindness was shown, we should not forget, toward soldiers of a foreign and possibly hostile government who, so far as the New Mexicans knew, were plotting an armed invasion.

And now, at San Juan, Baptiste La Lande re-enters the picture. " My friend," he said to Pike in his ingratiating manner, " I am very sorry to see you here. We are all prisoners in this country and can never return.

I have been a prisoner for nearly three years and cannot get out." But the Creole over-played his part, his questions excited the explorer's suspicion, and finally Pike made him admit that he had been sent by the Spaniards " to draw out who and what I was " and ended by throwing him bodily out of the room. There is some confusion here, for from other sources we learn that the Spanish knew well enough who and what Pike was; indeed, as we have seen, they knew his route and time of starting so well that Melgares came near intercepting him.

Pike could be firm with poor Baptiste, but he knew how to be tactful when necessary. The priest who was his host at San Juan was an amateur botanist — intelligent men needed such diversions in that lonesome country — and talked to the young officer by the hour about his favorite subject. Unhappily he talked in Spanish and Latin, of which Pike knew next to nothing, and had no knowledge of English. But Pike cultivated the good padre's respect and esteem by listening attentively for as much as two hours at a stretch. Some of the clergy had other hobbies. At Santa Cruz Pike observed a young priest " strutting about with a dirk in his boot, a cane in his hand, whispering to one girl, chucking another under the chin, going out with another, etc." But Pike was from a colder clime. Perhaps he misinterpreted this spiritual father's attitude toward his flock.

On the third of March the little cavalcade came in sight of something which reminded Pike of " a fleet of flat-bottomed boats which are to be seen in the spring and fall season descending the Ohio River." Santa Fe at last! He was not unduly thrilled, however, and as he came nearer he thought that the magnificence of the two church steeples " formed a striking contrast to the miserable appearance of the houses." But this was long before any American had discovered that adobe houses were picturesque and more than a century before American architects had fallen into the vogue of imitating them.

Governor Alencaster received the young officer with a severity and chilliness that at first led Pike to believe that war had already been declared between the United States and Spain. Under this impression he stoutly denied that Dr. Robinson had been a member of his party. He did not know how much the Spaniards had found out about the Doctor and he feared that they might shoot him as a spy. He also tried to conceal his more important papers, distributing them among his men and showing the governor the half-empty trunk in which they had been carried. But no sooner had he done this than he became worried lest the men should lose or reveal the documents under the influence of Santa Fe's genial wines, and put them back in the trunk. Next day the astute Alencaster again sent to fetch them, and this time Pike was to see no more of them. They lay gathering dust for three generations in the Mexican archives, until a twentieth-century American historian came upon the faded packet labelled "El Viagero Piake."

By degrees Alencaster thawed out, assured Pike that he was not a prisoner, though he would be obliged to present himself before General Salcedo, the commandant at Chihuahua, and ended by presenting the captive with a new shirt and neckcloth "made in Spain by his sister and never worn by any person." Thus arrayed Pike sat down to a dinner given in his honor by the governor. Clothes seem to have meant a good deal to the young explorer. His pride was hurt by the sartorial plight in which he had reached the New Mexican capital. "When we presented ourselves," he complained, "I was dressed in a pair of blue trousers, blanket coat, and a cap made of scarlet cloth lined with fox-skin. My poor fellows were in leggings, breech-cloths, and leather coats, and there was not a hat in the whole party. This appearance was extremely mortifying to us all, especially as soldiers; although some of the officers used frequently to observe to me that ' worth made the man,' etc., with a variety of adages to the same amount. Yet the first impression made on the ignorant is hard to eradicate, and a greater proof cannot be given of the ignorance of the common people than their asking if we lived in houses or in camps like the Indians, and if we wore hats in our country." But the dinner turned out well. It was "rather splendid, having a variety of dishes and wines of the southern provinces; and when his excellency was a little warmed with the influence of cheering liquor he became very sociable."

Next day, probably with a headache or two to recall the jovialities of the evening before, Pike and his men were sent south on their way to Chihuahua. He was now turning his back on the Trail but his casual comments on the country and the people make it worth our while to follow him. Pike's captor, now his warm friend, Don Bartholomew — or, if one prefers the Spanish spelling rather than the one Pike uses, Bartolomé — Fernandez went part of the way. After the bibulous old gentleman who commanded the escort had drunk himself peacefully to sleep Pike and Fernandez would spend an evening in deep conversation. The Mexicans, Fernandez would say, desired " a change of affairs and open trade with the United States." Then Pike would get eagerly down on the floor and " point out to him with chalk the geographical connection and route from New Mexico to Louisiana " — another indication, by the way, that he knew the

difference between the Red River and the Rio Grande.
If the two young men could have spoken for their countrymen there would never have been another cross word
between the United States and Mexico. But say what
he could Pike could not convince his friend that the
Americans would not invade New Mexico by the next
spring at the latest. This fear was present all through
the Spanish provinces. It lasted for forty years and then
was amply justified. It accounts for much of the bitter
opposition that Pike's successors on the Trail were to
meet with. But Pike and Fernandez parted with brotherly tears. " He embraced me," the lieutenant wrote in
his diary, " and all my men."

The journey was made by way of Santo Domingo,
thence to Albuquerque and Isleta, and so down the Rio
Grande Valley. Pike had always an eye for the picturesque and a liking for fine phrases. At San Felipe he
was delighted with a concert of " bass drums, French
horns, violins and cymbals." At Albuquerque Father
Ambrosio Guerra brought into the room " his adopted
children of the female sex . . . Indians of various nations, Spanish, French, and finally two girls who from
their conversation I concluded to be English." " Waited
on by half a dozen of these beautiful girls," Pike goes on,
growing more and more rhapsodical, " who, like Hebe
at the feast of the gods, converted our wine to nectar
and with their ambrosial breath shed incense on our
cups " — in short, a pleasant, though perfectly proper,
time was had by all. It will be evident that the young
explorer had a truly discriminating taste in such mat-
ters. And he saw New Mexico at its best. The spring
irrigation was going forward and " everything appeared
to give life and gaiety to the surrounding scenery."

The journey continued as merrily as wedding bells.

Near Atrisco the Americans were entertained with "supper, wine, and a violin, with a collection of young people to a dance." Melgares, leader of the expedition which had been sent out to capture Pike near the beginning of his journey, now turned up as commander of the escort and proved to be as amiable and amusing an enemy as one could wish, with "much of the urbanity of a Frenchman." It is sad to think that a few years later Pike, killed in the assault on York, now Toronto, Canada, would be lying in his grave, and that Melgares would have degenerated into a fat and arbitrary governor. But the future troubled no one during this memorable holiday captivity. The policy of making life agreeable for the Americans was continued with more gusto than ever. At one point Melgares dispatched a messenger ahead, with a note saying, "Send this evening six or eight of your handsomest young girls to the village of San Fernandez, where I propose giving a fandango for the entertainment of the American officers arrived this day." And when Pike and his comrades reached San Fernandez they found "really a handsome display of beauty."

In Chihuahua, which was reached after a few weeks of this happy travelling, Pike was cordially received by General Salcedo, though the general politely but firmly refused to return the explorer's confiscated papers. Again the Americans were treated almost as guests of honor, and everything was done to make their stay a pleasant one. They were set free after their interview with Salcedo and sent back to the United States by the Texas route. At San Antonio Governor Cordero gave them a dinner, at which toasts were drunk to the President of the United States, the King of Spain, General Wilkinson, and "these gentlemen, their safe and happy arrival in their own country, their honorable reception and the continuation of the good understanding which exists between the two countries." With this charming gesture — the more charming because the " understanding " between the United States and Spain was anything but good at the moment — the Spaniards sent Pike on the last leg of his long journey, and on the first day of July, almost a year from his departure from St. Louis, he walked into the American fort at Natchitoches.

Of course the mutual expressions of good will fooled neither Pike nor his hosts. Pike, in his private letters and in his reports, frankly anticipated an American invasion of Mexico in the near future. He saw signs, he was sure, of Mexico's coming independence of the Spanish " ligatures of restrictions, monopolies, prohibitions, seclusions, and superstitions." What was good in New and Old Mexico he credited to the inhabitants, what was bad to Spain. In case of a revolt, he asked, should not the United States help their Mexican brethren to throw off the Spanish yoke? " Twenty thousand auxiliaries from the United States, under good officers," he argued, " are at any time sufficient to create and effect the revolution. These troops can be raised and officered in the United States but paid for and supplied at the expense of Mexico. Should an army of Americans ever march into the country and be guided and governed by these maxims they will only have to march from province to province in triumph and be hailed by the united voices of grateful millions as their deliverers and saviours, while our national character resounds to the most distant nations of the earth." Poor Pike! He had not learned that when a courtly Spanish gentleman offers a friend his house and gardens he does not expect the tender to be taken too literally.

To Wilkinson privately Pike wrote from Natchitoches, four days after his arrival, "I yet possess immense matter, the results of one year's travel . . . results which in our present critical situation I do conceive to be immensely important, and which open a scene for the generosity and aggrandizement of our country, with a wide and splendid field for harvests of honor for individuals." The last phrase would have appealed to Pike's fat-souled patron. There was nothing Wilkinson would have liked better than the prospect of a wide and splendid field for a harvest of honor for an individual of exactly his own dimensions. But he wrote, with a smile as innocent as that of any cat with a canary inside, "They have asserted that your and Lieutenant Wilkinson's enterprise was a premeditated co-operation with Burr. . . Let it then suffice for me to say to you that of the information you have acquired and the observations you have made you must be cautious, extremely cautious, how you breathe a word, because publication may excite a spirit of adventure adverse to the interests of our government or injurious to the maturation of those plans which may hereafter be found necessary and justifiable by the government."

Pike's confiscated papers, found in the Mexican archives some years ago by Dr. Herbert E. Bolton, strengthen the conviction that Pike and his patron believed an early war with Mexico probable and that Pike at all times had military considerations in mind. But this expectation was not clearly betrayed in the papers which fell into Mexican hands. Pike's official instructions were as pure as the driven snow — as pure as though they had been written to be captured. "You must indeed be extremely guarded," Wilkinson had written, in July 1806, "with respect to the Spaniards.

Neither alarm nor offend them unnecessarily." Some of Pike's notes, from which his report was later compiled, he succeeded in carrying away with him, rolled small and crammed into musket barrels. And, as he relates, he had a devil of a time afterwards in sorting them out and reading them.

Pike's soaring ambitions were doomed to be buried in an early grave. But his narrative, published in 1810, is a landmark of outstanding importance in the history of the Southwest. It aroused at once in those who read it the desire for profit and the yearning for romantic adventure — two strands which are interwoven throughout the whole history of the Santa Fe Trail. The romance was there abundantly — the naked plains, the savage mountains, the women and the wine that were to be had at the end. But the profit motive, or excuse, for wandering southwestward was also present, in Pike's description of the needs and products of the country and his account of the trade between Old and New Mexico. From New Mexico, in his day, went sheep, tobacco, dressed skins, furs, buffalo robes, salt, and "wrought vessels of a superior quality." The New Mexicans manufactured for their own uses a rough species of leather, cigars, pottery, and some cotton goods and blankets. But these were so poor and so costly that they might easily be displaced by competition from better and cheaper imported goods. Already the Spaniards were bringing to Santa Fe dry goods, confectionery, arms, ammunition, iron, steel, gold, and silver, and — of all things! — cheese. The caravans were then taking five months to fetch and carry between Santa Fe and Mexico, though the custom had grown up of making El Paso a division point, where the caravans from north and south met and exchanged goods. On his journey south from Santa Fe Pike passed a caravan of three hundred men, guarded by thirty-five or forty soldiers, and driving fifteen thousand sheep. But the Trail to the Missouri was far shorter than that to the principal markets of Mexico.

After Pike's narrative was published New Mexico had for American adventurers something of the appeal that the golden cities of Cibola and Quivira had had for the Spanish pioneers. Only this gold was real. Pike described no land of dreams. He gave statistics. He mentioned the fact that high grade imported cloth sold in Santa Fe for between $20 and $25 a yard, linen for $4 a yard and other dry goods in proportion. Traders who had access to New England textiles watered at the mouth at such figures. Only the prospect of Spanish dungeons kept them away from the New Mexican market, and even that, as we shall see, was not always successful. But though dollars and cents are henceforth to play a large part in the story of our Trail we must not fall into the error of thinking that they were everything. Not while the love of danger, of strange places, and of freedom survives even as a memory can the story of the Santa Fe Trail be written in purely economic terms. Pike stirred men's imaginations. He made them restless to be up and going. His prairies and his mountains called to them as the sea calls to predestined sailors.

For this his reward was such as those who serve republics — or, for that matter, kings — may well expect. That is to say it was precisely nothing, except fame. Neither he nor his widow nor any of his men, not even those who were crippled by the hardships they underwent, received, so far as can be ascertained, a single penny from the government in addition to their ordinary soldier's pay. A proposal to reward them was favorably reported by a House committee in 1808, but like so many similar proposals it died a-borning.

But now a new chapter opens — a chapter Pike did not foresee, whose possibility he even deplored.

CHAPTER V

DESERTS AND DUNGEONS

FROM these immense prairies," Pike had written, "may arise one great advantage to the United States, viz., the restriction of our population to some limits, and thereby a continuation of the Union. Our citizens, being so prone to rambling and extending themselves on the frontiers, will through necessity be constrained to limit their extent on the west to the borders of the Missouri and the Mississippi, while they leave the prairies incapable of cultivation to the wandering and uncivilized aborigines of the country."

This opinion was common enough at the time and for many years thereafter. The prairies, as we now know, were anything but incapable of cultivation, and as for the rambling propensities of our citizens they were as impossible to check as the westward movement of the sun or the eastward drift of the prairie winds. The very year of Pike's return Manuel Lisa and Jacques Clamorgan of St. Louis sent Louis Baudouin toward New Mexico with a load of trade goods. He was arrested by Lt. Melgares in October and taken captive to Santa Fe. Even before Pike set out Lisa had been gazing with speculative eyes across the plains to Santa Fe. In a letter to Pike in the summer of 1806 General Wilkinson had declared that Lisa " and a society of which he is the ostensible leader have determined on a project to open some commercial intercourse with Santa Fe," adding

" that as this may lead to a connection injurious to the United States you must do what you can consistently to defeat the plan." Just what harm the Lisa expedition could have done is hard to say. Lisa did not easily give up the idea. He mentions it in a letter written as late as September 1812. Perhaps he was ultimately discouraged by the hostility of the Spanish authorities or by the manifold risks, not so much to life — the plainsmen were accustomed to risking their lives — as to property, which the long journey involved. But in 1809 Lisa and Pierre Chouteau incorporated the St. Louis-Missouri Fur Company, and it was not long before the fierce rivalries of the northwestern fur trade drew their attention away from the New Mexican market. Nevertheless, we must enter the names of Bàudoin and his patrons, even with a question mark, on the list of the very earliest of the Santa Fe traders.

Unless we accept as gospel truth the account which John Shaw wrote of his trip with two youthful companions, Peter Spear and William Miller, in the summer of 1809, to a point " beyond all the western headwaters of the Mississippi except the Missouri and the Arkansas " — and there are some reasons for doubting Shaw's narrative — the next expedition westward along our Trail was by three Missourians, Joseph McLanahan, Reuben Smith, and James Patterson, under the guidance of a Spaniard named Emanuel Blanco. "We presume," said the Louisiana *Gazette,* which announced their departure in its issue of December 28, 1809, " their objects are mercantile; the enterprise must be toilsome and perilous, the distance being computed at five to six hundred miles, altogether through a wilderness heretofore unexplored." It is interesting to note how naïvely the American assumption of " a wilderness heretofore unexplored " persisted. More than a generation later it won John C. Frémont the title of " Pathfinder," although Frémont's achievement was not so much in finding paths as in writing about them. McLanahan and his friends had obviously kept close-mouthed as to their plans.

However, they went hopefully on their way, jogging across the plains with no serious mishaps until they reached the headwaters of the Red River. There they were picked up by a Spanish detachment, taken to Santa Fe, haled before the governor for examination, and sent to Mexico to lie for two years in prison. No word came back and their friends believed them dead. A wave of indignation swept over the frontier. The editor of the *Gazette* waxed wroth. " The assassins of Mexico," he growled, in an article published on October 4, 1810, " have ere this butchered three respectable citizens of Louisiana. Yet a little while and a day of terrible retribution will arrive." In March 1811, he wrote: " Three hundred men, well equipped, from Kentucky, Tennessee, and the Illinois territory were expected to rendezvous at the Canadian fork of the Arkansas by the twenty-fifth of this month. The object is said to be the release of Messrs. Smith, M'Clanahan, Patterson, and others ; and to bring off what gold they can conveniently seize ; or, if such a course offered fairer prospects of success, to join the revolutionary party." This was published exactly a week before the revolutionary movement under Padre Miguel Hidalgo, who had set out in September 1810, to free Mexico from the Spanish yoke, collapsed with Hidalgo's capture. Apparently the three hundred heroes never assembled and never marched, but we have here, fully a generation before the Mexican War, a sample of the temper that made that war possible.

The captured traders were liberated in 1812 and came back to the United States. A letter of McLanahan's to Governor Howard of Louisiana, dated at St. Louis on June 18, 1812, tells the story of the expedition and its martyrdom. The party had gone out, McLanahan says, for the innocent purpose of securing " geographical and commercial information." While thus harmlessly engaged they were seized and led in irons to Chihuahua. From Chihuahua they were sent separately into the interior of Mexico, " under circumstances of suffering and privation which we feel unwilling to detail and of ignominy from which we would equally banish reflection." Incidentally, the man who rounded off this last phrase was far from being an ignorant and unlettered frontiersman. After the first year the captives were allowed to return to Chihuahua, and in another twelve months were turned loose to make their way home as best they could.

McLanahan's experiences are in sharp contrast to those of Pike. We shall find these sharp contrasts all through the early history of the Trail. The Spaniards and Mexicans could be nearly as cruel as the most savage Indians, and almost as gentle as angels. Their natural impulses toward the stranger within their gates were generous and hospitable. It was only when their interests were at stake or their distrust aroused that they turned vindictive. McLanahan had, of course, run counter to the policies of the official and trading classes of New Mexico, whose pocket-books would be threatened by any infringement upon the Chihuahua trading monopoly. But McLanahan was not in the least discouraged. He believed that the people of the Spanish provinces were friendly to the Americans, no matter what might be said and done by their captains and their governors. The lowlier Mexicans had been kind to him. He had eaten their bread and drunk their wine. " We have no hesitation," said he, remembering, perhaps, the women coming to their doors in the evening, " in avowing that the conduct exhibited us was condemned by all but the immediate dependents of the government." He ended by announcing that he intended to risk the deserts and the Spanish dungeons again, explaining: " We think we can calculate the amount of opposition, we feel that we can justly appreciate the glowing reception we shall meet from the unfortunate, the embruted American Spaniards." But he seems never to have set out. Before his time came to do so another group of Americans had gone to Santa Fe and met a fate harder to bear than his had been.

This was the Robert McKnight party, who went up the Missouri river in April 1812, and across country to New Mexico, using Pike's report as a guide, just as many years later the California emigrants used Frémont's narrative. Apparently they started out in the belief that Hidalgo had overthrown the Spanish rule and that Americans would be welcomed in Old and New Mexico. But Hidalgo's bullet-pierced body had been almost a year in the grave. They learned their mistake too late, when Governor Manrique confiscated their goods and threw them into prison. They had passed over the Trail successfully, with none of those fearful misadventures that were to befall those who followed it in later years. But their skill and courage were of little use to them when they stood before a hostile autocrat. Like the members of the McLanahan party they were sent to Chihuahua, and some did not see their home again until their release was ordered after Iturbide's successful uprising against the Spaniards in 1821. Their

imprisonment was made the subject of a message of
the President of the United States, and of diplomatic
representations both to the Viceroy of Mexico and to the
King of Spain. Just why these efforts accomplished
nothing between 1812 and 1821 is something of a mystery and perhaps also something of a scandal. The suffering and loss of the members of the party could hardly
be expressed in money terms, though it is on record that
McKnight's sequestered goods, the proceeds of which
were used to pay for the prisoners' maintenance, were
sufficient to support them a good part of the nine years
at a rate of eighteen and three-fourths cents a day for
each man.

It is a curious fact that the hardships and injustices
from which these men suffered did not embitter them
against the Mexicans or against the strange, wild, glamorous land of Mexico. Something alluring in land and
people held them more firmly than any Spanish prison.
Robert McKnight after his release returned to Chihuahua, where Kit Carson once hired out to him as a
teamster. He is said to have made a fortune working
the copper mines of Santa Rita, and trading when the
Apaches would let him with the Chihuahua outposts.
James Baird and Samuel Chambers, two other members
of the party, engaged in the Santa Fe trade as soon as
they were liberated and the Trail was open. Baird
subsequently became a Mexican citizen and settled in
El Paso. In 1826, the year of his death, he wrote a letter
to the chief Mexican official of the El Paso district urging that " foreigners " be excluded from Mexico, so that
" we Mexicans may peaceably profit by the goods with
which the merciful God has been pleased to enrich our
soil."

Nor did the misfortunes of the McKnight party altogether keep Americans out of New Mexico during the next few years. There was probably a good deal more trapping by Americans on Spanish soil than was ever set down in print, and some printed references do indicate that a few trappers reached Santa Fe. Thus the St. Louis *Inquirer,* in September 1822, observed that " it is becoming a familiar operation for our citizens to visit " New Mexico. Seemingly the phrase refers to a period of some duration and not merely to the expeditions of 1821 and 1822, to which we shall shortly come. The western fur traders and Indian traders were not easily daunted, nor did they pay over-much attention to international boundaries. And they had a hearty contempt for Mexicans, except in overwhelming force. It was a contempt often mingled with friendliness, but the friendliness was the lordly gesture of a haughty race toward one which it considered inferior.

A few definite accounts of Anglo-Saxons in New Mexico between 1812 and 1821 we do have. In 1814, after McKnight and his associates had been brutally laid by the heels, Joseph Philibert went with a party to hunt on the upper Arkansas. Next year he returned alone to St. Louis for supplies. He was delayed in getting back, and his men, after waiting for him for a time at the appointed rendezvous, were driven by hunger to throw themselves on the mercy of the Spaniards at Taos.

Meanwhile Philibert, having collected the goods and horses he needed, fell in with Jules De Mun and Auguste Pierre Chouteau, who were organizing a fur-hunting expedition, and agreed to join forces with them. Chouteau was a member of the great fur-trading family of St. Louis. The combined party made the journey safely to Huerfano Creek, where Philibert had his rendezvous, and there learned from some Indians that the missing trappers were at Taos. De Mun was sent to find them. His letter to Governor William Clark, in which these events are related, makes no mention of any difficulty in getting over the mountains. It was not geography that worried the trappers at that moment, it was politics. Happily there had been a change of governor since the imprisonment of the McKnight party, and De Mun met with a pleasant reception.

"I arrived at Taos," says De Mun, "where I found the men, who had been received with the greatest hospitality and allowed to pass the winter there. I went on to Santa Fe, to explain to the Governor the reasons of my coming into the country. As soon as I alighted in the capital I was presented to the then Governor, Don Alberto Mayenz, who at first expressed his surprise to see me; but no sooner had I told him the circumstances under which I came than he treated me very politely."

De Mun, Chouteau, and Philibert returned reassured to their trapping enterprises, and for about a year their routine was broken only by trips to the American settlements and a brush or two with the Pawnees. Probably they had adventures enough to fill a five-foot shelf. But these adventures were part of the day's work. A trapper came to take them for granted. But meanwhile Governor Maynez, as the name is more correctly spelled, had been superseded by Pedro Maria de Allande who did not like Americans. De Allande brusquely ordered the trappers to leave Spanish territory, and they accordingly retired to the eastern slope of the range, which they believed to be American soil. But this did not satisfy the suspicious Spaniard. In March, when De Mun went into Taos to learn how the land lay, he was told that wild rumors were afloat in New Mexico.

"It was said," he relates, "that at the first fork of

the Arkansas [the Rio de las Animas, Purgatoire or
Picketwire] we had built a fort; that we had there twenty
thousand men, with many cannon and ammunition,
and other such idle tales." Two days later a solemn
troop of two hundred soldiers arrived at Taos with
orders to take De Mun back with them and search for
the fabulous American army. De Mun led them to the
trappers' camp, which of course turned out to be like
all trappers' camps, with no trace of fort or invading
host. The Americans were nevertheless given peremp-
tory orders to clear out. Prevented from doing this by
the snow in the mountains, they were intercepted two
months later, probably on the American side of the line,
and haled before the governor at Santa Fe. That chol-
eric functionary immediately flew into a violent rage,
in the course of which he threatened to have their brains
blown out on the spot. He relented sufficiently to throw
them alive into the dungeons in front of the Palace,
where they were kept in chains for forty-four days. Little enough did they see during that period of the idyllic
life of the quiet little town; no one gave banquets in
their honor; no lovely senoritas washed their feet. But
they lived through the hard experience, being a tough
and seasoned lot. Finally they were brought before a
court-martial. The bearded Americans in their ragged
leather coats, blinking in the sudden light of day, faced
their inquisitors. It was an anxious moment.

" Many questions were asked," relates De Mun, " but
particularly why we had stayed so long in the Spanish
dominions. I answered that, being on the waters of
the Arkansas river, we did not consider ourselves in the
domains of Spain, as we had a license to go as far as the
headwaters of said river. The president denied that our
Government had a right to grant such a license, and

entered into such a rage as prevented his speaking, con-
tenting himself with striking his fist several times on the
table, saying, 'Gentlemen, we must have this man
shot!' . . He talked much of a big river that was the
boundary line between the two countries, but did not
know its name. When mention was made of the Mississippi he jumped up, saying that that was the river he
meant; that Spain had never ceded the west side of it.
It may be easy to judge of our feelings, to see our lives
in the hands of such a man."

They filed back to their dungeon and lay the night in
great suspense. Next day they were informed of the
verdict. All their possessions, amounting, as De Mun
estimated, to $30,380, were to be confiscated. They
were to be allowed one horse apiece with which to return
home — or at least relieve the Spaniards of their unde-
sirable presence. To add insult to injury they were
forced to kneel to hear the sentence read and then to kiss
the paper on which it was written. There was nothing
for them to do but make their miserable way back to
St. Louis, with nothing but a few equine scarecrows to
show for their original investment of capital and two
years of hard and dangerous living.

A few other names crop up during this period. There
was, for instance, Ezekiel Williams, who wrote the narrative of his wanderings not because he wished to enrich
the literature of his country but for the extremely practical purpose of clearing himself of the charge of murder-
ing one of his companions. Williams, if we are to believe
his story, became separated from his trapping party on
the Arkansas in 1812 and came four hundred miles down
the river alone. Perhaps he really did this and perhaps
he did not. Williams seems to have been one of those
tall liars whom the western country from time to time

developed. But trappers existed who were capable of such feats as Williams describes. Behind the thick curtain of our ignorance we can discern stirring events and fabulously romantic lives. Lone campfires rose on many a perilous spot. Gaunt forelopers of the westward movement were making sure the path that the great procession was to follow. They came like bees to honey, like moths to the flame.

To one man, David Meriwether, was reserved the distinction of being, so far as there is record, the last American trader to be imprisoned by the Spaniards on New Mexican soil. In 1819 Merriwether was travelling across the prairies with a party of Pawnees — a dangerous kind of vacation for any white man. Out of the mountains rode the Spanish Colonel Vizcarra with a swarm of cavalrymen at his heels; the Pawnees were beaten and scattered and Meriwether was captured and taken to Santa Fe. The Spaniards were in constant fear of American aggression. They accused Meriwether of being a spy. The governor at this time was Melgares — that same Melgares whom Pike had described as " having much of the urbanity of a Frenchman." He had little enough urbanity as he glared at poor Meriwether. His first impulse was to strip the American, and a black servant whom Meriwether had with him, of all their belongings and turn them loose in the wilderness. Merriwether coolly pointed out that winter was coming on and that the governor's proposal was equivalent to murder.

There was a flicker of the old urbanity. Melgares gave orders that the two intruders should be given a mule, a gun, and a little ammunition apiece. The Spanish horsemen rode with them into the mountains beyond Taos, then left them to find their way home if they could—or perish if they could not. Meriwether was a man of grim resolution. When the Spaniards had attacked the Pawnees he had named a rendezvous for such members of the party as might manage to escape. He went there, found three Pawnees, and in their company managed, after incredible adventures, to get back east to the United States. Thirty-four years later Meriwether returned to Santa Fe, this time not as a wretched captive but as governor of the American Territory of New Mexico. The old *carcel* in which he had been confined was still standing, but it is soberly stated that at the very moment he took his oath of office the roof fell in.

Two years after Meriwether's imprisonment the revolutionary army under Iturbide marched into the City of Mexico, and the power of Spain in Mexico was for ever at an end. The reverberations of that great event were soon felt in Santa Fe. Never again, except for a single brief period and for a plausible reason, was the New Mexican frontier to be closed to American trade.

The tides of destiny had turned. The Trail, that had been so long quiet, flowed with eager life. First came a sprinkling of men on horseback, with pack animals, then the wagons began to roll westward, and every year, until the coming of the railroad, the procession grew longer and more dense. Long before the discovery of gold drew multitudes to distant and romantic California the road to Santa Fe was as familiar to the traders as the main streets of their native villages. The Americans were to be held back no more. Their dust was to blur the clear horizon for ever and ever.

CHAPTER VI

THE TRAIL MAKERS

OF ALL the things done that cannot be undone, the opening of a backward country to civilization is the most irretrievable. Of all who ride under the pointing finger of fate the men who break new Trails have the mightiest monuments. Such a man was Captain William Becknell, whom Hiram Martin Chittenden has justly called the " Father of the Santa Fe Trail." It is true that in a sense the Trail had many parents, beginning with the Conquistadores, or with the ghostly Indians who first moved across the plains in search of buffalo, and including an unnumbered caravan of Spanish, French, and Yankee trappers and traders. Becknell, as should now be apparent, did not actually " discover" the route. He may have been the first trader to cross the fearful desert of the Cimarron. He certainly was the first to use wagons. But his chief distinction is that after he opened the Trail it stayed open. Where his horses' prints and wagon ruts led, the westward surge of travel followed — great portions of his route it follows to this day.

But Becknell had no such glittering prospect in mind on the first day of September 1821, when he and his party set out from Arrow Rock, near Franklin, Missouri. His diary shows he headed for Santa Fe, not merely to trade with the Indians in the Rocky Mountains. But his route to the mountains did lie very near the subsequent main line of the Trail, through the site of Osage City to the Arkansas. October 21st found the Becknell party leaving the main river and turning up what he describes as the left fork of the Arkansas. A little later they were struggling through what must have been the Raton Pass. For two days they labored prodigiously rolling away great rocks before even attempting to take the horses over. They got across and came down on the plateaus on the other side, reaching the Canadian and, on November 12th, Rock River.

On the thirteenth they watched with some apprehension the approach of a small body of Mexican troops. But if they expected harsh treatment they were agreeably surprised. The Mexicans not only greeted them in a friendly fashion and indicated they should go on Santa Fe. They rode onward through towns that were suddenly all smiles. It was the honeymoon of liberty. All men, even the Mexicans and the Americans, were brothers. Or, as Becknell says, the traders were received " with apparent pleasure and joy," and their little stock of goods was soon sold at profitable prices. They had reached Santa Fe on November 16th — a date to be remembered in any history of the Trail. Early in December they turned their backs on the little city which had turned so warmly hospitable. They had news to carry back to the Missouri. Seventeen days after leaving Santa Fe they were on the Arkansas. In forty-eight they were home. The gods of the Trail sped them on their way.

" My father saw them unload when they returned," says H. H. Harris, as quoted by George P. Morehouse, " and when their rawhide packages of silver dollars were dumped on the sidewalk one of the men cut the thongs and the money spilled out and clinking on the stone pavement rolled into the gutter. Everyone was excited and the next spring another expedition was sent out. To show what profits were made I remember one young lady, Miss Fanny Marshall, who put $60 in the expedition and her brother brought back $900 as her share."

Word ran along the border and things began to happen. But meanwhile another American trader, Thomas James, had blundered into Santa Fe. James himself believed that he was the first to reach the city after the revolution of 1821. "I commanded the fourth expedition to Santa Fe from the United States," he wrote in his book entitled "Three Years among the Mexicans and Indians," "and I was the first American that ever visited the country and escaped a prison while there." James does not mention Becknell, nor does either Becknell or Josiah Gregg (the latter being the leading authority on the first period of the Trail) mention James. But since Becknell's account makes November 16th the date of his arrival in Santa Fe, whereas James does not claim to have arrived until December 1st, it seems necessary to give Becknell the honors.

The two dates hint at a curious little personal drama. Becknell left San Miguel, some fifty-odd miles from Santa Fe, on December 13th, on his way home, and must have been still in Santa Fe when James arrived. As it would have been absurdly impossible for the two men to have been in the little capital at the same time without knowing of each other's presence, the only presumption possible is that each did know and that each chose to suppress the fact. James had suffered heavy losses on the way and was in a touchy state of mind when he arrived. Perhaps he took a dislike to Becknell, his successful rival, and for that reason deliberately left him out of the story. In the end the issue comes down to one's belief in the veracity of the two traders. The internal evidence of James's book leads an unprejudiced reader to believe that if either James or Becknell was a liar the distinction belongs to James. In any case James did not open the Trail, for he came in by a route which never became popular.

As James tells his story he left St. Louis on May 10th, in company with John McKnight, a Spanish guide, and a party of about a dozen men. John McKnight was on his way to Mexico to find his brother Robert, imprisoned since 1812 in Chihuahua and released amidst the jubilations of Iturbide's success. With this following of "young and daring men, eager for excitement and adventure," James loaded ten thousand dollars' worth of biscuit, whiskey, flour, lead, and powder into a keel boat, and set off down the Mississippi. At the mouth of the Arkansas the party turned up that stream, first to "Au Poste," or Arkansas Post, then to Little Rock, Fort Smith, and the spot where Fort Gibson was to be erected three years later, thus crossing the present state of Arkansas and entering Oklahoma. Here, probably near the mouth of the Cimarron, they found the water too shallow for their boats and bought horses of the Osage Indians with which to pursue their journey overland.

Near the site of Fort Gibson, James, who had gone ahead of his companions, came upon Hugh Glenn, getting ready to go into the Indian country with twenty men and an outfit of trading goods. We shall return a little later to Glenn, and to Jacob Fowler, his guide and probably one of the world's worst spellers. James proposed that the two parties join forces and travel together toward the Spanish settlements. Glenn refused, and this was the beginning of the intense dislike and suspicion which James felt toward him. The two men bade each other a not too affectionate farewell and parted, to meet again some months later in Santa Fe.

James waited for the rest of his party to catch up and resumed his journey, along the Cimarron and later the North Fork of the Canadian River, and into what is now the Texas Panhandle. Here the Comanches got upon the traders' trail and robbed them of a part of their goods. This was hard enough luck. But the news ran round the prairie that there were still rich pickings to be had. A second time the Comanche feathers quivered behind the sagebrush. This time there were only two thousand Indians, in an ugly mood. Only one among them, a chief named Cordaro, who had visited the American post at Natchitoches and carried with him a sheet of paper testifying that he was a good Indian and a friend of the Americans, seemed to have a spark of human kindness in his breast. His eagerness to live up to his testimonial perhaps saved the lives of James and his companions.

The Americans lay sleepless all night in the heart of the Indian camp. At dawn they faced the mob of savages, who seemed about to attack them. The signal for the assault, as they afterwards learned, was to be the striking of the first tepee. Cordaro had postponed the tragedy but was now powerless to avert it. James and the rest resolved to sell their lives at a stiff price. They waited, standing behind their piled-up saddles, muskets loaded, ready to fire at the first hostile move. Suddenly a commotion began in the rear of the Indian camp. There was a cry, in the Comanche language of "White men! White men!" Through the crowd came riding six Spaniards, like messengers bearing reprieves. No modern scenario writer could have imagined a more dramatic moment. The Indians fell back, spears were lowered. The Spanish prestige, even at that remote spot in the prairies, was enough to save the Americans' lives.

The Indians did not give up their plunder without grumbling. They had orders from the New Mexican government, they said, to stop all Gringos from passing. But the new arrivals replied that " This was under the government of Spain, but that they were now independent and free and brothers to the Americans." Cordaro, a James Fenimore Cooper Indian if ever there was one, refused at first to be reassured. He was as unwilling to trust his friends to the Spaniards as to his own people. "They will imprison you," he protested to James, " as they have imprisoned all Americans that ever went to Santa Fe." And he did come into Santa Fe a few weeks later to make sure that this calamity had not occurred.

After this hair-raising adventure the travellers continued with only the ordinary ups and downs of prairie life and went into Santa Fe by way of Pecos and San Miguel. Once arrived, James sold the sad remnant of his noble barge-load of goods. It had cost him ten thousand dollars and he realized a scant twenty-five hundred. Two hundred of this James gave to John McKnight, who had heard that his brother Robert had gone to Durango, sixteen hundred miles south of Santa Fe. It is pleasant to know that the brothers were happily reunited. But John was destined to fall victim to a Comanche arrow, after all. He returned safely to St. Louis, but next year went with James to establish a post on the North Fork of the Canadian, and there, in 1823, was killed.

Meanwhile, the party headed by the haughty Colonel Glenn packed its doll rags and turned westward, still

ignorant, as James had been, of the Mexican revolution
and the new complexion of affairs at Santa Fe. Fowler,
who kept a journal [since edited with its original spelling intact by Dr. Elliott Coues], was perhaps the most interesting member. He was a native of New York, a
resident of Covington, Kentucky, and a seasoned wilderness traveller. His wife, a woman of French birth who
tradition says was most charming, sometimes went with
him, carrying along as many of the Parisian refinements as she could. One wishes she had gone on the trip
now in prospect, but unfortunately the sunset trails at
the time, though they had heroes enough, had few
heroines. Fowler left Fort Smith on September 6, 1821,
and met Glenn at the latter's cabin on the Verdigris
River. We must not think of Glenn as an uncouth Indian trader because he made his headquarters in this
remote spot. He was a civilized and keen-minded business man who made money in the southwestern trade
and later in life owned thousands of broad acres in
Missouri.

The Glenn-Fowler party, instead of going directly
west, as James had done, headed north, went across the
present Oklahoma line into Kansas, and crossed the
Arkansas River — and the Santa Fe Trail that was soon
to be — near the site of Cimarron, west of Dodge City.
Following a friendly tribe of Indians, as was customary
among traders, they wintered in the Rocky Mountains
among the Kiowas and Arapahoes. In the course of
their wanderings one of the party was fatally clawed by
a bear. On November 28th they were within " six days'
easy travel of Taos," though they did not venture in.
However, the mention of this fact shows how well they
knew the region. On November 30th they encountered
a party of " Creoles of that country," who " seemed well

disposed " — but, to the husband of the surpassingly neat Esther de Vie, far dirtier than was necessary. One of the Indians asked the Spanish captain to show him how he prayed. " It is only necessary to judge of them," observes Fowler. " The captain and all his party were painted like the Indians the day they traded and during his prayer the Captain caught a louse on his shirt and ate it." But the romanticist on the frontier has ever needed a strong stomach.

" Conl Glann," as Fowler calls him, was sufficiently reassured by his meeting with the Spaniards, lice not-withstanding, to take four men and go into Taos. Fowler, left behind for the time being, occupied himself and the men with building a fort near the present site of Pueblo, Colorado. This was a wise precaution, for, as he jotted down in his diary, " we are now in the Hart of the Inden Cuntry and Emeditly on the Great Ware Road." On January 28, 1822, word came from Glenn that all was well. " We now under Stand," wrote Fowler next day, " that the Mackeson provence has de Clared Independence of the Mother Cuntry and is de-sirous of a trade with the people of the United States. Conl Glann also advises me that he has obtained premi-tion to Hunt and trap and trade in the Spanish prov-ences." The bars were down at last! Soon after this Fowler and the rest of the company also went down to Taos. On the crest of the Sangre de Cristo the wind " was so cold we Scarce dare look Round." Fowler calls the road to Taos the " Old Taos Trail " — old, indeed, even in 1822.

The dawn of a new epoch was at hand. The Chinese wall that had surrounded New Mexico was collapsing like stage scenery at the end of an act. But the Glenn party were slow to realize the full import of what had happened. They still thought of themselves as trappers and hunters, not as Santa Fe traders. So, instead of idling in lovely Taos, they spent most of the winter hard at work in the mountains. The winter was so severe that it was hard enough merely to keep alive. The party killed some elk and took some beaver, but they also lost some of their horses. In the spring Glenn went into Santa Fe, though the others seem not to have gone beyond Taos. In June the whole party started back for the States. This time their company included not only John and Robert McKnight, and James Baird, who had returned from Mexico with the McKnights, but in addition the unfortunate and indignant James. For James there was no poetry in Santa Fe, though he left it in its warm and blooming season, when the sunshine struck across the low house-tops and the land was drowsy and fruitful. " I now," he writes, " on the first of June 1822, bade adieu forever to the capital of New Mexico, and was perfectly content never to repeat my visit to it or any other part of the country." In this mood James could not have been the most genial of travelling companions. Glenn's prosperity had been too great, and James attributed it to the fact that he had hypocritically turned Catholic in order to curry favor with the Spaniards. James also asserted later on that Glenn borrowed money of him and never paid it back, and in short he regarded the colonel as a " sordid miscreant." So we may think of the party as jogging homeward across the lovely green prairies of late spring and early summer, and at night assembling around the campfire of glowing buffalo chips to discuss one another's failings.

But greater events were stirring than anyone's private faults and quarrels. The year 1822 was a momentous one in the history of the Trail. Every trapper and trader along the Missouri and Arkansas Rivers, and their branches and headwaters, now knew that at last the New Mexican frontier was open. On the 12th of June, not far east of Syracuse, Kansas, the travellers met a party of sixteen men, headed by Colonel Benjamin Cooper and his two nephews, Braxton and Stephen. The Coopers had heard the news from Santa Fe, but they, too, were still trappers rather than traders. Somewhere along their route they had met another party headed by Captain Joseph Walker, and Walker and his men were going with them to Taos. Glenn and his companions continued eastward for sixteen days longer. Then something happened that probably made them forget their disputes for at least a few minutes. They found upon the prairie something that had never been seen there before since the beginning of time. They came upon wagon tracks! They could not have witnessed anything more significant had they encountered an army with banners. Here, at last, was the great Trail subdued to the uses of man. Neither wind nor rain nor snow, nor the trampling feet of the bison, were ever permanently to wipe those tracks from the face of the land.

To understand how these first ruts came to be there we must return to Becknell, who had got back to Franklin on January 29, 1822, eager to take advantage of the new opportunities which had so suddenly and splendidly opened up in the southwest. He had travelled light, with only one companion, a man named McLaughlin. When he reached Missouri he had a story to tell — a story so glowing that when spring came two expeditions were ready to try their fortunes in New Mexico, his own party and one headed by the Coopers. Cooper, as his friend Alphonso Wetmore testifies, was " an old and very respectable inhabitant" of Missouri. The Coopers, with a party originally numbering sixteen, and using pack horses, went across country to the Arkansas River, then up the river and over the "Old Taos Trail." They carried between $4,000 and $5,000 worth of goods.

Becknell and the Coopers probably started about the same time, but the Coopers, having no wheeled vehicles, made better speed. Wetmore, writing on August 9, 1824, testifies that Becknell "took with him a wagon, as did two or three of his associates." There seem, in fact, to have been three wagons in the Becknell party. But the use of wagons was not Becknell's only innovation. The year before he had had great difficulty in getting even his horses over Raton Pass, and he knew that the passage of the mountains with wagons was utterly impossible for a small party. He had in mind a shorter route, over more level and also more perilous country, and one over which the great mass of the travel to Santa Fe was to follow him for many years to come.

The Becknell company, numbering twenty-one, left Arrow Rock, Missouri, Becknell's starting point of the previous year, on May 22nd. They had not gone far toward the Arkansas when they ran into a band of Osage Indians, and would have lost their horses and their goods had not one of the Chouteaus, who had long traded with this tribe, interceded for them. It will be remembered that James, the year before, had *bought* horses from this tribe. The Osages, though never so savage as some of the more western Indians, were quite capable of stealing horses from one trader and selling them to another. Safe out of this scrape Becknell and his followers went their way and presently were joined by a company headed by a trader named John Heath. These chance encounters are among the most fascinating and

baffling features of some of the early narratives of the
Trail—they hint much and tell little. Little is known of
Heath's trail years. Becknell says, "the hiliarity
[Becknell's spelling] and sociability of this gentleman
often contributed to disperse the gloomy images which
very naturally presented themselves on a journey of such
uncertainty and adventure." Maybe this tribute is fame
enough for Heath. Maybe it is better to be " hiliarious "
under difficulties than to discover new rivers and
ranges.

Becknell and his men followed the route up the Arkansas to a point about five miles west of Dodge City, which
for reasons we shall perceive a little later was afterwards familiar to Santa Fe traders as "The Caches."
So far they had met with no serious hardships, though
hauling wagons across a roadless country deeply cut in
many places by streams was certainly no holiday excur-
sion. But now they left the river and boldly turned
south across the desert toward the Cimarron. They had
only the amount of water that could be carried in their
canteens and for guidance they had but a pocket compass and the stars. For two days they found no water.
They plodded in the blinding heat and saw mirages of
lakes, streams, and golden cities. They cut off the ears
of their mules and sucked the blood. At last, when they
had almost lost hope, they came upon a buffalo which
they were able to kill and whose stomach proved to be
filled with water. One of those who were present told
Josiah Gregg, years later, " that nothing ever passed his
lips which gave him such exquisite delight as his first
draught of that filthy beverage."

Knowing that water must now be close at hand the
stronger of the travellers pushed on, came to the Cimarron and returned in time to save the lives of their weaker

companions. Such, at least, is the accepted story of
the trip. It happens that Becknell's journal does not
describe the experience in the desert. " Our greatest difficulty," he there states, " was in the vicinity of Rock River,
where we were under the necessity of taking our wagons
up some high and rocky cliffs by hand." It is barely
possible that the near-tragedy in the desert happened,
not to Becknell but to Cooper the next year, 1823. It
is also possible that Becknell suppressed the adventure
because he did not want to be too discouraging. The
" Father of the Santa Fe Trail " must necessarily emphasize his offspring's virtues, not its faults.

But the early Santa Fe traders were not easily
daunted. They were what we would now call gluttons
for punishment. James Baird, whom we have just seen
returning with Colonel Glenn and the two McKnights
after his nine weary years in Chihuahua, had scarcely
reached St. Louis when he persuaded some merchants of
that city to finance himself and Samuel Chambers, another one of the original McKnight party, in a new venture to Santa Fe. Baird and Chambers were so eager
to hear the sound of Spanish again that they would not
wait for spring but set out in the fall of 1822. Near the
site of Dodge City the snow came upon them, too deep
for travel, and they were forced to go into winter quarters.
They made their camp on an island in the river, for
safety against the Indians, and managed to keep themselves alive. But their pack animals wandered off and
died. When spring came they " cached " their goods
and made their way to Taos to get mules with which to
complete the journey. The holes in the ground which
were left when the goods were taken out were still visible
nearly a quarter of a century later and the place was
called from that time forward The Caches. " Few

travellers," wrote Gregg, about 1844, "pass this way without visiting these mossy pits."

Unless we count the Baird party, which actually reached New Mexico in the spring of 1823, there was only one recorded expedition to Santa Fe during that year. This was led by Major Stephen Cooper, who had gone out with his uncle, Colonel Benjamin Cooper, the year before. The Cooper family were pioneers and Indian fighters in the Boonslick country. Sarshall Cooper, the Major's father, had been killed by an Indian as he sat at his own fireside with his wife and children. Consequently a little thing like a jaunt to Santa Fe was not likely to intimidate the Coopers. They had been going west for a long time — over the Alleghenies into Kentucky, from Kentucky into Missouri. It had got to be a habit with them.

Cooper organized a company of thirty men, with a stock in trade consisting mostly of dry goods. On the Little Arkansas the Indians ran off all but six of his horses. Cooper was a man of unshakable determination. He went back to Missouri and procured more horses. "We pursued our journey," he continues in his diary, "without any further molestation from Indians, but sometimes suffered severely from want of water. On one occasion eight of our men gave out entirely on that account and were unable to travel. The rest of the company, with the exception of myself, cut the lash ropes from their packs, scattered the goods upon the ground, took the best horses and scattered off like crazy men for water, leaving me and the eight men behind. Some of those who were leaving us fell on their knees and pled with me to go with them and save my own life; urging as reason that the men were bound to die and that I could do them no good by staying. I said I would not leave

them as long as a breath of life was left in one of them;
that if they found water they should return to us.

"This was one or two o'clock in the afternoon. When
it became dark I built a fire of buffalo chips and fired
guns in the air as a signal to guide them to us. About
midnight four men returned with water and we were all
saved. The others had drank so much water that they
were unable to return and remained by the water-hole.
We were lost in attempting to reach them, and it was
four days before we found them. From this time on to
the end of our journey we had no further difficulty."
Perhaps they had had sufficient difficulty for one trip!

Cooper seems not to have taken wagons on this expedition, though Becknell had showed their practicability the
year before. But even though the amount of goods the
party could carry was limited to what could be loaded on
horses the journey proved richly profitable. Each member had invested about $200. They returned in October
1823 with four hundred "jacks, jennies, and mules,"
furs, and some articles of a miscellaneous nature —
enough, certainly, to pay rich dividends. Their four-
legged booty was apparently the beginning of the now
world-renowned Missouri mule. This notorious beast
was a New Mexican product. He invaded Missouri
from the west, filling a need which the rush of settlement
into the river country was just beginning to create.
From 1823 on he formed a conspicuous article of commerce. Gregg, the principal source of information for
this period of the Trail's history, gives the cost of the
goods taken by Americans to New Mexico in 1823 as
$12,000, the number of proprietors, or independent
traders, as thirty, and the total number who went out
as fifty. But he may be referring to some expedition of
which no account survives, or to the Baird party, which

as we have seen did not get to Santa Fe until 1823. And the time was coming when journeys to Santa Fe would be remembered only when something happened out of the normal course of events.

On April 1, 1824, a rude tavern in the thriving young town of Franklin echoed to the shouts and boisterous conversation of a group of plainsmen who had gathered there to plan another caravan to Santa Fe. It was agreed that the rendezvous should be at Vernon, Missouri, that the date should be May 5th, and that each man should " come equipped with one good rifle, one pistol, four pounds of powder, eight pounds of lead, and twenty days' provisions." The start was actually made on May 16th — eighty-one traders, one hundred and fifty-six horses and mules, twenty-five wagons and a small piece of field artillery with which to scare the Indians. The wagons included one or two stout road vehicles, two carts, and Dearborn carriages.

In the group were Augustus Storrs, who next year went as American consul to Santa Fe, and M. M. Marmaduke, subsequently governor of Missouri. Both of these men wrote useful accounts of the Trail and of their experiences on it. They came and went uneventfully, as events were then counted in the western country. On the Big Blue they had to let their wagons down by ropes. On the *Jornada,* that fearful stretch of desert between the Arkansas and the Cimarron, they were without water from four in the morning until four in the afternoon. One of their dogs lay down and died of thirst. The men were not much better off. " I never in my life," Marmaduke confesses, " experienced a time when such general alarm and consternation pervaded every person on account of want of water." But finally they came upon a little ravine, in the bottom of which was a blessed trickle. And on July 28th, seventy-three days after leaving Franklin, they came over the last hill and saw the roofs and heard the bells of Santa Fe.

They did not dally long amid the delights of the little capital, for on the 24th of September they were back in Franklin. With them they carried $180,000 in gold and silver, and $10,000 in furs — a tidy profit on an investment of between $30,000 and $35,000. A few, impatient at the slow sales in Santa Fe, had gone south and hawked their wares in El Paso, Chihuahua, Sonora, and even Durango, sixteen hundred miles from Santa Fe. Their journeys were comparable with those of Ulysses, though they navigated land instead of sea. They were men of the utmost enterprise and hardihood, fearing neither God nor man, nor devil, nor an unfriendly Nature. The details of their journeys are often bare — so many men, so many wagons, so many mules, so many silver dollars. But through the naked narratives throbs a great, exultant energy.

Braxton Cooper, whom we met on the plains with his Uncle Benjamin in the spring of 1822, was another one of those who made the Santa Fe venture in 1824. But he waited until November, and about all we know of his adventures is that two of his men were killed, one by the Osages and one by the Comanches, and that he probably did not return to Missouri until the spring of 1825. A little later in that same year another event of some importance occurred. Twenty-six New Mexicans came to Council Bluffs, conferred with Major O'Fallon, the United States Indian agent, and made a treaty with the Pawnee chiefs stipulating that the Pawnees should not molest caravans. The significant feature of this incident was not the treaty, which the Pawnees broke, but the fact that the government of New Mexico was for the first time in history actually encouraging trade between the Rio Grande and the Missouri. The New Mexicans were soon to discover that they were as good at desert freighting as the Americans. They should have been, for they had been doing it for two and a half centuries. They were to gain for themselves some of the profit from the great carrying trade across the plains and add not a little to the life and gaiety of the caravans.

With 1825 we come to the end of what may be called the period of trail-making, for that year saw the first (and only) government survey of the route. After 1825 there was a recognized " trace " to Santa Fe, though occasional parties could and did succeed in getting lost. From this time on it would be tiresome to give the incidents of every trip — though it is well to remember that for years to come, indeed almost until the coming of the railroads, every trip had its elements of danger and adventure. In 1825 between $65,000 and $75,000 worth of goods were taken out; there were, according to Gregg, ninety proprietors, and altogether one hundred and thirty men made the trip. There must, therefore, have been forty men who worked for wages alone. As time goes on the number of proprietors in proportion to the number of employees will steadily diminish until in 1843 only one man out of every eleven will be a trader in his own right. Most men will then embark for Santa Fe, like sailors for the China ports, not in the hope of fabulous gain but because they are wanderers, because they cannot help themselves but must fly like moths toward the western sun.

CHAPTER VII

BENTON'S "ROAD"

NOW, as the third decade of the century goes by, the prairie mists begin to lift from the Trail. Starting from the Missouri river and following the hoof-prints and wagon ruts of the many who have travelled these plains and deserts and mountains before us, we need not lose ourselves. We may lose our horses and be left afoot in the wilderness, we may die of thirst, we may lose our scalps — but that is another story. Let us see how the Trail was marked and what it was like a little more than a century ago.

We have seen that William Becknell is plainly entitled to be called the Trail's father, but to be strictly fair we must give that famous westerner, Senator Thomas Hart Benton, credit for playing the important rôle of consulting physician both before and after the happy event. As editor, in his youth, of the St. Louis *Inquirer*, Benton had ardently advocated the opening of trade with Mexico across the plains. As a Senator, after the opening of the Mexican frontiers in 1821, he pushed the project with renewed enthusiasm. The time was ripe. Western Missouri was fast being settled. The former territory had become a state in the very year of Becknell's first journey. The same year had seen steamboats wriggling upstream over the snags and sand-bars of the Missouri. The frontier counties were full of active and ambitious men, who could no more stand still on the

verge of the prairies than water could pause at the brink
of Niagara. As for Benton, the spokesman for these
restless frontiersmen, he had, as always, his dream of a
United States extending to the Pacific — preposterous
though such a dream was. In the summer of 1824,
therefore, we find him taking up the Santa Fe trade with
characteristic enthusiasm. Governor Alexander Mc-
Nair of Missouri had sent a petition to Washington in
April, asking Congress to encourage and protect the
newly born " commerce of the Prairies." Benton went
west to get first-hand information and interviewed many
of the traders. Among them was Augustus Storrs, who
drew up, at Benton's request, a statement concerning
the " origin, present state, and future prospects of trade
and intercourse between Missouri and the Internal
Provinces of Mexico."

Storrs wrote with a loving hand. First he describes
the route which his party followed. " From the western
limit of Missouri, near Fort Osage [Sibley, Missouri],"
he explains, " our course to the Arkansas River was
west-southwest; thence up the river considerably north
of west 240 miles; then 40 miles due south to the Semarone [Cimarron] river; thence up the Semarone nearly
a due west course 100 miles; thence southwest to Taos."
He goes on encouragingly. " The face of the country,
through which the route passes, is open, level, and free
to the base of the Rocky Mountains." There were many
little watercourses to be crossed, but all one had to do
was to " dig the banks down with spades and hoes and
in some instances to cover the bottom with saplings and
brush." He lifted his eyes, as all but the most coarse-
grained travellers had to do, to the loveliness of the
plains. " The prairie here, in the month of May, is
adorned with a great variety of flowers, and probably

presents some of the most distant and beautiful views on earth." So lushly did the grass grow, and this Storrs notes with delight, that when he returned at the end of the summer the tops were in places as high as the head of a man on horseback.

Now and again he strikes out a phrase that makes us see with his own eager eyes. He speaks of the first sight of the sand belt in the valley of the Arkansas, a strip then seven miles wide and hard to travel through, as resembling " a dim flame of fire, fifteen or twenty feet in height." Always he is an optimist. The passage of the Arkansas he had not found difficult. It was true that the bottom was often full of quicksand, but a wagon could be gotten across if plenty of horses or mules were attached and it was driven smartly. He speaks of crossing " a high and perfectly level plain to the Semarone," but makes no particular point of danger from lack of water. Yet, as the diary of his companion, Marmaduke, shows, his expedition had twelve bad hours on this plain, the terrible *Jornada*. He constantly emphasizes the ease and practicability of the journey. " Thus far," he declares, as he stands at the foot of the snow-crowned Sangre de Cristo range, " there is not a single hill of consequence, or which presents difficulties to the progress of a wagon."

He speaks with justified enthusiasm of the game along the road. " There is probably no equal extent of wilderness in the world so well supplied. Deer are scarce, but buffalo, elk, and antelopes are abundant." " The common tall grass of Missouri," he was one of the first to note, did not extend beyond the Arkansas. But past that point there grew the shorter, tougher buffalo grass, rich brown in July, as richly green after the rains of August. On the strength of the facts he had set forth he

recommended that a road be surveyed from Fort Osage
to the Arkansas River, the line to be marked by mounds.
The Arkansas River was of course chosen because its
southern bank was then the boundary between the
United States and the young Republic of Mexico.
There was need also, he pointed out, for treaties with
the nine tribes of Indians through whose hunting
grounds the Trail passed.   Even as Storrs pictured it
the road to Santa Fe was no boulevard for weaklings.
But the men of the west trod it unafraid.   To them
Storrs pays a tribute that might well be carved upon a
monument: " Danger, privation, heat, and cold are
equally ineffectual in checking their career of enterprise
and adventure."

Benton went back to Washington to propose a bill for
government improvement of the route to New Mexico.
He called it a " road " and in after years seemed to think
that he more than any other man was responsible for its
being " built."   As a matter of fact, it was never a road
that any highway engineer would care to put his name
to, nor did anyone build any considerable portion of it.
Like Topsy, it just growed.   But Benton went into the
subject with all the fine warmth of his nature.   " The
road which is contemplated," he declared, " will trespass
upon the soil or infringe upon the jurisdiction of no
state whatever.   It runs a course and a distance to avoid
all that; for it begins upon the outside line of the outside State and runs directly toward the setting sun, far
away from all the States."

The Little Americans of the day asked whether the
United States had a right to make roads upon the territory of another nation, as it would have to do if the road
went beyond the Arkansas.   But no such right was in
question.   The road was to go to the Arkansas.   Beyond

that point, with the approval of the Mexican government, the surveyors would set up markers. The bill
passed both houses after some debate but by a good
majority, and was signed by President Monroe two days
before Inauguration Day, 1825. It carried the modest
appropriation of $30,000. Only $10,000 of this was to be
used to mark the Trail. The rest was to be spent in buying rights of way from the Indians. President Adams,
on taking office, promptly appointed a commission of
three to superintend the work — Benjamin Reeves,
formerly state auditor and lieutenant-governor of Missouri; George C. Sibley, a fur trader of high standing
and large experience; and Pierre Menard, another fur
trader and first lieutenant-governor of Illinois. Menard
could not serve, and his place was taken by Thomas
Mather. Joseph C. Brown was appointed surveyor.

The expedition left Franklin on July 4, 1825, amidst
the shouting and shooting appropriate to that day in a
frontier community, and a week later began running
its first lines at Fort Osage. The surveyors worked fast.
Exactly two months later they had reached the Arkansas. Here they waited for a time while permission was
sought from the Mexican government to continue on
the other side of the river. This was obtained after some
delay, and it was not until the next year that the survey
was carried into Taos. Meanwhile, the commissioners
had made a treaty with the Osage chiefs, on August 10,
1825, at a spot one hundred and forty-five miles west
of Independence. From this meeting lovely Council
Grove, later a very famous point on the Trail, took its
name. Six days later the commissioners smoked the
pipe of peace with the Kansas chiefs at McPherson.
Each tribe was to receive the princely sum of $800 in
cash and merchandise, in return for which it was to al

low the traders peaceable passage through its domains. These agreements were, on the whole, adhered to. But with the far more dangerous Pawnees and Comanches the commissioners did not consider themselves empowered to deal. The Pawnees, though they hunted and raided across the Trail, had no title to lands upon it. The Comanches had their habitat on Mexican soil. So the great troublers of traffic went unpropitiated — an omission which was to have evil consequences.

In this same year, 1825, President Adams appointed Augustus Storrs to be consul at Santa Fe and Joshua Pilcher at Chihuahua. Storrs accepted; Pilcher declined. These were moves to encourage the new western trade — though an ironically poor best when set beside the great destinies that were at stake. As for Surveyor Brown's conscientious labors they had curiously few results. No road was as much as scratched across the plains. The mounds were soon demolished or blew away. Brown's notes, which were copious, would have been invaluable to all newcomers on the Trail for many years. They might have saved more than a few lives. But some thrifty official saved a few hundred dollars instead, by sticking them away in a pigeon-hole, where they remained unpublished and unread until they had no longer anything but a historical value.

But though Brown's report guided no one in his lifetime it may guide us now in a swift preliminary exploration of our route. The Trail had, as we shall see presently, several successive starting points. In Johnson County, Kansas, nearly all the resulting branches joined. Yet the main Trail, though it was definite enough, was never so exact as it would have had to be in a country with fences. It might shift a considerable distance to one side or the other according to the wetness

or dryness of the season or the friendliness or unfriendli-
ness of the Indians. Ingenious travellers, or very foolish
travellers, were continually experimenting with cut-offs,
sometimes successfully, sometimes not. The Trail had
never the rigidity of a railroad or a modern automobile
highway. It was a living thing, which changed and
wandered and grew. It was not names upon a map —
it was people; people travelling, singing, swearing,
sweating, fearing, fighting, going in clouds of dust by
day, plowing through quicksand and mud, sitting around
great fires at night, hunters, trappers, traders, soldiers,
emigrants, of all degrees of intelligence, virtue, and vice,
of most races, bound together only by a common hardihood and a common exposure to the vastness and desolation and beauty of the trans-Missouri wilderness. It
is a fabulous procession. When we point to a signpost
and read the faded inscription we see letters that burned
into men's memories like unquenchable flame.

At various times in the Trail's history we might have
set out on our journey from Franklin, Fort Osage, Independence, Westport, or Fort Leavenworth. Let us
assume that we have set out from Independence. Forty-
one miles out we shall come to the site of Gardner, where
the Oregon Trail branches off. We shall enter what is
now Douglas County near Black Jack and pass through
Palmyra — "Old Palmyra," now part of the modern
town of Baldwin, once a favorite spot for camping and
repairing wagons — and Willow Springs. In Osage
County we shall pass Flag Spring, Overbrook, 110-Mile
Creek, and at Burlingame we shall cross Switzler's or
Bridge Creek. In Lyon County we shall pass near the
sites of Waushara and Agnes City. In Morris County
we shall cross Rock Creek and make our first important
halt at Council Grove. Here ends the hardwood belt.

From this point until the Rocky Mountains are reached there will be nothing but cottonwood, which grows only in the river bottoms and is not much good for cooking and no good at all for repairing wagons. Its inner bark can be fed to stock in a pinch and on desperate occasions it has been eaten by human beings, but there its practical uses end.

Of Council Grove we shall hear much more, but now we must push on, near Helmick, near Wilsey, to the famous Diamond Springs, about four miles from the future village of that name. Diamond Springs, " Diamond of the Plains," was so named by " Old Ben " Jones of the Brown surveying party — " Old Ben," dead these hundred years, yet coming suddenly alive and genial into the circle of our campfire.

From Diamond Springs our oxen strain, our mules sweat, along a line running north of Burdick, near Herington, near Lost Springs, Ramona, and Tampa, all three in the future Marion County; we come to the damnable ford of the Cottonwood at Durham, with the teamsters swearing like mad as we slide down one bank and fight our way up the other; now we are in the cottonwood country, and much good may it do us. In McPherson County we cross Turkey Creek and go south of McPherson; we go through the center of Rice County, passing a little south of Lyons and crossing Cow Creek; we pass Ellinwood and Fort Zarah and come close to the river near Great Bend in Barton County. Here begins the " short grass " region. About here, too, the waters of the Arkansas, alkaline lower down, become drinkable.

Now we turn southwest with the river to Pawnee Rock, also sometimes called Painted Rock and Rock Point — a famous landmark. If we are typical travellers we carve our names on it. Beyond Pawnee Rock we

have two branches to choose from to reach the site of
Dodge City. One follows the river closely, passing near
the sites of the towns of Garfield and Kinsley. The other
avoids the sand-hills, running as much as ten miles from
the river. Both have to cross Coon Creek.

Now, near the site of Dodge City, we have to make
our choice between the Cimarron route, and the mountain or Pike's Peak division of the Trail. For the present
we shall follow the Cimarron cut-off. But this does not
quite end our problem. There are three crossings of the
Cimarron desert — the old *Jornada*. The first or lowest
of these leaves the Arkansas at Mulberry Creek, west of
Dodge City. It is the driest of the three and the most
dangerous. The so-called Middle Crossing is near the
site of Cimarron. It is the shortest route from the Arkansas to Santa Fe and the one generally followed for
many years after 1830. It is not, however, the one suggested by Surveyor Brown. Brown first examined the
Lower Crossing, at Mulberry Creek, found it " incom-
modious of water and timber for fuel " and lacking in
" such prominent land marks as will be a sure guide,"
and therefore rejected it. He also rejected the Middle
Crossing, which at the time was often made from the
Caches, five miles west of the site of Dodge City. He
conceded that in the spring and early summer it might
be safe enough " to those who may be acquainted with
it or may have a compass to direct them," and that it
was about thirty miles shorter than the upper route.
But he held that " the upper route is more safe for herd-
ing stock and more commodious to the traveller, as he
will always be sure of wood and water on the river and a
sure guide, and in general it is easier to kill buffalo for
provision."

He therefore went on to the Upper Crossing, going

over the river about six miles above the site of Garden
City, "just below the bend, at the lower end of a small
island with a few trees." Here the banks were low
enough to permit the wagons to get down easily. "The
river here," he commented, "is very shallow, not more
than knee deep in a low stage of the water. The bed of
the river is altogether sandy, and it is unsafe to stand
long on one place with a waggon [sic], or it may sink
into the sand. After passing a few wet places just beyond the river the road is again very good up to Chouteau's Island. Keep out from the river or there will be
sand to pass. At Chouteau's Island the road leaves the
river altogether."

This Upper Crossing was near the present town of
Hartland, Kearny County. We shall not follow it on
our present trip, but we can get a good idea of what
prairie travel in the Far West is like if we read some of
Mr. Brown's careful directions. "On Cow Creek or
Cold Water," he says, "short grass commences and the
short grass bounds the burnings of the prairie." He refers, of course, to the annual burning of the tall grass by
the Indians, or perhaps sometimes by fires set by lightning. He goes on: "This creek is almost as nigh home
as buffalo are found, and from this creek they may be had
at almost any place until within sight of the mountains
near Santa Fe. Before leaving the river, where fuel is
plenty, the traveller will do well to prepare food for
the next hundred miles, as he will find no timber on the
road in that distance, except at one place, which will
probably be one of his stages; at least he should prepare
bread. In dry weather buffalo dung will make tolerable
fuel to boil a kettle, but it is not good for bread baking,
and that is the only fuel he will have. After leaving the
river the road leads southward, leaving the two cotton-

wood trees on the right, which stand perhaps a mile from the river."

If a traveller followed Brown's directions he could hardly go wrong. But since the Brown report was not published no one had in his generation a chance to follow them, and since the Upper Crossing was soon superseded by the Middle Crossing, which Brown condemned, they might in any case have been superfluous at this point on the Trail. The fact was that even on a journey of nearly eight hundred miles the frontiersmen and freighters were unwilling to purchase additional safety by going an extra thirty miles. Thirty miles meant the loss of between a day and a half and two days. The caravan drivers had the same irresistible impulse to save time that makes a modern New Yorker break across the street while the traffic lights are against him. So Brown's excellent advice was bound to have gone unheeded. It would have been forgotten even before the winds and rains had obliterated his mounds. And nine years after his survey an incident occurred which made the Middle Crossing a little less dangerous. The year 1834 was unusually rainy, even in the desert, and wagons crossing the Cimarron wilderness made ruts which hardened during the next dry season and became permanent. After that no one needed to get lost on the *Jornada*.

The mountain route avoided the *Jornada* altogether. The traveller went up the Arkansas to Bent's Fort, on the north bank of the river, below the site of La Junta and some fourteen miles above the mouth of the " Picketwire." This fort was built in the years 1832-33 by the three Bent brothers, Charles, William, and George, and the two St. Vrains, Ceran and Marcellin. From Bent's Fort the mountain division followed Timpas Creek southward over the ragged heights of Raton Pass.

After getting over the pass the traveller could either
continue along the base of the mountains to Santa Fe,
or, on reaching a point opposite Taos, cross the range
to that place. Surveyor Brown's route to Taos followed
the road to Santa Fe up the Cimarron and as far as the
Canadian River. Then it turned west over two ranges
to the high and lovely plateau on which Taos lies. The
first of these ranges furnished " the worst part of the
road." The second, and main dividing ridge, was not so
hard to cross. Brown selected Taos rather than Santa
Fe because, as he said, it was " the nearest of the Mexican settlements, the most northern and the most abundant in provisions for man and beast." But though he
did not carry his survey into Santa Fe he did give some
directions, " not from observation but from information," for getting there by way of San Miguel. Let us
assume that we have safely made our way across the
Jornada, drunk our fill from the pools which we have
scooped out in the wet sand of the Cimarron, followed up
the Cimarron and crossed to the near-by Canadian.
Brown tells us what to do next.

We are to turn nearly south after crossing the Canadian. Then (substituting the first person plural for
Brown's third person singular) " after going a few miles
we will reach a bold running stream. We will cross it at
a fall or rapid, as below we cannot for its rocky cliffs and
above we cannot on account of mud and quicksand.
After crossing this creek we will continue forward in the
same direction, and, where convenient, will ascend the
high table-land which extends all along on the right, and
will proceed forward just by the east end of a small
mountain shaped like a shoe, with the toe to the
west. . . It may be a day's travel or more from the crossing of the Canadian. After passing it a longer mountain

will be sighted, leaving it on the left. This, too, is in sight as soon as the other, which is called the Pilot. After passing the long mountain on the left the directions are general. The mountain will be a guide on the right; some small isolated ones on the left. The road is level and generally good. Several small creeks will be crossed, and the road, bearing a little west of south, will lead to San Miguel, which is about forty-five miles southeast from Santa Fe, to which the road is plain."

At or near the site of Ulysses, in Grant County, Kansas, we will perhaps have seen the marks of the trails from the Upper and Lower Crossings joining with our own. In Cimarron County, Oklahoma, as the Trail developed, there were two routes, which reunited at Taylor's Springs on the Canadian. At Las Vegas, eighty-one miles from Santa Fe and six hundred and ninety-nine from Independence (by Gregg's measurements) all spurs and branches of the Trail came together. There, after our long and weary journey, we have our first taste of Mexican hospitality. Here are brown children, tumbling out of the adobe houses to stare at us, and becoming frightened running to hide behind their mothers' skirts; here are Mexican girls with more than half an eye for the *Americanos;* and here are sleepy, lounging Mexican men, half-resentful, half-friendly. The *posada* opens willing doors, we may drink the Mexican wines and cool ourselves in the shade. We can relax, for the dangers and hardships of our journey are over. We still have to swing some distance to the south, climb Glorieta Pass, a mile and a half above the sea, then, from the site of the future hamlet of Canyoncito, follow a rough path twelve miles more over the hills to Santa Fe, our journey's end. But we have no more misgivings now. We are through with perils for the time being. A little more and we shall see the flat roofs and the church towers, and the ancient capital will be at our feet.

Such was the skeleton of our Trail. We shall have need to traverse it many times before we are through, and in the end perhaps it will take on flesh and blood, and we shall smell it, hear it, taste it and feel it as though our feet had gone where now none but the ghosts of the valiant dead can pass.

We may pause for a moment to glimpse a picture of the Trail, as actually travelled between 1831 and 1844, from Gregg's table, in which the first column gives the camping places or springs, the second column the intervening distances, and the third the total distances, measured from Independence:

	MILES	MILES
Independence	0	
Round Grove	35	
Narrows	30	65
110-Mile Creek	30	95
Bridge Creek	8	103
Big John Spring	40	143
Council Grove	2	145
Diamond Spring	15	160
Lost Spring	15	175
Cottonwood Creek	12	187
Turkey Creek	25	212
Little Arkansas	17	229
Cow Creek	20	249
Arkansas River	16	265
Walnut Creek (up Arkansas)	8	273
Ash Creek	19	292
Pawnee Fork	6	298
Coon Creek	33	331

	MILES	MILES
Caches	36	367
Ford of the Arkansas	20	387
Sand Creek (leave Arkansas River)	50	437
Cimarron River	8	445
Middle Spring of the Cimarron	36	481
Willow Bar	26	507
Upper Spring	18	525
Cold Spring (Leave Cimarron River)	5	530
McNee's Creek	25	555
Rabbit Ear Creek	20	575
Round Mound	8	583
Rock Creek	8	591
Point of Rocks	19	610
Rio Colorado	20	630
Ocate	6	636
Santa Clara Spur	21	657
Rio Mora	22	679
Rio Gallinas (Las Vegas)	20	699
Ojo de Bernal	17	716
San Miguel	6	722
Pecos Village	23	755
Santa Fe	25	780

Let us now turn back for a little while to visit those places from which the adventurers on the Trail set forth — those riotous Anglo-Saxon frontier communities so strangely different from the ancient Mexican city at the Trail's end. For it was this difference, this passing through a wilderness from the front lines of one civilization to the outposts of another, that did most to give the Trail its glamour.

CHAPTER VIII

THE PRAIRIE PORTS

THE SANTA FE trade was on one side the offspring of the fur trade, and the fur trade at the
beginning of the second quarter of the nineteenth century centred in St. Louis. Hence St. Louis
was originally the starting point of the Trail. It was
from that city, or near by, that the first American explorers and trappers, as well as those Frenchmen who
made so desperate an effort to break into New Mexico,
naturally set out. The early years of the Trail were
years of strife and glory, with Americans and British
contending for the vanishing beaver and many a heroic
drama enacted in the vast arena formed by the great
plains and the Rocky Mountains. Not until men
stopped wearing beaver hats and the palmy days of the
fur trade passed did that enterprise cease to affect the
commerce with New Mexico. St. Louis merchants for
some time financed or outfitted the traders, just as for
some time the best wagons used in the trade came from
Pittsburgh. Why Pittsburgh? Because it was there
that the earlier westward migrations had outfitted, and
men were slow in losing the habit of looking upon it as
a jumping-off place.

But just as the expanding frontier overleapt Pittsburgh, so in time it left St. Louis, too, behind. The opening of river travel made the long haul to the frontier
obsolete. Until 1820 lively little Franklin, two hundred

and five miles up the river from St. Louis and eighty-seven miles below the mouth of the Kansas, had communicated with the metropolis only by means of saddle horses and pack animals. In that year a four-horse stage began to run between the two points. Next year the first commercial steamboat appeared. The trip could now be made for about $10.50 by either land or water, and freight could be handled for comparatively little cost. Franklin inevitably became what Gregg calls it, "the cradle of our trade." Established in 1817, it had immediately shown all the symptoms of becoming a boom town. Within a year it had one hundred and fifty houses, and lots which sold for $50 in 1817 were going at $600 in 1818. By 1819 the infant city had thirteen stores, four taverns, two billiard rooms, a post office, a jail, and a weekly newspaper — the first west of the Mississippi River outside of St. Louis. By 1820 flatboats from Franklin were going down the Missouri and Mississippi to New Orleans, and, as we have just seen, next year the steamboats came up. For a time it looked as though Franklin were to be the St. Louis of western Missouri, and perhaps were destined even to outstrip the mother city. It had its moment of high hope and dizzy prosperity.

"The town of Franklin, as also our own village," said the Fayette *Intelligencer,* on May 2, 1828, "presents to the eye of the beholder a busy, bustling, and commercial scene, in buying, selling, and packing goods, practising mules, etc., etc., all preparatory to the starting of the great spring caravan for Santa Fe. A great number of our fellow citizens are getting ready to start. . . They generally purchase their outfits from the merchants here at from twenty to thirty per cent advance on the Philadelphia prices, and make from forty to one hun-

dred per cent upon their purchases." It was at Franklin, it will be remembered, that Becknell's expedition of
1821 had its rendezvous. It was at Franklin, about
1825, that fifteen-year-old Kit Carson, apprenticed to a
saddler, first heard of the Far West from the lips of men
who knew it like a book; and it was from David Work-
man's shop in Franklin that he ran away, in September
1826, with a Santa Fe caravan. But Franklin, though
it pulsated with vigorous life for a few mad, hopeful
years, died young. The founders had made the unhappy
mistake of building on an alluvial bottom which the
whimsical Missouri began suddenly to undermine. It
was in 1828, the year when the Fayette *Intelligencer*
spoke so glowingly of its prospects, that the little town,
then numbering between 1500 and 1700 inhabitants, collapsed and slid into the water. The citizens who had
remained loyal to the old spot retreated two miles back
from the stream and built a town which they called New
Franklin, and later on the still existing village of Boon-
ville was established on the more stable opposite bank.
But no artificial respiration could save Old Franklin.
It had been hopelessly drowned. Steamboats could go
further up. Why walk or drive mules overland when a
steamboat could do the work more easily and cheaply?
So the echoes of the laughter in the taverns, of the shouting of the drivers, died away forever from the site. Only
the graveyard remained, with its tombstones grass-
grown and askew.

But though one town or a dozen towns might die the
frontier was youthful and alive. Independence, a few
miles below the future Kansas City, was established in
1827, the year before Franklin perished. Soon steamboats began to tie up at its wharves and before long it
was the leading outfitting place, not only for the Santa

Fe traders but for the Rocky Mountain fur traders and
Indian traders.   Later great numbers of the emigrants
who went over the Oregon Trail outfitted there. " Independence in those early days," says John C. McCoy, an
old settler of Jackson County, Missouri, quoted by
Ralph Emerson Twitchell, " was selected as a place of
arrival and departure and as an outfitting place for trappers and hunters of the mountains and western plains.
It was well worth while to witness the arrival of some of
the pack-trains.   Before entering they gave notice of
their arrival by the shooting of guns, so that when they
reached Owens and Aull's store a goodly number of
people were there to welcome them.   A greasy, dirty
set of men they were.   Water, surely, was a rare com-
modity with them.   They little cared for it except to
slake their thirst.   Their animals were loaded down
with heavy packs of buffalo robes and peltry.   Occasionally they had a small wagon which, after long usage, had
the felloes and spokes wrapped with rawhide to keep the
vehicle from falling to pieces.   So accustomed were they
to their work that it took them little time to unload their
burdens from the backs of the animals and store the
goods in the warehouse.   The trappers let the merchants
attend to the shipping.

" The arrival in Independence was always a joyous
ending of a hazardous trip, and when once safely over
it they were always ready for a jolly time, which they
had to their hearts' content.   They made the welkin
ring and filled the town with high carnival for many
days.   The mountain trade at length gave way to the
Mexican trade, this being on a much larger scale.   Pack
mules and donkeys were discarded, and wagons drawn
by mule and ox teams were substituted.   Such men as
David Waldo, Solomon Houck, William and Solomon

Sublette, Josiah Gregg, St. Vrain, Chaves, and others of like character were early adventurers and as the governor gave them permission to enter and trade with the people they ventured across the plains regardless of the dangers. Samuel C. Owens, it is said, was the first trader in Independence. He came to Missouri from Kentucky when he was a young man. He was the first clerk of the circuit court of Jackson County. John Aull, his business partner, had owned a store in Lexington, Missouri. Owens and James Aull lost their lives while with Doniphan's expedition in Mexico." Owens died in a battle; Aull was killed in a robbery of his store in Chihuahua. McCoy erred in naming Owens the first trader in Independence, but he was prominent there.

In its wilder moments Independence was no place for those who loved peace and quiet. Here, says Ruxton, writing in 1846, "the wild and dissipated mountaineers get rid of their last dollars in furious orgies, treating all comers to galore of drink, and pledging each other in horns of potent whiskey to successful hunts and ' heaps of beaver.' " Of course the glory of the fur trade was long past when this was written, but the traditions of the wild and reckless breed who carried it on were slow in dying.

Independence, like Franklin, suffered from the misbehavior of the river, though by no means so severely. In 1833, only six years after the town was founded, its steamboat landing was washed away, and it became necessary for pilots to go further upstream to find another and more permanent bank to tie to. This they did at Westport Landing. Some authorities give Isaac McCoy, a pioneer Baptist missionary, credit for the first actual settlement of the town of Westport, which lay at some distance back from the landing. The town site lay in the midst of a fertile prairie, and near by there were springs of good water and excellent camping grounds for parties en route for the west. Soon a Frenchman named Pierre Roi built a road down to the boat landing. The river craft used also to touch at Blue Mills and at Wayne City, six miles below Independence. But though Independence did not fade completely out of the picture Westport took a firm grip on destiny and grew. Its ultimate fate, which is a long way ahead of the present stage of our story, was to be first a rival of Kansas City, established in 1839, and finally, two decades after the last freight wagon had rolled and rumbled into Santa Fe, to be absorbed into the greater city and sink its picturesque identity in the prosaic title of the Fourth Ward. During the Civil War, as we shall see, Leavenworth, as a military post well out of reach of rebel raids and influences, was a vital branch terminus of the Trail. Heavy trains left with military supplies, but the fort can hardly be classed in importance, for us, with Franklin, Independence, or Westport.

To these jumping-off places came the fantastic population of the great frontier — Indians, gamblers, merchants in broadcloth and tall hats, tavern-keepers, French-Canadian voyageurs, river men, traders, trappers, soldiers, drivers, conversing in a mixture of three European languages and a score of dialects. The towns were like seaports or mining camps or the neighborhoods of barracks or cattle towns of the later days. Astute and unscrupulous trading went on side by side with wild revelry. Men spent their wages or their profits in a night and returned again to the Trail. Very few of the refinements of civilization had reached the frontier. These were growing, unsettled, raw and tumultuous communities. Nearly every man there, and some of the women, too, were playing against destiny for high stakes. The atmosphere was feverish and dynamic. The frontier towns were aggressive. They were the outposts of an attack. When we follow the caravans into Santa Fe presently we shall see how different was the aura of that little capital, how deeply plunged in peace it was. The traders made noise enough, but the desert peace was always audible behind the shouting and carousing.

Between the ports on the Missouri and the havens in arid New Mexico flowed that traffic which came to be known as the Santa Fe trade. We must consider the economics of this traffic, for had not the Trail been a source of profit only the pure romanticists, of whom there are never very many, would have traversed it. But while we are making ourselves a picture of sales, purchases, and profits let us bear in mind that this is not the whole picture. It was because the Trail offered a hazardous and exciting rather than a dull and certain way of earning a living that it drew to itself certain types of men, and these men lent to it their own gaiety, youth, and daring.

As far back as the time of La Lande's journey to Santa Fe in 1804, and probably even further back, it had been apparent that goods could be carried eight hundred miles from the Missouri River to New Mexico more cheaply than two thousand miles through Old Mexico from Vera Cruz. But the postponement of this geographically logical trade because of Spanish exclusiveness and jealousy was nevertheless a good thing. It brought industrial and commercial America nearer the Missouri River. It made the Americans so strong that the traders of Chihuahua and the south of Mexico could less than ever compete with them. On the contrary the Americans were able to invade Mexican territory and compete with the native merchants. The New Mexicans and some of the Old Mexicans were eager for Yankee notions. Their own countrymen, as has been seen earlier in these pages, had not always dealt too scrupulously with them. The Americans may not have been at heart more honest. But they were less given to killing the geese that laid their golden eggs.

"An idea prevails among the people there," said Captain Becknell, in speaking of his first trip to Santa Fe, "which certainly is a very just one, that the goods hitherto imported into their country were the remains of an old stock and sometimes damaged. A very great advance is obtained on goods and the trade is very profitable; money and mules are plenty, and they do not hesitate to pay the price demanded for an article if it suits their purpose or their fancy." The brave captain advised his fellow countrymen in the trade to "take goods of excellent quality and unfaded colors." Augustus Storrs, in his venture of 1824, carried "cotton goods, consisting of coarse and fine cambrics, calicoes, domestic shawls, handkerchiefs, steam-loom shirtings and cotton hose," and "a few woolen goods, consisting of super-blues, stroudings, pelisse cloths and shawls, crepes, bombazettes, some light articles of cutlery, silk shawls and looking glasses."

Articles of feminine luxury, such as silks and velvets, never lost their popularity in the trade. Hardware, with iron selling originally at a dollar a pound, naturally commanded fancy prices. The New Mexicans had literally no manufacturers, and attractive machine-made goods almost sold themselves. The bulk of the cargoes remained for a long time domestic cottons, although after the first decade a good deal of English cotton goods was also brought in. At first some of the traders also carried powder, knives, traps, blankets, and trinkets for trading with the Indians whom they always met along the way. Merchants in St. Louis, Franklin, Independence, and Westport used to make up goods " expressly for the Santa Fe market," as the newspaper advertisements expressed it.

As early as 1825 Senator Benton was able to say that the New Mexican trade " had grown up to be a new and regular branch of interior commerce, profitable to those engaged in it, valuable to the country from the articles it carried out and for the silver, furs, and mules it brought back, and well suited to the care and protection of our government." There was other testimony to the same effect. Said the Missouri *Intelligencer,* in February 1830: " The inland trade between the United States and Mexico is increasing rapidly. This is perhaps one of the most curious species of foreign intercourse which the ingenuity and enterprise of American traders ever originated. The extent of country which the caravans traverse, the long journeys they have to make, the rivers and morasses to cross, the prairies, the forests and all but African deserts to penetrate, require the most steel-formed constitutions and the most energetic minds. The accounts of these inland expeditions remind one of the caravans of the East. . . The dangers which both encounter — the caravan of the East and that of the West — are equally numerous and equally alarming. Men of high chivalric and somewhat romantic natures are requisite for both."

No balance can be struck between danger, hard labor, and deprivation on the one hand and chivalry and courage on the other. All we can be sure of is that the men of the Santa Fe Trail showed a profit in these intangibles as well as in the more substantial rewards which, under the strict economic interpretations of history, explain their comings and goings. The best, indeed the only, estimate of the quantitative growth of the trade between 1822 and 1843 is that of Gregg. Where his figures can be checked with other sources of information they are usually found accurate, and we may assume a fair degree of accuracy in all of them. Here is Gregg's table:

Year	Cost of Goods in the U. S.	Proprietors	Total Number in Party
1822	$15,000	60	70
1823	12,000	30	50
1824	35,000	80	100
1825	65,000	90	130
1826	90,000	70	100
1827	85,000	50	90
1828	150,000	80	200
1829	60,000	20	50
1830	120,000	60	140
1831	250,000	80	320
1832	140,000	40	150
1833	180,000	60	185
1834	150,000	50	160
1835	140,000	40	140
1836	130,000	35	135
1837	150,000	35	160
1838	90,000	20	100
1839	250,000	40	250
1840	50,000	5	60
1841	150,000	12	100
1842	160,000	15	120
1843	450,000	30	350

The second column of figures represents what was taken to Santa Fe. What came back, in a profitable year, was considerably more. Operations in some of the earlier years were a good deal like taking candy from a child. For the $35,000 worth of goods taken out in 1824, $190,000 in furs and specie was, as we have seen, brought back. In 1825 the traders did almost as well. From the gross profits large expenses naturally had to be deducted. A trader might charge the New Mexicans twice as much as would be paid at retail for the same goods in the United States, but his actual net profit might be from ten to forty per cent, or, if the market soured on him, he might have to take a loss. In 1830 the sixty proprietors are said to have spent $175,000 for all expenses and to have earned gross profits of $200,000, leaving only $25,000 to be divided among them.

We shall have to consider the quaint ways of the Mexican customs a little later. They added a good deal to the cost of doing business. During the years covered by Gregg's table the average total yearly tariff paid at Santa Fe by Americans was between $50,000 and $80,000. Sometimes the whole matter of tariffs degenerated into a game of wits, with the Mexican officials working for their own pockets as well as for their government, and the Americans doing their best to circumvent them. Thus, in 1839, when Governor Armijo imposed a special tax of $500 on each wagon, the Americans merely piled more goods on their wagons and brought bigger ones. Or they halted just outside the city, at the top of the last grade, burned or abandoned part of their wagons and loaded everything on those that remained. The traders may sometimes have been, as a St. Louis newspaper put it, " confessedly smugglers and bribers." If there was corruption — and there was — it is impossible to say who began it. But the traders soon made themselves a necessity, and though New Mexican officialdom was jealous and suspicious of them it could not do without them.

We have already made note of some of the goods which the returning caravans brought back, notably the Missouri mule. For the first fifteen years of the trade furs were important, and few caravans crossed the plains eastward bound without at least some packs of them. Beaver and otter skins sold at from $8 to $12 each, buffalo robes at about $3. Storrs brought back " Spanish milled dollars, a small amount of gold and silver in bullion, beaver furs and some mules." The mules and precious metals remained important. Some copper was carried out, and a little very poor tobacco. Sometimes sheep were driven across the plains, though the danger of loss en route was great. Mr. F. F. Stephens credits the Spanish silver with having done much to establish and strengthen the monetary system of Missouri. It began to come in at a time when sound money was so scarce as to be almost non-existent. In 1839 the Santa Fe traders are said to have saved the Bank of Missouri from a dangerous run by sending to its vaults some $45,000 in specie. Said Captain A. Harris, writing in 1840 to Representative Cross of Arkansas: " The State of Missouri is at this day the soundest in the Union in her monetary affairs. She is filled with specie; and the interior Mexican states have supplied it."

For many years the traders tried to have established on the Missouri River a port of entry, from which imported goods could be sent into New Mexico free of duty. This measure would have especially relieved the merchants who dealt in English cottons. In 1845 Independence was actually named as an entry port, but the outbreak of the Mexican War in the following year and the subsequent pushing back of the Mexican frontier made the action of little practical importance.

Modern Americans, accustomed to thinking of commerce in terms of millions and hundreds of millions of dollars, will not be unduly impressed by the statistical picture of the Santa Fe trade, either in the years at which we have already glanced or in the years to which we have still to come. The amounts involved were small, even for a generation whose ideas of fortune were far simpler than our own, and they were but little companies of valiant men who crossed deserts and mountains to earn them. But these men were carrying America to the Southwest, they were conquering an empire, they were evolving a western culture which knew few books, yet which was powerfully to affect their country's civilization. We may take off our hats to these gaunt brown figures, now growing so ghostlike against the western horizon.

In another chapter we shall look at life on the Trail as it developed during the quarter century between Becknell's first expedition and about the time of the Mexican War. Some of the conditions we shall encounter were present from the first. Others changed with the passage of time, notably — and disastrously — the relations between the white men and the Indians. The war itself, as it bore upon conditions in Santa Fe and along the Trail, will deserve special consideration later on. It will not always be possible to say precisely when a certain feature of Trail life appeared or disappeared. The traditions and technique of the trade developed slowly over a stretch of years. In some instances the changes were abrupt, but more often they were gradual. We cannot easily make a complete description which will be true of the Trail in every respect for a selected year. But we can arrive at a conception which is as true of the Santa Fe Trail during its early flowering as, for instance, are the accepted historical accounts of the age of chivalry.

We can see the pageant pass — Indians and buffalo, Mexicans, Frenchmen, and Yankees, wagons covered with Osnaburg sheeting, sometimes a trim-looking carriage, oddly out of place in the wilderness, rolling westward, rolling eastward, in clouds of dust, through seas of mud, plunging across fords, struggling through the passes, a great procession linking every year more closely the land of the Anglo-Saxon with the land of the Spaniard, until at last the prairie, the desert, and the quiet, dreamy towns along the Rio Grande are all American, and the rest a story that is told.

CHAPTER IX

THE RED BROTHER

THE TRADERS going to Santa Fe faced a number of elemental dangers — the danger of hunger and thirst; the danger from flooded rivers and quicksands; the peril of winter storms if they travelled late in the season, and the ordinary risks in hunting, especially among herds of buffalo. But the deadliest of their perils was that of Indian attacks, less in some years than in others, yet never wholly absent, particularly from the country beyond the Arkansas, so long as the Trail existed. Indeed, the Indians grew more and more menacing. In the days of the fur trade the white man was a customer who bought their furs, a storekeeper who sold them powder, whiskey, and blankets, sometimes an associate who hunted and trapped with them and married their women. It was to the trapper's interest that the Indians should keep to their old modes of life and be protected in their old hunting grounds. He did not want their land. He was willing enough that everything west of the Missouri should forever remain what Jacob Fowler called The Inden Cuntry. He knew that there was always a chance of his being robbed by the Pawnees or scalped by the Comanches, or despoiled and murdered by any one of a dozen other tribes, but these were the chances traders took.

As the Trail developed and as population began to dam up behind the great bend of the Missouri, two things happened. First the Indians began to realize that their hunting grounds were in danger of being overrun by white men as those of the eastern tribes had been long before. Second the Santa Fe trade produced a regularity, both as to season and as to route, in the white man's journeys across the plains. Before the Trail became a live thing the Indians *might* come upon parties of trappers or traders and rob them, as they did the James party. But after the route was definitely established they could be *sure* to intercept richly laden caravans if they lay in wait long enough at the strategic points.

By an unhappy coincidence one of these strategic points was in the desolate stretches of the *Jornada,* which Nature had done her best to make formidable. "Keep your eyes skinned," said an old trapper to Wetmore, as they headed south after crossing the Arkansas in 1828. "We are now entering upon the most dangerous section of the Trace." There had been trouble with the Indians along the Trail in 1826, when a band of Arapahoes surrounded twelve men encamped on the Cimarron and drove off five hundred of their horses, mules, and burros. But in 1828, the year of Wetmore's journey, came grim tragedy — the first of its sort reported among the caravans. A party including two young men, Daniel Munroe and a son of Samuel G. McNees of Franklin, whose first name seems not to have been remembered, was returning from Santa Fe. They had gone as far as a little tributary of the Canadian, about twenty-five miles southwest of the Cimarron, and near mile-post 555 in Gregg's itinerary. Here Munroe and McNees, becoming separated from the others and fearing no danger, lay down and slept. The Indians stole upon them, shot them with their own guns, and escaped.

The sound of the firing brought the other members of the party to the spot. But they were too late. The Indians had vanished, McNees was already dead and Munroe was gasping from a mortal wound. McNees was buried where he had fallen and the near-by stream was for a long time known as McNees' Creek. Munroe was carried forty miles along the homeward journey, when he too died and was buried beside the Trail. But this was not the end of the story. In fact, this was one of those stories that never had an end as long as the Indians roamed at large in country which the white man wanted. Gregg tells us what happened next.

"Just as the funeral ceremonies were about to be concluded," he says, "six or seven Indians appeared on the opposite side of the Cimarron. Some of the party proposed inviting them to a parley, while the rest, burning for revenge, evinced a desire to fire upon them at once. It is more than probable, however, that the Indians were not only innocent but ignorant of the outrage that had been committed, or they would hardly have ventured to approach the caravan. Being of quick perception they very soon saw the belligerent attitude assumed by some of the company, and therefore wheeled around and attempted to escape. One shot was fired, which wounded a horse and brought the Indian to the ground, when he was instantly riddled with balls. Almost simultaneously another discharge of several guns followed, by which all the rest were either killed or wounded, except one, who escaped to bear his tribe the news of their dreadful catastrophe.

"These wanton cruelties had a most disastrous effect upon the prospects of the trade; for the exasperated children of the desert became more and more hostile to the pale-faces, against whom they continued to wage a cruel war for many successive years. In fact, this same party suffered very severely a few days afterwards. They were pursued by the enraged comrades of the slain savages on the Arkansas river, where they were robbed of nearly a thousand head of mules and horses. But the Indians were not yet satisfied. Having beset a company of about twenty men, who followed shortly after, they killed one of their number and subsequently took from them all the animals they had in their possession. The unfortunate band were now not only compelled to advance on foot, but were even constrained to carry nearly a thousand dollars each upon their backs to the Arkansas River, where it was cached . . . till a conveyance was found to convey it to the United States."

This second incident also occurred in the Comanche country, and not far from McNees' Creek, at the Upper Springs of the Cimarron. A party of twenty-five, according to some accounts, with five wagons, one hundred and fifty mules and some specie, were coming back from Santa Fe. They were surrounded by the Indians, who ordered them to halt for the night. Since this would have been to put themselves wholly in the power of the savages they kept on their way. At the rear, behind the wagons, rode Captain John Means and two other men. They had to ride coolly, not too fast, with their backs toward the Indians — a feat requiring consummate courage. Any other attitude was sure to invite instant attack. But the Indians fired upon them just the same. Means was shot off his horse and scalped before he had drawn his last breath. The other two, Ellison and Bryant, clapped spurs to their beasts and got away. The Indians, in hot pursuit, charged in upon the main party, followed them for a considerable distance and seriously wounded one other man. The situation was now desperate. The traders decided to abandon their wagons, hide part of their specie, and slip away under cover of darkness. The Indians, listening for the creak of wagon wheels, heard nothing. All night the fugitives travelled across the ghostly desert, and all the following day. On the second night they reached the Arkansas, cached the rest of their burden of silver, and went on toward the settlements, on foot. The remainder of the journey was one of those terrible prairie nightmares that befell men turned loose without horses, sufficient food or means to kill game. At Walnut Creek, three hundred miles from Independence, five of the stronger members pushed on ahead and reached the settlements. A rescue party found the other survivors nearly at the point of death from hunger and fatigue.

News of these events caused a furor in the Missouri settlements and an insistent demand was made that the federal government send troops to protect the caravans. Accordingly, in the spring of 1829, shortly after Andrew Jackson became president, Major Bennet Riley was ordered to take four companies of the Sixth Infantry and accompany the traders as far as the international boundary. It is said that Riley was the first to employ oxen on the Trail. He was probably also the first to use Fort Leavenworth, established in 1827, as a starting point. Unfortunately, Riley's men, being on foot, were in no position to catch mounted Indians. But this folly of sending infantry on such an errand was unavoidable. The United States army had no cavalry in 1829, nor did it have any until 1833, when the first regiment of dragoons was mustered into service. Riley's usefulness was further limited by the fact that he was ordered to halt at Chouteau's Island, where the Trail crossed into

Mexican territory and where the most dangerous portion of the journey began.

All went well until this point was reached, the troops went into camp, and the traders continued across the sand-hills on the Mexican side. Three men rode ahead of the caravan, supposedly keeping a sharp lookout for Indians. One of them, a Mr. Lamme, was " the largest capitalist and owner of the company." The three had gone six or seven miles from the river and were considerably in advance of the caravan when they dismounted at a spring and stooped to drink — a wantonly reckless thing to do under the circumstances. The war cry of the Kiowas suddenly shattered the desert stillness and the Indians swooped from behind the sand-hills. All three of the white men managed to mount and ride for their lives. Lamme, unhappily, was mounted on a slow-going mule which not even an Indian attack could spur to great activity. He was overtaken, shot out of his saddle, and scalped. His companions succeeded in regaining the main body of the caravan, where they were safe for the time being. But the situation was unpromising. All around them were low sand-hills and in the sand-hills were the Kiowas.

The attack had occurred late in the afternoon. Toward dusk a messenger slipped out of camp and succeeded in making his way to Riley's camp. Riley did not pause to unravel red tape, but broke camp and marched with all speed to the rescue. Perhaps this was the first time that an armed American force of such a size had entered Mexican territory. Plodding through the soft sand in the darkness, with orders given in low voices, and the jingle of accoutrements silenced as much as possible, the troops succeeded in reaching the beleaguered traders about one o'clock at night. The In-

dians were expected to attack at dawn, as was their custom. Unfortunately a stupid American bugler sounded
the reveille in the darkness of early morning, and the
surprise party which had been planned for the Kiowas
did not come off. Riley marched with the caravan to
Sand Creek, forty miles further on, and then, seeing no
more Indian signs, returned to his camp on the Arkansas. The traders went on to Santa Fe without further
trouble.

The summer passed. The Kiowas remained in the
vicinity of Riley's encampment, never giving him an opportunity for a pitched battle, but running off his stock
and sniping at his outposts. October came and no caravan. Riley had already broken camp and was about to
set off for Fort Leavenworth when news reached him
that the traders were at last on the way, this time under
guard of a Mexican escort commanded by Colonel Antonio Vizcarra, a seasoned Indian fighter. On the way
they had had a little excitement. They had fallen in
with a large band of Arapahoes and Comanches, who had
approached them in friendly fashion and then, at least
so the traders said, had treacherously opened fire upon
them. The fire was instantly returned, and the Indians,
their ammunition soon exhausted, broke and ran. After them swarmed the furious traders. The pursuit
became a massacre. Some of the Indians, falling
wounded from their horses, were scalped alive, as Lamme
had been. Even the Mexican regulars, who were by no
means mollycoddles, are said to have been aghast at the
savage cruelty displayed by the Yankees on this occasion. According to General Philip St. George Cooke,
who was at this time a junior officer under Major Riley,
they " undoubtedly took the skin from some of the bodies
and stretched it on their wagons." With these grue-

some trophies they resumed their march, and the two
little armies, Mexican and American, met and frater-
nized at Chouteau's Island.

The spectacle was one of the most picturesque in the
long history of a colorful frontier. The island itself, as
Surveyor Brown said, was "the largest island of timber
in the river." Along the south side and on the lower
end was a "thicket of willows with some cottonwood
trees." The camp was probably on the edge of the woods,
in the open spaces, facing north and west. Here, with
punctilious courtesy, Major Riley played host to Colonel
Vizcarra and several of the Mexican officers, the guests
squatting on a green blanket. The menu was one to
make a prairie traveller's mouth water — bread, buffalo
meat, and, as a delicacy fit for kings, salt pork. To give
a guest salt pork on the Arkansas River was a compli-
ment as great as feeding him on nightingale's tongues in
Rome. To make the feast complete Viscarra had
brought a large raw onion, and the whole was topped off
with plenty of whiskey, served in tin cups. But the feast
which Vizcarra gave in return far outdid Riley's best. In
Vizcarra's commodious tent the sixteen officers present
sat around a table, glistening with silver, ate fried ham
and cakes and drank chocolate and Mexican wines.

"On this occasion," says Twitchell, "there were gathered upon the frontier in all probability the strangest
collection of men and animals ever assembled. There
were a few Creoles, polished gentlemen, magnificently
clothed in Spanish costume; a larger number of grave
Spaniards, exiled from Mexico, on their way to the
United States, with much property in stock and coin,
their entire equipage being Spanish; there was a company of Mexican regulars, as they were called, in uniform, hardly up to the standard as soldiers; several

tribes of Indians and Mexicans, much more formidable as warriors, who stood about in groups, along with their horses, each man armed with a lance and bow and arrows; there were many Frenchmen; added to these were the American command of about one hundred and eighty men, hardy veterans in rags, but well armed and equipped for any service; four or five languages were spoken, and to complete the picture was the *caballada* of more than two thousand horses, mules, and burros, which kept up an incessant braying. . . In the dusk of the evening a large group of the Mexican Indians came into camp, bearing aloft on their lances the scalps which had been lately taken, and all singing Indian songs; dark figures, with matted hair streaming over their shoulders, uttering the wild notes of their deep-toned choruses, they resembled demons rather than men. Suddenly an Indian would enter the circle and indulge in an extravagant display of grief, beating his forehead and breast and howling like a famished wolf; and then, dashing the scalps to the ground, would stamp upon them and fire his gun at them. After this propitiatory lament to the manes of a departed friend, or relative, he would burst forth, along with the others, into the wildest and most unearthly song of triumph and exaltation."

On October 14th the assembly broke up, Colonel Vizcarra leading his motley crew back toward Santa Fe, the friendly Indians and the trappers scattering to their hunting grounds, and Major Riley heading the march of the caravan toward the Missouri River. The traders got home safely and without further incidents. But though the soldiers had shown themselves eminently useful the sending of military escorts along the Trail never became a government policy. Only twice before

the Mexican War, once in 1834 and again in 1843, was
the experiment repeated. At least these are the only escorts of which the War Department records afford evidence.

In 1834 Captain Clifton Wharton was sent out with
his shiny new Company A of the First Dragoons. Wharton was ordered to conciliate the Indians if he could. He
left Fort Gibson on May 13th and had friendly talks
with both the Pawnees and the Comanches. But this
was not accomplished without difficulty. The traders
were imbued with the frontier conviction that the only
good Indian was an Indian with an ounce of lead
through some vital spot. They had with them a small
cannon, and it was all that Wharton could do to prevent
them firing on the chiefs who were coming to the parley.
Wharton went as far as the crossing of the Arkansas.
Perhaps his report had as much as anything to do with
the decision of the War Department not to send escorts
in the eight years that followed. In this document he
stated that he did not believe troops were needed between
Walnut Creek, 273 miles from Independence and the
Arkansas, 115 miles further on. He added that "past
experience shows that any organized regular attack is
not to be apprehended on the American side." This was
probably true at the time — that is, as long as the Indians of the central plains were friendly.

There is a curious detail in connection with the next
military escort, which was sent out in 1843. The traders, it is said, wanted the news of their movements kept
from "Bent and his people," for fear of "the nests of
semi-trappers and semi-brigands who harbor not very
far from Bent's establishment." This was probably no
reflection on the Bents, who stood high throughout the
West. Yet we do not hear of highway robberies along

the Trail during this period, except as an incident of the hostilities between Texas and Mexico. Perhaps the allusion quoted had something to do with the rumors of the activities of the three bands of Texans commanded by Colonel Warfield, Colonel Snively, and Captain McDonald who were loose along the Trail that summer. It may seem a little strange that organized brigandage, with no veil of pseudo-patriotic motives, did not begin sooner. But though the western wilderness was vast a highwayman would have found it hard to bring his plunder out to civilization, where alone it could be of much use to him, without being caught. All the trails converged and ran into what we should now call bottle-necks.

The escort of 1843 was commanded by the same Cooke, now a colonel of the Second Dragoons, who had been with Riley in 1829. He was a man of distinct individuality, as his diary shows. " Delightful, truly," he comments on this occasion, " to escort two hundred wagons with twelve owners, independently disposed and sharply interested in carrying out different views of emergencies — the failure of water, grass and fuel." This may hint at another reason why troops did not more often accompany the caravans. An army officer on such duty naturally wanted to command. And traders were loath to be commanded, except by officers of their own choosing. But Cooke did his duty, as diplomatically as he could, and that year there were no serious Indian troubles.

Such is the brief record of military protection on the Trail. There are references in some of the contemporary narratives which suggest that detachments on duty along the frontier did go with the caravans on a few other occasions. The Mexicans seem to have sent escorts more frequently than did the Americans, no doubt with the double purpose of protecting the traders from the Indians and preventing smuggling. But the traders soon learned that no one cared as much for their skins as they did themselves. Their occupation made them good shots and superb riders, they were fiercely self-reliant, and they knew the ways of the Indians. In effect they became soldiers in their own defence — better soldiers than the government could have enlisted and sent into the field.

The fatalities on the Trail up to the time of the Mexican War were not many in proportion to the number of men engaged in the trade. But they were dramatic, terrible, and long-remembered. After 1829 the next killing by the Indians was that of Jedediah Smith, one of the most noteworthy explorers and fur traders of his time. Smith had gone out with General Ashley's expedition to the Rocky Mountains in 1822; he had, as Edwin L. Sabin says of him, " been as far north as the present city of Spokane; he had carried beaver to the British and the Bible to the Flathead, and by his explorations of the country of the Snake and the Columbia, as transmitted to the war department, had supplemented the information previously supplied by the routes of Lewis and Clark and the Astorians; he had been as far south as San Diego, he had thrice crossed the Great Basin, and with Ewing Young had investigated California from the south to the extreme north." He is said to have been the first white man to cross the Sierras into California. In 1826, with David E. Jackson and William L. Sublette, both noted Westerners, he had bought out General Ashley's fur business, which in turn was resold four years later to the Rocky Mountain Fur Company. In 1831, still only thirty-three years old, with a boundless fund of energy, he turned his attention to the Santa Fe trade. The caravan with which he set out in the spring of that year was one of the best-equipped that had ever taken the sunset trails. Twenty fine new wagons bumped along the rough roads and eighty picked men guarded them.

But though Smith was probably as good a pathfinder as ever stood in moccasins his party, like several before it, ran into desperate trouble in the *Jornada*. This, it should be remembered, was before the rains of 1834 had melted the desert's surface into mud and enabled the wagons to carve a lasting highway across it. There was little trace to follow. For three days the traders wandered, hopelessly lost. Their animals began to die, and the men were not much better off. Then those who could be spared from attending to the wagon train scattered to look for water. Smith came upon a buffalo trail and followed it until at last he came to the valley of the Cimarron. The river bed was dry, as it often was, and he probably stooped to scoop out a hole in which the underground water might collect. One can imagine with what joy he bent his head to the muddy trickle and the wet sand. The party was saved!

The rest of the story has to be pieced together from the narrative of his companions, who followed his tracks and found his body, and from the account of the tragedy later given some Mexican traders by the Comanches who ambushed him. He was either lanced or shot as he rose to remount his horse after satisfying his thirst. Yet he held himself erect, jerked his pistols from their holsters and killed two of his assailants before he died. By the grim mathematics of the frontier he had made the Comanches pay twice over for their victory. So, with blood on his hands, died one of the gentlest of men and

one of the best friends the Indians ever had. "He was,"
says William Waldo, a fellow trader, "a bold, outspoken
and consistent Christian, the first and only one among
the early Rocky Mountain trappers and hunters. No
one who knew him well doubted the sincerity of his
piety. He had become a communicant of the Methodist
church before leaving his home in New York, and in
St. Louis he never failed to occupy a place in the church
of his choice, while he gave generously to all objects connected with the religion which he professed and loved.
Besides being an adventurer and a hero, a trader and a
Christian, he was himself inclined to literary pursuits
and had prepared a geography and atlas of the Rocky
Mountain region, extending perhaps to the Pacific, but
his death occurred before its publication." Though he
spent eight or nine years in the wilderness he did not
have an unmixed affection for the life men led there.
"Instead of finding a leather stocking," said a young
man who saw him in St. Louis in November 1830, " I
met a well-bred, intelligent and Christian gentleman,
who repressed my youthful ardor and fancied pleasures
for the life of a trapper and mountaineer by informing
me that if I went into the Rocky Mountains the chances
were much greater in favor of meeting death than of
finding restoration to health, and that if I escaped the
former and secured the latter, the probabilities were
that I would be ruined for anything else in life than
such things as would be agreeable to the passions of a
semi-savage." His was a fascinating career, and a rare
one. Had he lived he doubtless would have figured
largely in the later history of the Trail.

Two years after this, in March 1833, two hundred
Comanches surrounded a party of twelve who were on
their way from Santa Fe to Independence, near what

is now Taylor Springs on the Upper Canadian River. One man fell at the first volley. The others took cover. A second trader was killed as the Indians crept in from all sides. All day and all the following night the fight went on. At daybreak, the dreaded hour of the attack as practised in Indian warfare, the traders waited, their ammunition nearly exhausted, prepared to sell their lives at as high a price as they could. Unexpectedly an Indian called out to them from the waning darkness that they might now proceed. They took him at his word, broke camp in haste and went on unmolested. But many of them were wounded, their horses and mules had all been driven off, it was the dead of winter and they had little food and not much chance of getting more. But they were a tough breed. Three who became separated from the rest lost their way and starved to death somewhere near the canyon of the Canadian River, but the other seven survivors reached the border in safety.

The romantic type of western literature has left the impression that nearly all Indians encountered in the wilderness were hostile, and that the white man was commonly the innocent victim of their savagery. This is just as great an error as are some of the idealizations of James Fenimore Cooper. The Indians were not always the aggressors. Except for a few tribes like the Apaches, who had lived for generations by raiding their neighbors' camps and towns, the Indians were never the aggressors, for they fought as a rule only when the white men invaded their hunting grounds. When the white came solely as hunter and trapper, and in not too great numbers, he could be assimilated easily enough into the Indian scheme of life.

There were as wide variations among the tribes as

there are among modern European states. Close to or within the frontier were the civilized or semi-civilized nations, such as the Cherokees, Choctaws, Chickasaws, Creeks, Seminoles, Delawares, and Shawnees. The Kansas and Osage Indians, though given to stealing any little things they could lay hands on, were not dangerous to life after the treaty of 1825. Most annoying, perhaps, among the prairie tribes were the Pawnees, who were specialists in horse stealing but would kill if there were anything to gain by the act and not too much risk were involved. In 1828 the Pawnees spread the report that they had a war party of fifteen hundred men in the field, sworn to kill and scalp any traders they could lay hands on. But considering their numbers they did little damage that year.

The Grosventres of Saskatchewan, cousins of the Arapahoes and allies of the Blackfeet, are said to have made their debut on the Trail in 1831. The Cheyennes and the Sioux sometimes came down to the caravan track, though not always in a warlike mood. The Kiowas, who attacked the 1829 caravan, and were in alliance with the Comanches, we have already met. The Arapahoes were another menace. The Comanches — the "Arabs of the Plains" — were believed to be about 20,000 strong in the early days of the Trail, and, as events showed, were distinctly unfriendly and aggressive. The Utes, Navajos, and Apaches, all warlike tribes, were not finally subdued until long after the Mexican War, though they frequently made treaties with the whites.

Yet despite the swarms of savages perhaps no more than a few men were killed by Indians during the first decade after Becknell's journey. Very often the redmen were content to drive off horses, and though few caravans went through without an exchange of shots the damage to human life and limb was usually slight. Property losses, on the other hand, were often serious enough. In the bad year of 1828 they amounted to $40,000, or nearly one-fourth of the total amount of goods taken west from the Missouri River.

The wrongs done the Indians by the whites were probably quite as grave as those done the whites by the Indians. The Indians very naturally took the view that the western country, which they and their fathers had hunted over and dwelt in for uncounted generations, was their homeland, and that it was being ruthlessly invaded. Their methods of warfare were brutal, but except for the torturing of prisoners no more so than those to be witnessed on another western front in the civilized second decade of the twentieth century.

But questions of abstract right and wrong are academic when an industrialized race comes into contact with one which is still in the pastoral stage. The pioneers were not philosophers. The attitude they often took toward the Indians was very often like that expressed by a trail-hardened mountain man to Captain R. B. Marcy. Said he: "They are the most onsartainest varmints in all creation, and I reckon tha'r not mor'n half human; for you never seed a human, arter you'd fed and treated him to the best fixins in your lodge, jist turn round and steal all your horses, or ary other thing he could lay his hands on. No, not adzackly. He would kinder feel grateful and ask you to spread a blanket in his lodge ef you passed that-a-way. But the Injun don't care shucks for you, and is ready to do you a heap of mischief as soon as he quits your feed.

" No, Cap., it's not the right way to give um presents to buy peace; but ef I war governor of these yeer United

States I'll tell you what I'd do. I'd invite um all to a big feast and make b'lieve I wanted to have a big talk; and as soon as I got um all together I'd pitch in and sculp about half of um, and then t'other half would be mighty glad to make a peace that would stick. That's the way I'd make a treaty with the dog'ond varmints; and as sure as you're born, Cap., that's the only way. Tain't no use to talk honor with um, Cap.; they hain't got no such thing in um. They won't show fair fight and they kill and sculp a white man whan-ar they get the best on him, and ef you treat um decent they think you are afeard. No, Cap., the only way is to whip um and then the balance will sorter take to you and behave themselves."

There were treaties enough, first and last, but in the end it was the mountain man's brand of " statesman-ship " that prevailed. There were honorable individuals on both sides, but it was not in the nature of the situation that either white man or red man should long keep faith. The innocent suffered for the sins of the treacherous and the blood-thirsty. A special Indian commission which reported in 1868 estimated that in half a century the United States spent half a billion dollars and lost twenty thousand lives in Indian war. Most of this fighting took place west of the Missouri River and much of it in the regions traversed by the Santa Fe Trail. And this con-stant menace lent the Trail some of its darker romance and gave it some of its most hideous chapters.

Yet, in spite of all, the white men and the red man mingled their strains and to some degree their cultures. In time white men came to be proud of having Indian blood in their veins. White men borrowed from the In-dians the rich lore of the wilderness. Something of the Indian way of thinking probably crept into their minds, even without their knowing it, and went to make that characteristic attitude which we call western. The Southwest was a melting pot, into which were thrown Indians, Spaniards, Mexicans, Frenchmen, and Americans. The great mountains and the great plains moulded them. Something new came out, something different from the pioneer strain of the eastern streams and woods. And in this new mixture was a considerable dash of the despoiled and defeated, yet perhaps in the end invincible Red Brother.

CHAPTER X

ON THE MARCH

FIRST came the patient pack-horse, the faithful companion of the fur trader in every western journey. The pack-horse could go almost anywhere a man could go. But he was not so good for carrying heavy burdens on a long and relatively easy trail as was the mule. Besides, the mule was abundant in New Mexico. He had his faults, to be sure. Sometimes his energy would display itself at inopportune moments, as when, after having walked four or five hundred miles, he would suddenly "take fright from a profile view of his own shadow and run like an antelope of the plains." But very often the mule outfits would come into Santa Fe, after eight hundred miles or more of travel, in pretty good condition.

But though the mule may have seemed the ultimate solution of the prairie transportation problem he was not. When Major Riley's experiment with oxen proved successful, in 1829, his example was soon followed by the freighters. Soon at least half the animals used were oxen. Now, whereas New Mexico was long the home of the mule, oxen could be had only in Missouri, and consequently many caravans must have gone west under ox-power and come back under mule-power. This was the more likely to be the case, since oxen usually arrived at Santa Fe in no condition to make a return trip. They were not as adaptable as mules, and it was hard to get them to eat the buffalo grass or gamma grass which was the only forage beyond the Arkansas River. The oxen were sometimes shod with raw buffalo hide, but mules frequently made the whole trip on the hoofs with which nature had provided them. In later years mules gradually went out of fashion in the freighting business, and the ox became the standard draught animal of the plains.

Although the first wagons to which these faithful beasts were hitched came from Pittsburgh, they were soon succeeded by the famous "Murphy wagons," made by a gentleman of that name in St. Louis. Later still, wagons were manufactured for the New Mexican trade in Independence and in the final years in Kansas City. A loaded wagon was no trifle — it might weigh anywhere from three to seven thousand pounds. The average weight, after the trade had fallen into regular habits, was about five thousand pounds. If oxen were used about six yoke would be needed for each wagon, with an equal or greater number held in reserve to take the places of those that gave out. Hundreds and thousands of ox skeletons went to join those of the buffalo all across the prairie. If mules were employed, ten or twelve would be required for each wagon.

The drivers were a mixed breed. As early as 1826 a Mexican, Don Manuel Escudero, led an outfit from Franklin, and by the early forties half the trade was in Mexican hands. In Gregg's time the Mexican muleteers, or *arrieros,* worked for a wage of from $2 to $5 a month, and lived on corn and frijoles, plus what game they could shoot. These men packed their goods on mule back, about three hundred pounds to a mule, each muleteer acted as chaperon to about eight mules, and a caravan, consisting of from fifty to two hundred mules, travelled between twelve and fifteen miles a day. As it happened, this was also about the standard speed of the ox teams of later years.   As the trade developed and wagons supplanted the pack saddle wages rose, and in the thirties and forties packers and drivers were receiving between $25 and $50 a month and " found."   The American muleteers and ox drivers came from the Missouri country, as a rule.   It soon became quite the custom for young men to make a trip or two to Santa Fe before settling down.   If they had a little money they went as traders; otherwise they hired out.   The food provided for the Trail became standardized, like everything else.   The usual allowance for each man was fifty pounds of flour, fifty pounds of bacon, ten pounds of coffee, twenty pounds of sugar, and a little salt.

The ox drivers, who walked beside their teams, employed a vicious-looking implement consisting of a whip with a stock from sixteen to twenty inches long and a lash ten to sixteen feet long.   Though they did not have the finesse of the stage-drivers, who could flick a lagging horse precisely and delicately on the exact spot intended, they did have to be both strong and skilful. The caravans were organized on lines similar to those in the great emigrant trains which tramped the trails to Oregon and California, but because they usually had a majority of seasoned plainsmen a far better discipline was maintained.   Santa Fe freighting was a business which appealed to men with a passion for freedom and independence, but there were times during every trip when the individual temperament could not be given free rein — too much was at stake.

The usual procedure was to organize at Council Grove, since the Trail east of that point was safe from Indian attacks and no great degree of vigilance was required.   Here the company would elect a captain, a first lieutenant, a second lieutenant, a clerk, a pilot, a court of three members, a commander of the guard and perhaps a chaplain. The caravan captains were commonly men of standing and experience. For instance, Charles Bent, grandson of the Captain Silas Bent who had a leading part in the Boston Tea Party, builder with his brothers and the St. Vrains of Bent's Fort, and destined to be killed by the insurgents while governor of New Mexico, was captain of the caravans of 1828, 1829, 1832, and 1833. Next to the captain in importance was the commander of the guard. West of Council Grove no caravan dared relax its vigilance for a moment, for even though lives were not constantly in danger livestock always was. Every able-bodied man, even though he were only a "passenger," had to stand guard regularly. There was no excuse from this duty, and unrelenting watchfulness was expected. The property and perhaps the lives of all were at stake.

The average day's journey was from fifteen to eighteen miles, though this might be lengthened or shortened to fit the distances between good springs and camping places. These were established at an early date, so that an experienced prairie traveller knew his camp-grounds about as well as a railway trainman knows his station stops. Wet or dry seasons of course made changes in the ease or difficulty of traversing certain portions of the Trail. A rainy month might make travelling heavy along the Narrows, east of Council Grove, but rain in the desert might besprinkle the *Jornada* with little ponds and bring dried-up water courses to life.

Bad weather sometimes caused disaster to caravans setting out too late in the year. In 1841 a party under Don Manuel Alvarez lost two men and all its mules in a snow-storm not far from Council Grove. In 1844 a party lost three hundred mules in an October storm on the Cimarron. In 1848 a government freighting company lost eight or nine hundred head of cattle and had to abandon its wagons. Next year a party caught on the *Jornada* at the beginning of winter lost all its animals and had to camp in the snow till spring. A thousand head of cattle perished in 1850 between the Cimarron and San Miguel. In 1851 one man was frozen to death and three hundred mules were lost in a storm on Cottonwood Creek, thirty-seven miles west of Council Grove.

At first the caravans travelled in a single column, sometimes as much as a mile long. As this formation exposed them to attack, the plan was soon adopted of breaking the line into four sections, which travelled abreast. When night came, or when there was danger of an attack, the sections were quickly wheeled about so as to form a hollow square, into which the livestock was driven. The traders could then fire from the shelter of the wagons. A large caravan in hollow square was well-nigh invulnerable to attack by any force of Indians likely to be encountered. With such organization as this the " infinite peril " with which, as Wetmore said, the earlier expeditions were attended, was reduced to something like reasonable limits. " On the whole," declares Gregg, writing in 1844, " the rates of insurance upon adventures in this trade should hardly be as high as upon marine adventures between New York and Liverpool." Just as the caravan formation was not generally adopted until Council Grove was reached, so it was usually broken up at the Upper Canadian River — the Rio Colorado, as Gregg called it — some 140 or 150 miles east of Santa Fe.

The personnel of the caravans would be worth a volume by itself. These infinitely picturesque characters were the successors of the hunters and trappers, the predecessors of the cowboys. The Mexican and American drivers did not make up the whole roster. The French-Canadian, descendant of the old *voyageur,* was still to be found on the Trail, singing the songs his ancestors had sung on many a long and lonesome trip on wilderness rivers and across strange mountains. And then, as there are many witnesses to testify, there were " besides traders and tourists a number of pale-faced invalids generally to be met with." Gregg adds that many chronic diseases, especially of the liver and the digestive apparatus, have been cured by a trip over the Santa Fe Trail. Perhaps the cause lay in the prairie air, perhaps in the simple food, perhaps in the discovery that there were graver dangers and more serious discomforts than dyspepsia.

Then there began to be, as our revered authority again says, " a little sprinkling of the softer sex." Gregg himself encountered, in 1831, " two respectable French ladies " and a Spanish family. Sometimes well-to-do people journeyed in style, and " handsome pleasure carriages with elegant horses " might be seen jogging genteelly over the boundless plains. It was a long trip for elegance to make, for until the time of the American occupation there was not a single permanent human habitation between the Missouri River and the first Mexican settlement, at San Miguel, by the route ordinarily followed. If the traveller went by way of the upper Arkansas, it is true, he found a semblance of civilization at Bent's Fort. But the fort only served to emphasize the vast loneliness and savagery of the surrounding mountains and plains. That we shall see when we come to visit it.

We are fortunately able to follow some of the caravans

as they make their way along the Trail, though in order
to do so we must resign ourselves to a rate of travel which
according to twentieth-century standards is maddeningly slow. But we shall see and experience things which
are forever denied to those who ride the limiteds or soar
in airplanes. We shall have a sense of mystery and
strangeness that America will never know again. Let
us join Josiah Gregg's caravan as it sets out from Council Grove in 1831:

"Early on the 26th of May we reached the long-
looked-for rendezvous of Council Grove; here we joined
the main body of the caravan. Lest this imposing title
suggest to the reader a snug and thriving village it should
be observed that on the day of our departure from Independence we passed the last human abode upon our
route; thenceforth from the borders of Missouri to
those of New Mexico not even an Indian settlement
greeted our eyes. This point is nearly a hundred and
fifty miles from Independence and consisted of a continuous strip of timber nearly half a mile in width, comprising the richest varieties of trees, such as oak, walnut,
ash, elm, hickory, etc., and extending all along the valleys of a small stream known as Council Grove Creek,
the principal branch of the Neosho river . . .

"'Catch up! Catch up!,' the familiar note of preparation, was now sounded from the captain's camp, and
re-echoed from every division and scattered group along
the valley. On such occasions a scene of confusion
ensues, which must be seen to be appreciated. The
woods and dales resound with the gleeful yells of the
light-hearted wagoners, who, weary of inaction, and
filled with joy at the prospect of getting away, become
clamorous in the extreme. Scarcely does the jockey on
the race-course ply his whip more promptly at the magic

word 'Go!' than do these emulous wagoners fly to
harnessing their mules at the spirit-stirring sound of
'Catch up!' Each teamster vies with his fellows who
shall be soonest ready; and it is a matter of boastful
pride to be the first to cry out, 'All's set!'

"The uproarious bustle which follows, the halloing
of those in pursuit of animals, the exclamations which
the unruly brutes call forth from their wrathful drivers,
together with the clatter of bells, the rattle of yokes and
harness, the jingle of chains, all conspire to produce a
clamorous confusion which would be altogether incom-
prehensible without the assistance of the eyes; while
these alone would hardly suffice to unravel the laby-
rinthine manœuvres and hurly-burly of this precipitate
breaking-up.

"'All's set!' is finally heard from some teamster,
'All's set!' is directly responded from every quarter.
'Stretch out!' immediately vociferates the captain.
Then the 'heps' of drivers, the cracking of whips, the
trampling of feet, the occasional creak of wheels, the
rumbling of wagons, form a new scene of exquisite confusion which I shall not attempt further to describe.
'Fall in!' is heard from headquarters, and the wagons
are forthwith strung out upon the long inclined plain,
which stretches to the heights beyond Council Grove."

Gregg first went west because he was suffering from
ailments the doctors did not know how to cure. He
started in a carriage, carrying with him a number of
civilized dainties with which to tempt a jaded appetite.
Within a week he had exchanged the carriage for a
saddle and was eating buffalo meat and camp bread with
the rest of the crew. Apparently he completely recovered, for he lived many years actively engaged in the
New Mexican trade, succumbing finally to hunger and

possible illness during a tragic trip, in 1850, through the forests of northern California.

His journey in the halcyon days of 1831 followed what had already become the customary route of the Trail, as we traversed it in a preceding chapter. In 1839 he tried an alternate route which he believed to be better, though it was never very generally adopted. This was approximately due west from Van Buren on the Arkansas River, a little north of the 35th parallel of latitude, which is about that of Santa Fe. Gregg crossed the Arkansas near the mouth of the Canadian, then travelled between the Canadian and its north fork. James, it may be recalled, had taken a somewhat similar course in 1821. Gregg was greatly impressed by the magnificent canyon of the Canadian, with its surrounding broken mesa and fantastically shaped rocks, as he now saw them for the first time. Riding ahead across country, while the main body of the caravan swung south around the *Cerro de Tucumcari*, near the present town of that name, he entered the little old capital on Independence Day.

From Santa Fe, after a breathing space, he went on to Chihuahua, across the *Jornada del Muerto*, and along the route followed by the Mexican *arrieros* for nearly three centuries. The journey took him forty days. He started back to the States on February 25, 1840, with forty-seven men, including sixteen Mexicans and a Comanche interpreter. This last individual, called Manuel El Comanche, had married a Mexican girl and was living a sober, righteous, and altogether un-Comanche-like life in San Miguel. From time to time, perhaps more frequently than we have record of, the Indians did blend into the Mexican communities in this fashion. The caravan had a *caballado* — in later

years the Americans sometimes twisted this word into
" cave-yard " — of two hundred mules and nearly three
hundred sheep and goats. Though it arrived safely there
were some alarums and excursions. Once Indians were
prowling near by in the dead of night, and Gregg and
his companions heard the eerie " Pawnee whistle." Once
they were chased by a prairie fire, which came near
being the end of them. Once there was a great storm of
wind and dust, during which their sheep and goats were
lost on the borders of the *Llano Estacado*.

But the journey had its delicate moments. Out of
the somewhat matter-of-fact account of distances covered and landmarks observed there sometimes emerge
bright pictures worth travelling far to see. For instance:
" The watch tried to comfort themselves by building a
rousing fire, around which they presently drew and commenced spinning long yarns about Mexican *fandangos*
and black-eyed damsels." It is not much. But swiftly
the flames leap upward, men's faces glow and fade as the
light touches them, voices come out of the darkness, the
livestock can be heard ruminating near by, with an occasional braying and whinnying and stamping. Over-
head, as one lies on his blanket afterwards, the stars
wheel and blaze.

They came upon strange lives. On the Canadian
River they met a white woman " from the neighborhood
of Matamoras, who had been married to a Comanche
since her captivity." She " did not entertain the least
desire of going back to her own people." Another captive of the Indians was a Spanish boy of twelve, who
had been taken from his home near Parral. He, too, was
sadly reluctant to go back. " *Yo soy demasiado bruto
para vivir entre los Cristianos,*" he told them. " I am
too wild to live among Christians any more."

Sometimes the Indians entered the camp to trade. This practice the caravans did not encourage — there was too much chance for treachery. The good will of a Comanche was never to be relied upon, however amiable he might seem at the moment. If all went well, as it did on this trip, the Indians trickled away in little groups, after a few knick-knacks had been disposed of, " *sans ceremonie* and as silently as possible." Indian trading had fallen into the hands of a class of Mexicans known as *Comancheros,* belonging to the " indigent and rude classes of the frontier villages." These men took out a few dollars' worth of goods, sometimes not more than twenty dollars' worth, and bartered with the Comanches. They were reasonably safe because they did not have enough to make it worth while to murder them, while at the same time they supplied certain real wants. After the Mexican War they incurred the hostility of American settlers by selling weapons and ammunition to the Navajos and Apaches. They could often go freely among the savages when no other white men's lives were worth a moment's purchase.

It is not easy to say why Gregg's route, which was shorter than the one over the Kansas plains, did not become popular. Years later some altruist or another would occasionally announce this route as a new and shining discovery of his own, pointing out that the pasturage was better, the Indians more friendly, and the terrain easier to travel over. But the new road never caught on. The route had become fixed. It was almost as rigidly determined, in its general trend though not in its details, as though it had been a railroad. The towns on the Missouri held their own as starting points.

Having made two trips with Gregg and accustomed ourselves somewhat to the hardships and allurements of the Trail let us follow Thomas Jefferson Farnham, in the year 1839, from Independence to Fort Bent. Farnham, too, is good company. " It is quite amusing to greenhorns, as those are called who have never been engaged in the trade," he writes, " to see the mules make their first attempt at practical pulling. . . The team is straightened and now comes the trial of passive obedience. The chief muleteer gives the shout of march and drives his long spurs into the sides of the animal that bears him; his companion follows his example, but there is no movement. A leer, an unearthly bray, is the only response of these martyrs to human supremacy. Again the team is straightened, again the rowel is applied, the body-guard on foot raise the shout, and all apply the lash at the same moment. The untutored animals kick and leap, rear and plunge and fall in their harness. After a few trainings, however, of this description, they move off in fine style." Still, one begins to see why Major Riley preferred oxen.

A few miles west of Independence " a skirt of black oak timber occasionally lined the horizon or strayed up a deep ravine near the Trail." Farnham notes with a not unpleasant thrill that " the extreme care of the pioneers in the overland Santa Fe trade was everywhere noticeable in the fact that the track of their richly loaded wagons never approached within musket-shot of these points of timber." Maybe this was a greenhorn's romantic illusion. After 1825 there never was much danger east of Council Grove — at least not until the Civil War set white men to preying on one another.

Farnham gives a vivid picture of the guards at night, motionless and stooping or squatting in order to catch the movements of possible lurking Indians against the sky. He, too, makes us understand why the plainsman's heart leapt at the sight of Council Grove. " The trees, maple, ash, hickory, oaks of several kinds, butternut, and a great variety of shrubs clothed in the sweet foliage of June, a pure stream of water murmuring along a gravelly bottom, and the songs of the robin and thrush, made Council Grove a source of delight to us, akin to those that warm the hearts of pilgrims in the great deserts of the East when they behold from the hills of scorching sand the green thorn-tree and the waters of the bubbling spring." How much more lovely the Grove must have seemed to those coming home, out of the deserts and the dangers of the Trail! But if one set one's face westward, as we do as we travel with Farnham, there came " the shrubless plains again," though in June everywhere a foot deep in tender grass.

Violent thunder-showers roll over the prairie. The caravan struggles with difficulty over the famous and hated ford of the Cottonwood. Far out on the plains it meets a caravan returning from Bent's Fort, thirty men, ten wagons loaded with furs, and two hundred sheep for the Missouri market. Horsemen ride to greet one another and to exchange news, like captains of ships hailing at sea. At the Little Arkansas we are held up by rain and flood, but as the storm abates the waters fall fifteen feet in twelve hours, and we cross and go on. At the parent Arkansas we find banks of " sand and loam as hard as a public highway and generally covered with a species of wiry grass that seldom grows to more than one and a half or two inches in height " — that is, of course, the gamma grass. This useful plant, as a later traveller, Alexander Majors, said, " grew almost as thick in places as the hair on a dog's back," and the buffalo's teeth and lower jaw were so arranged by a benevolent Nature that the animal could eat it easily.

The valley of the Arkansas could be dreary enough. "The sunflowers of stunted growth and a lonely bush or willow or an ill-shaped, sapless cottonwood tree, whose decayed trunk trembled under the weight of the years, together with occasional bluffs of clay and sandstone," so Farnham finds, "form the only alluring features of the landscape." The river itself, where the caravan first comes upon it, is about three-fourths of a mile wide, three and a half to four feet deep, and running with a five-mile-an-hour current. As one goes upstream it grows shallower. The alkaline water is of a "chalky whiteness" and "so delicious" that some of the men "declare it an excellent substitute for milk." Some of these details have not altered with time. But that in these days of the railroad, the automobile, and the airplane we can see them with Farnham's eyes is much to be doubted. For the prairie when Gregg and Farnham went west was bathed in an absolute and crystalline loneliness, in which all experiences, of terror, of beauty, of creature comfort, and of dreadful suffering, were magnified. There is upon the prairies, in the twentieth century, no such loneliness. It is a wild thing that could not bear civilization.

But let us go on. Every morning whips crack, teamsters yell, and the process of 'catching up' is renewed. "A noble sight these teams were, about forty in number, their immense wagons still unmoved, forming an oval breastwork of wealth, guarded by an impatient mass of near four hundred mules, harnessed and ready to move along their solitary way. But the interest of the scene was much increased when at the call of the commander the two lines, team after team, straightened themselves into the Trail, and rode majestically away over the undulating plain." Then, three hundred miles

west of Council Grove, according to Farnham's
calculations, come the buffalo, thousands of buffalo,
buffalo so thickly spread over an area of fifteen miles on
either side of the Trail that "when viewed from a height
it scarcely affords a sight of a square league of its
surface."

As he is going to Bent's Fort Farnham does not have
to cross the *Jornada* to the Cimarron. We may go with
him up the Arkansas because after a time most people
did go that way. Bent's Fort has been, in 1839, for
nearly a decade a memorable landmark. Here the trails
leading down from the Platte to Taos, eighty miles away,
and to Santa Fe, at twice that distance, join with those
running from the Missouri into the mountains. Here,
too, or close by, pass the great seasonal migrations of the
principal Indian tribes of the western plains. So, though
the fort lies in the midst of a seeming desolation, it is
actually at a veritable wilderness cross-roads. Stay here
long enough and every famous trapper, hunter, and
trader, and most of the famous chiefs of the day will
come and knock at the gate.

The structure, as Farnham sees it in 1839, is built
around a hollow square, entered through a double gate,
with a corral for animals and an enclosure for wagons
adjoining. The walls are six feet thick at the base and
from seventeen to eighteen feet high. On the northwest
and southeast corners are bastions, where sentinels keep
watch. About sixty men are needed to maintain the
establishment, of whom fifteen or twenty do the freighting between the fort and Independence, while most of
the others hunt or guard stock. The chief hunter at this
time, that is, from 1838 to about the end of 1841, is a
man named Kit Carson. At the other end of the social
scale — the lower end, according to frontier notions —

are " a few young gentlemen from the cities," who act as clerks.

The Bent brothers probably wear beaver hats, high stocks, and broadcloth coats when they are playing the rôle of respectable merchants in St. Louis. At the fort respectability demands a different garb. "Two of them," says Farnham, " were there when we arrived. They seemed to be thoroughly initiated into the Indian life; dressed like chiefs, in moccasins thoroughly garnished with beads and porcupine quills, in trousers of deerskin, with long fringes of the same extending along the outer seam from ankle to the hip, in the splendid hunting shirt of the same material, with sleeves fringed on the elbow seam from the wrist to the shoulder, and ornamented with figures of porcupine quills of various colors, and leather fringes around the lower edge of the body; and chiefs they were in the authority exercised in this wild and lonely fortress.

" A trading establishment to be known must be seen. A solitary abode of men seeking wealth in the teeth of danger and hardship, rearing its towers over the uncultivated wastes of nature, like an old baronial castle that has withstood the wars and desolations of centuries; Indian women tripping around the battlements in their glittering moccasins and long deer-skin wrappers; their children with most perfect forms and the carnation of the Saxon cheek struggling through the shade of the Indian; the grave owners and their clerks and traders, seated in the shade of the piazza, smoking the long native pipe, passing it from one to another, drawing the precious smoke into the lungs by short hysterical sucks till filled, and then ejecting it through the nostrils; or it may be seated around their rude table, spread with coffee or tea, jerked buffalo meat, and bread made of unbolted

wheaten meal from Taos; or, after eating, laid comfortably upon their pallets of straw and Spanish blankets
and dreaming to the sweet notes of a flute; the old
trapper, withered with exposure to the rending elements,
the half-tamed Indian and half-civilized Mexican servants, seated on the ground around a large tin pan of dry
meat and a tankard of water, their only rations, relating
adventures about the shores of Hudson's Bay, on the
rivers Columbia and Mackenzie, in the great Prairie
Wilderness, and among the snowy heights of the mountains; and delivering sage opinions about the destination of certain bands of buffalo; or the distance to the
Blackfoot country . . . present a tolerable picture of
everything within its walls.

"If we add the opening of the gates on a winter's
morning — the cautious sliding in and out of the Indians whose tents stand around the fort, till the whole
area is filled six feet deep with their long hanging black
locks and dark watchful flashing eyes; and traders and
clerks, busy at their work, and the patrols walking the
battlements with loaded muskets; and the guards in the
bastions standing with burning matches by their car-
ronades; and when the sun sets the Indians returning
again to their camp outside to talk over their newly-
purchased blankets and beads, and to sing and drink
and dance; and the night sentinel on the fort that treads
his weary watch away, we shall have a tolerable view of
this post in the season of business."

The "season of business" is not always a safe or
secure one. "The country in which the fort is situated
is in a manner the common field of several tribes, unfriendly alike to one another and the whites. The
Eutaws and the Cheyennes of the mountains near Santa
Fe and the Pawnees of the Great Platte come to the

Upper Arkansas to meet the buffalo in their annual migrations to the North; and on the track of these animals follow up the Comanche, and thus in the months of June, August and September there are in the neighborhood of these traders from fifteen thousand to twenty thousand savages ready and panting for plunder and blood. If they engage in battling out old causes and contentions among themselves the Messers. Bent feel comparatively safe in their solitary fortress. But if they spare each other's property and lives they occasion great anxiety at Fort William [the original name for Bent's Fort]; every hour of day and night is pregnant with danger."

Such was the grim background of the old Indian traders and trappers, inherited in large measure by those who used the Trail to Santa Fe. It was an atmosphere of fear and struggle from which no one who ventured far out upon the plains could wholly escape. There was no certainty, west of Council Grove and east of the Canadian. The Indians who traded for the white man's beads and blankets one day might be after his scalp the next. The white man might shoot down friendly Indians in the belief that they were hostile and receive by his campfire hostile Indians in the belief that they were friendly.

Yet into this deadly arena there sometimes came women, young, delicately nurtured, beautiful. Seven years have gone by since Farnham went to Bent's Fort. The summer of the Mexican War has arrived. Susan Shelby Magoffin, nineteen years old, not long married to her big, handsome trader husband, sets forth gaily and romantically from Independence in the month of June in a "Rockaway carriage." Though the war drums are beating it is not chiefly of war that Susan thinks. She is to have her troubles. She is to sacrifice her baby to the rigors of the Trail; it is to die at birth. But she is young, she knows she is beautiful, and she is ever so much in love with her husband, and all these things throw a glamour over a journey which even hardened plainsmen, grown grey on the prairies, swore foully at — and loved!

"The teamsters were just ' catching up,' " says Susan in one of the first entries in her diary — how faithfully she noted down the lingo of the Trail! — " and the cracking of whips, lowing of cattle, braying of mules, whooping and hollowing of the men was a novel sight, rather." But, dear, well-brought-up girl that she was, she did find it " disagreeable to hear so much swearing." She had not learned that mules could no more be driven without swearing than wagons could roll without wheels. One wishes she had had the bad taste to set down some of the rich and picturesque profanity of the Santa Fe Trail, so much of which, couched in three or four languages and born of constant toil and danger in a vast and dazzling and also irritating scene, has now been lost from the memory of man.

The Magoffins travelled in grand style, with a conical tent, a table, a fully equipped bed, a carpet and stools, which, since this was Susan's wedding journey, was all as it should have been. In a prairie rain-storm, however, she found that the only way to keep dry, even under the conical tent, was to stay in bed. The rain left the road so muddy that they made only a mile an hour. A wagon which got mired in Cottonwood Creek — how blue the air must have been sometimes at that loathsome crossing! — would not budge until eleven yoke of oxen were hitched to it. But Susan liked most of her experiences. She had, without knowing quite what had happened, escaped almost completely out of her native Victorian period. " I breathe free," she confided to her diary, " without that oppression and uneasiness felt in the gossiping circles of a settled home."

The prairie grass came up to her waist. Raspberries and gooseberries were growing in profusion. True, there were green bugs, snakes, and " musquitoes," but after a dinner of boiled chicken, soup, rice, and dessert of wine and gooseberry tart one didn't mind. It should not be necessary to add that this was not a typical Trail dinner, even for a bride.

They came to Cow Creek, 249 miles from Independence. All day the men worked to get the wagons across and they made but three miles from camp to camp. A dozen miles further on they reached the Arkansas, three weeks out of Independence, and Susan marked how much " shorter and finer " the grass was, and how the winding paths made by the buffalo cut innumerable lines across the plains. At Pawnee Rock, trembling for fear a savage head might suddenly pounce at her from behind a boulder, she cut her name, along with hundreds of others, on the soft surface. The carriage was wrecked crossing Ash Creek but they got it rolling and went on. Susan, having used up the picnic supplies she had brought from the States, learned the charms of real prairie cooking. " Such soup as we have made of the hump ribs, one of the choice parts of the buffalo! I never ate its equal in the best hotels of New York and Philadelphia, and the sweetest butter and most delicate oil I ever tasted, 'tis not to be surpassed by the marrow taken from the thigh bones." On Sunday there was a halt, and she heard the teamsters " singing the hymns perhaps they were taught by a good pious mother." And yet it may not have been so much the pious mother as

the pious but lovely young bride who set those rough
tongues to such unaccustomed exercises.

The Magoffins went to Bent's Fort, where there was
now a billiard room and a race track. At the fort they
waited while Kearny's troops went ahead of them on
the famous march to Santa Fe. After a while the caravan proceeded. The dust was now " very great and the
vegetation so perfectly parched by the sun that not a
blade of green grass was to be seen." They saw mirages,
or, as they called them, " false ponds." They paused
and admired the Hole in the Rocks, an apparently bot-
tomless spring, filled with cold, clear water. Then came
tall rocks covered with cedar trees and again there were
birds and green grass. Above loomed Raton Pass, over
which they now began to move at a rate never exceeding
half a mile an hour. In one entire day they advanced
only six or eight hundred yards. The wagons had literally to be hauled by hand over the great rocks. It
took them five days to cross. Then they came down to
Mora, " a thriving village with its nice little cottages and
court house in the centre." And, cried Susan, snatching
a human personality out of the hundreds who had
travelled and were to travel the Trail, " Oh, the everlasting tongue of that boy Comapee! He is eternally
singing."

So, to the tune of Comapee's chanting — stilled these
eighty years, and yet audible, too, if one listens attentively — they went their way, down to Las Vegas, where
people drank copiously of *aguardiente* and stared at the
Yankee woman who had come so far over such a perilous
route; where matrons sat around with shamelessly
bare arms and necks, and children were running
about naked; in short, where it was most embarrass-
ing " to pass with gentlemen." We shall hear more

of Susan a little later when our own caravan arrives in Santa Fe.

Thus rolled the wagons, year on year, laden with human interest, charged with manifold destinies. Not one person went over the Trail, we may well believe, but had a story to tell. Multiply Gregg, Farnham, and Susan Magoffin by some hundreds or thousands and we might begin at last to understand what the Trail meant. But most of those who passed, though they swore and sang, and hoped and feared, and raised the very devil when they got into " port," have long been voiceless. They have gone where the game went. Once there were antelope and buffalo in profusion. The wild mustangs sometimes came in droves of a hundred or more, " gambolling and curvetting within a short distance of the caravans." There was a story of a beautiful " medium-sized mustang of perfect symmetry, milk-white save a pair of black ears, a natural pacer and so fleet it has been said as to leave behind every horse that has tried to pursue it, without breaking its pace." The " long and doleful bugle-note " of the grey wolf, king of the prairie, could be heard in the darkness. Elk and deer in great numbers frequented the Arkansas bottoms. There were black bear in the " Cross Timbers." The prairie dogs lifted their heads out of countless holes; bad luck to the man whose horse, galloping after the buffalo, caught a hoof in one of them. Rattlesnakes and horned toads harmonized with the hideousness of the desert, and mirages mirrored its beauty. The coyotes barked like a myriad of lost souls in hell. The big horns or mountain sheep hopped nimbly about the rocks beyond the Cimarron. Gregg found along the Canadian more wild turkey than he had powder to shoot.

It was a golden age, to be ended by war and ever-increasing floods of traffic. But if the golden age passed something vaster and more meaningful came in its place. America was marching jubilantly westward. The Trail was to become a thoroughfare, hard beaten, following the sun. It was to be the road of empire, it was to give us the Southwest, it was to speed westward the troops who were to bring harsh awakening not only to New Mexico but to that other dreamland, California.

The first discordant rumblings, the thunder with which the new day dawned, were heard from the direction of Texas, out of the line of our main Trail, yet bound to have a profound influence upon it. But before we listen to the rattle of the drums let us go with our own caravan, past San Miguel, past Pecos, over the last ridge, and down into Santa Fe. Let us see what it was that lured the Americans and what it was that they came in large measure to destroy.

CHAPTER XI

A CARAVAN ENTERS SANTA FE

ALONG the fifty-eight miles between San Miguel and Santa Fe ran what might be called a highway. According to George Wilkins Kendall, the historian of the Texan Santa Fe expedition, which passed that way in 1841, it had been built " at the expense of the St. Louis traders," and was at that time the only part of the Trail upon which attention had been so lavished. It led the travellers past the ruins of Pecos Pueblo, lying in a lordly site, with far vistas of many mountains, through Glorieta Pass, then turned left at Canoncito and went the final twelve miles northwest over the Glorieta range to Santa Fe. At the top of the last rise the worn and dusty newcomers caught sight of the city, lying at the foot of the Sangre de Cristo mountains, on the edge of a great plateau rolling westward toward the valley of the Rio Grande and the distant Sandias and Jemez mountains.

This was perhaps the greatest moment of life upon the Trail. It was a greater moment than the one which occurred when the returning pilgrims first saw the scraggly outposts of Independence lying in the distance and clapped spurs to their jaded horses. For Santa Fe had always the lure of strangeness and adventure. It was not a peaceful coming home, it was an excitement which set men's hearts thumping, made them throw their hats in the air, made them stand up in their stirrups, and yell like wild Indians and shoot off their fire-arms.

156

At first sight the town was not much to look at. It was possible to be utterly disgusted with it at first sight, second sight, and last sight. To enjoy it thoroughly one had to have a flair for such things. Literal-minded persons did not, puritanical persons usually did not, neat and methodical persons did not. But there were those who longed for it as a sailor longs for the sea. For some men, perhaps, it was an antidote for the smugness, hypocrisy and over-fastidiousness they hated in the American civilization of their day. But for all who came it was at least rest and food and the end of peril. The joy of the seasoned plainsmen, with forty days of uninhabited wilderness behind them, could not have been much greater if this indeed had been Cibola, the shining city, or Quivira, in which everyone ate from dishes of gold and the women fastened their hair with diamonds.

"I doubt," says Gregg, "whether the first sight of the walls of Jerusalem were beheld by the crusaders with much more tumultuous and soul-enrapturing joy. . . The wagoners were by no means free from excitement on this occasion. Informed of the ' ordeal ' they had to pass they had spent the previous morning in ' rubbing up,' and now they were prepared, with clean faces, sleek-combed hair and their choicest Sunday suit, to meet the ' fair eyes ' of glistening black that were sure to stare at them as they passed. There was yet another preparation to be made in order to ' show off ' to advantage. Each wagoner must tie a brand-new cracker to the lash of his whip, for on driving through the streets and the *plaza publica* everyone strives to outvie his comrade in the dexterity with which he flourishes his favorite brand of authority."

The city of the days preceding the American occupation was far from being the clean, well-watered, well-planted spot which delights the tourist today. It centred, as it does now, about the plaza, but the plaza was almost treeless, flowerless, shadeless, an extent of hard-packed adobe in the dry season, of mud in the wet season. The principal building was the *Palacio*, the seat of government, on the north side of the square. The greater portion of it may be seen to this day, almost as it appeared in Spanish times, a long, low building with a portico or arcade running along the whole front. It was started in 1610, three years after the founding of Jamestown, and had been in use ever since. It had seen the first Spanish settlers breaking the iron soil, it had heard the shouts of the revolting Pueblo Indians in 1680 and had been the scene of their councils, it had slumbered during warm afternoons and cool, mysterious nights for two hundred years before any Anglo-Saxon ever saw it.

The *Presidio*, of which the *Palacio* was architecturally a part, ran about four hundred feet east and west and about twice as far north and south. As it was originally planned as a place of defence, it was enclosed by an adobe wall. Within the enclosure, or forming parts of the wall, were not only the Palace but the quarters of the garrison, the prison, a chapel, a small cemetery and the *plaza de armas*, or drill ground. The main building was roofed with pine or spruce logs, many of which have withstood the weathering of three centuries and are still in place.

"Here, within the walls fortified as for a siege," says L. Bradford Prince, "the bravest Spaniards were massed in the revolution of 1680; here on the nineteenth of August of that year was given the order to execute forty-seven Pueblo prisoners in the plaza which faces the building; here but a few days later was the sad war council held which determined on the evacuation of the city; here was the scene of triumph of the Pueblo chieftains as they ordered the destruction of the Spanish archives and the church ornaments in one grand conflagration; here De Vargas gave thanks to the Virgin Mary, to whose aid he attributed his triumphant capture of the city; here, more than a century later, on March 3, 1807, Lieutenant Pike was brought before Governor Alencaster as an invader of Spanish soil; here, in 1822, the Mexican standard, with the eagle and the cactus, was raised in token that New Mexico was no longer a dependency of Spain; from here, on the 6th day of August 1837, Governor Perez started to subdue the insurrection in the north, only to return two days later and to meet his death on the 9th, near Agua Fria; here on the succeeding day Jose Gonzales, a Pueblo Indian of Taos, was installed as governor of New Mexico, soon after to be executed by order of Armijo; here, in the principal reception-room, in 1844, Governor Martinez killed the chief of the Utes by one blow with his chair; here, on August 12, 1846, Captain Cooke, the American envoy, was received by Governor Armijo, and sent back with a message of defiance; and it was here, six days later, General Kearny formally took possession of the city and slept, after his long and weary march, on the carpeted earthen floor of the Palace."

So there was history enough for one small building in a remote city in the hills — history made and in the making. The later events mentioned in Mr. Prince's resounding prose were not yet foreseen when the first American caravans entered the city. But New Mexico was ripening like a plum, for the invaders to pick.

On the south side of the plaza was a large military

chapel, with two low towers, in which hung bells. There were also the Chapel of Our Lady of Guadalupe and the parochial church. James, in 1821, speaks of " five very splendid churches." The present cathedral, though it contains many relics of the older days and looks venerable enough, was not begun until 1869. Those portions of the streets facing on the plaza which were not filled by the official buildings, churches, or the residences of the priests were occupied by the houses of the wealthier citizens. An *acequia,* or irrigation ditch, ran on two sides of the plaza. The first attempts at beautifying the town seem to have been the planting of cottonwood trees along these ditches. From the plaza radiated and straggled the lesser streets, where the poorer inhabitants lived. But before diving into the by-ways we must not overlook one other important though not very showy building — La Fonda, the inn which marked the end of the Trail. La Fonda did not have a bath connected with every room, but when the traders were in town it sheltered a vivid and dramatic life. For variety and picturesqueness its guests were probably not to be matched in any hostelry on earth.

When one went into the side streets one found the domestic style of architecture extremely simple, though not altogether bad. James, who was as glad as any man ever was to see the last of Santa Fe, says that " the houses were all white-washed outside and in and presented a neat and pleasing sight to the eye of the traveller." Lewis Garrard, writing of a similar kind of house at Taos, speaks of walls " mica limewashed to a dazzling whiteness." Pike says that the houses " had a very mean appearance on the outside but some of them are richly furnished, especially with plate." No doubt the time of year at which the visit was made had something to do with the visitor's impression of the outsides of the houses, for the New Mexicans, like the inhabitants of southern Spain, had the habit of whitewashing anew at regular intervals. The fact that there was no sewer system, and that the streets were unpaved and filthy may have done a good deal to detract from an exterior architectural charm. At best one could not afford to be squeamish. Old Santa Fe was in no respect chemically pure. Nevertheless, it had an enchantment. One walked along a continuous and forbidding wall, often arcaded to keep off sun and rain, with barred windows, wooden shutters and large doors which could be securely closed. But behind the walls and within the doors life was going on, with a dreamy perfection all its own.

If the visitor entered he came upon a *patio* or enclosed courtyard, upon which opened the various rooms of the house. The floors of these rooms were of adobe, which was firm and satisfactory so long as it did not get wet; the walls were plastered with adobe and covered with gypsum, which, because it rubbed off at the least touch, was in the better houses covered to the height of a person's shoulder with calico. Occasionally a coarse domestic fabric called *xerga* was spread upon the floor. The ceilings were commonly of uncovered beams, though muslin was sometimes tacked across them; or the interstices were filled in with small sticks, or *latias*. Sometimes the beams and *latias* were painted. The fireplaces, as is still the case today in many modern New Mexican houses, were so constructed that the sticks had to be placed upright against the back. The furniture was as simple as furniture could well be, and still merit the name. The rich, says Becknell, had " a rough imitation of our settee, which answers the treble purpose of chair, table and bedstead." Cooking was done in earthen vessels, and bread was baked in outdoor ovens. Mattresses covered with blankets served as seats as well as couches. Utensils of iron were rare, except among the very rich. Carpenter work was too costly and carpenters too scarce to permit much woodworking to be done.

In short, the physical apparatus of life was reduced to a minimum. It is possible that we obtain a better conception of what the externals of Santa Fe were like by visiting the Indian pueblos of today than by going to Santa Fe itself. Even in the matter of education the New Mexican during the 1820s did not stand far above his Pueblo Indian neighbor. There were no newspapers and no public schools. Few could read. News of the outer world was brought in by the caravans, from Mexico or Missouri, mainly by word of mouth. Aside from the spontaneous amusements of the inhabitants the church was the centre of cultural life. By modern standards the little city was dull. There was no organized apparatus of recreation.

But to understand old Santa Fe we must not picture it as we would a modern American town suddenly deprived of its motion picture theatres, its radios, its telephones, its phonographs, and its automobiles. Santa Fe had many beauties and graces of existence which we who live in a more complicated civilization may envy. It perhaps came as near to giving human life significance as New York or London or Paris does today. Courtesy which might put drawing-rooms to shame was found among the lowliest. Again and again we hear tributes to the unfailing hospitality of the common people — a hospitality so instinctive and so warm that it was often mistaken for a desire to conciliate. It was difficult for some Americans, even then, to understand a willingness on anyone's part to give something for nothing. We hear, too, of a natural gaiety which is like a far echo of Arcadia.

Indeed, a thing which puzzled and even irritated many American visitors was that though the people were so poor, so dirty, and so ignorant that they ought not to have been happy, yet none the less they stubbornly insisted on being so. To a traveller who had come from those thrice-blessed regions of North America where there were stoves, carpets, glass windows, lace curtains, antimacassars, railways, frock coats, front parlors, crinoline skirts, daily newspapers, flowered wallpaper, what-nots, feather beds, and spittoons, this attitude of the New Mexicans was almost insulting. It raised doubts in the visitor's own mind. What was the use of belonging to a superior race and having a superior civilization if the lesser breeds were not unhappy and envious?

" The inhabitants appear to me to be a miserably poor people, but perfectly happy and contented," wrote Marmaduke at San Miguel. A few days later, at Santa Fe, he repeated himself. " The inhabitants appear to be friendly and some of them are very wealthy; but by far the greater part are the most miserable, wretched poor creatures that I have ever seen; yet they appear to be quite happy and contented in their miserably priest-ridden situation." We must, of course, expect a slight religious bias in the puritanic northerners. The sentiment represented by Native-Americanism, Know-Nothingism and in the later days by the A.P.A. and the Ku Klux Klan was often carried across the plains with the caravans. Fortunately the religious emotions of the men of the prairies and mountains were commonly in an embryonic state, and they were not given to abusing their neighbors in the name of brotherly love.

Because the customs of the New Mexicans were different from those of the American borderers much misunderstanding was to be expected. The Missourians never did learn to comprehend the Latin frankness in dealing with some of the intimate and sinful aspects of life.

" I do not believe," Marmaduke observes indignantly, " there is a people on the globe so destitute of correct moral principles as the inhabitants of New Mexico. I scarcely know a single vice that is not indulged in by them to very great excess, except that of intoxication, and the absence of this is due to the scarcity of ardent spirits. In justice to them, however, I cannot forbear to remark that there does exist among them one single virtue, and that virtue is hospitality." But, he adds, with a sad shake of the head, " the men and women will indiscriminately and freely converse together on the most indecent, gross and vulgar subjects that can possibly be conceived, without the least embarrassment or confusion." Apparently the New Mexicans had reached that point of easy frankness which was not attained in polite society in the United States until after the World War.

James is even more severe, as severe as only a man with a strong moral sense and a personal grievance — the two so often go hand in hand — can be. " I had not supposed it possible," he declares, " for any society to be as profligate and vicious as I found all ranks of that in Santa Fe. The Indians are much superior to their Spanish masters in all qualities of a useful and meritorious population." James was present during the five-day carousal, early in January, 1822, in honor of Mexico's newly-won independence of Spain. He was disgusted beyond measure at what he saw.

"All classes," he tells us, "abandoned themselves to the most reckless dissipation and profligacy. No Italian carnival ever exceeded this celebration in thoughtlessness, vice and licentiousness of every description. Men, women and children crowded every part of the city, and the carousal was kept up equally by night and day. There seemed to be no time for sleep. Tables for gambling surrounded the square, and continually occupied the attention of the crowds. Dice and faro banks were all in constant play. I never saw any people so infatuated with the passion of gaming. Women of rank were seen betting at the faro bank and dice tables. They frequently lost all their money; then followed the jewelry from their fingers, arms, and ears, then the ribose [Spanish, *rebozo*] or sash edged with gold which they wear over their shoulders was staked and lost, when the fair gamesters would go to their homes for money and to redeem the last pledge and if possible continue the play. Men and women on all sides of me were equally absorbed in the fluctuating fortunes of these games. The demons of chance and avarice seemed to possess them all, to the loss of what little reason Nature had originally made theirs."

Incidentally it may be recalled that James himself was — and very naturally — in a bad humor because he had staked all and lost nearly everything in his commercial venture. He goes on: "Freedom without restraint or license was the order of the day; and thus did these rejoicing republicans continue the celebration of their independence till nature was too exhausted to support the dissipation any longer. The crowds then dispersed to their homes, with all the punishment of excess with which pleasure visits her votaries. I saw enough during those five days' revelry to convince me that the republicans of New Mexico were unfit to govern themselves or anybody else. The Indians acted with more moderation than the Spaniards."

We hear a juvenile echo of the same comment nearly thirty years later in Lewis Garrard's remarks about the girls of Taos. "How dulcet-toned," he cries, "are their voices, which, sirenlike, irresistibly draw the willing victim within the giddy vortex of dissipation." But, he adds, "we look in vain for the true woman's attraction — modesty, the attribute which encircles as a halo the intelligent, virtuous and educated woman." So many things were wrong, as a pure young man saw them, about the Mexican girls! Their skirts were so short that there was a positively shameless display of ankles. Their "chemises" were "too low-necked." Some of the traders, it is to be feared, found the temptations too great. The Missouri *Republican,* in February 1830, sarcastically remarked that the Missourians who went over the Trail "improved their habits and morals among the, in every way, vicious and lascivious inhabitants of New Mexico."

Susan Magoffin, being youthful and happy, was more inclined to see the good in her fellow creatures, though, as we have seen, she was capable of being shocked. The ladies, she noted, "dressed in the Mexican style; large sleeves, short waists, ruffled skirts and no bustles — which latter looks exceedingly odd in this day of grass skirts and pillows. All danced and smoke cigarettes, from the old woman with false hair and teeth to the little child." Unlike some American visitors, Susan was aware of the errors of her own people as well as of those of the New Mexicans. "I think," she remarks, referring to some officers of the army of occupation in 1846, "some of my countrymen are disgracing themselves here." She might easily have thought so. Two American officers in uniform called on her and made love to her while drunk. Perhaps it was the climate that did it, or the elevation, or something more subtle still. There is no question that Santa Fe did go to some people's heads.

Gregg, that cool and dispassionate observer, confirms without the hysterical adjectives much of what James and a few other moralists said. The people were certainly poor. There were many beggars, who were cherished as being good for people's souls. There was much petty thieving and no end of gambling. All grades of society, from the governor's wife down, visited the gaming tables without the least embarrassment. Señora Doña Gertrudes Barceló, a successful woman whose manners ran counter to the strict Puritan standards of the early Anglo newcomers to Santa Fe, came down from Taos, her lovely eyes flaming with ambition, got a place in a gambling house, made some lucky bets on the side, purchased a gambling business of her own, and became a prominent figure in the city's social life. Beautiful in her youth, she wore false teeth and a wig in her old age, but maintained to the last very much of an air. The élite of Santa Fe thronged her elegantly fitted monte rooms. She was, everyone admiringly conceded, the most skilful monte card dealer in the whole world. She gave balls, to which, unlike the common run of balls, only those who were invited could come. It is related that during the early days of the American occupation one Colonel David A. Mitchell, being ordered to open communications with Chihuahua, found himself without the necessary funds to supply his troops. Doña Gertrudes —she was also often referred to by the diminutive of Doña Tules—lent him a thousand dollars on condition that he enter the room at a formal ball with her on his arm. The gallant colonel, it is said, did his duty as an officer and a gentlemen, and Doña Tules received the final social *cachet*. She lived until 1851, and when she died was widely mourned and had a sixteen-hundred-dollar funeral, with all the honors of her church.

There was cock-fighting on Sundays and feast days, this, too, inevitably accompanied by gambling. " The church, the ball-room, the gambling-house and the cock-pit," Gregg tells us, " look like so many opposition establishments, for nothing is more common than to see people going from one place to another by alternate fits, just as devotional feeling or love of pleasure happens to prompt them." There was no bull-fighting, but there was bull-baiting. In *el coleo* the wild bull was pursued on horseback, and the *vaquero* who won the race seized the animal by the tail and tried to overturn it by a dextrous twist. The New Mexicans also played *pelota*, which may have been the game of the same title played to this day in the Basque provinces of Spain and southern France and in parts of Latin America.

There were dances of all sorts, formal and informal, respectable and less respectable. Gregg gives the name of *fandango* to the commoner sort and that of *baile* to the more pretentious. The *fandango* is, of course, the correct designation of a particular kind of dance, and Twitchell questions Gregg's use of it. But there is con-temporary justification for the usage. Thus one finds in the Santa Fe *Republican* for October 9, 1847, the an-nouncement: " Something New. Hovey and Co., at the Billiard Saloon, east end of Main street, will give a Fandango on Tuesday evening. Good music, good wine and pretty girls." This, though patently Anglo-Saxon, was in the traditional New Mexican vein. Everyone

danced. No one objected to good music, good wine, or
pretty girls.

" From the gravest to the buffoon, from the richest
nabob to the beggar, from the soberest matron to the
flippant belle, from the governor to the *ranchero,* from
the grandest senora to the *cocinera,*" so Gregg assures
us, " all partake of this exhilarating amusement. To
judge from the quantity of tuned instruments which
salute the ear almost every night in the week one would
suppose that a perpetual carnival prevailed everywhere.
The musical instruments used at the *bailes* and *fandangos* are usually the fiddle and the *bandolin* or *gui-
tarra,* accompanied in some villages by the *tombé,* or
little Indian drum. The musicians occasionally acquire
considerable proficiency in the use of these instruments."

The dances were of several sorts. There was an ordinary waltz, a slow waltz, which may have resembled
the tango, and the *cuna,* or cradle dance, in which there
was a beautiful figure danced with arms locked and
heads thrown back. A functionary called the *bastonero*
was master of ceremonies, and sometimes a privileged
jester sat on the platform with the musicians and ex-
temporized verses about prominent persons on the floor.
Often the dances were open to everyone and were announced by a parade of the musicians around the plaza.
There were some pretty customs associated with the
bailes. One of these, which may also be found in descriptions of Spanish-American life in early California,
was that of breaking egg-shells filled with cologne over
the heads of ladies or gentlemen whose attention a friend
of the opposite sex wished to attract.

Despite the free and easy manner which marked certain aspects and certain strata of New Mexican life the
relations between the sexes were as carefully regulated

among the wealthier classes as they are in all Spanish
countries. Marriages were arranged only by the consent
of the parents, and sometimes the desires of the young
people were treated as of minor consequence. Gallantry
was carried to a great extreme. Usually men and
women did not eat together — a custom which annoyed
the sociable Susan Magoffin excessively. The marriage
ceremonies were so expensive that often the poorer people omitted them altogether. As Susan said, everyone
smoked. Women as well as men invariably carried the
little sack of powdered tobacco, and everyone could roll
a cigarette with quick and skilful twists of the fingers.
Pueblo Indians may sometimes be seen doing the same
thing with the same materials today. To offer a woman
a cigarette was as common an act of courtesy as it has
been in most American cities since the World War.
Fastidious women often carried little golden pincers,
with which they held the cigarette and so avoided soiling
their fingers. Everyone drank, yet there was, as James
says, little or no drunkenness. Here again there is a
similarity with what we are told of the early days in
California. Hard liquor was scarce until some enterprising Americans set up a distillery in 1824. The coming of the American saloon meant, of course, the
introduction of American drinks and styles of drinking,
including the habit of imbibing until the imbiber became
pie-eyed.

To the picturesqueness of manners which has already
been indicated may be added a picturesqueness of costume. Against the glaring white walls even the poorest
people moved in splashes of brilliant color. Barbaric
jewelery was much in evidence. James saw women who
were said to have on their persons as much as $500 worth
of jewelery — not a great deal for New York or Paris in

now but a fortune in Santa Fe in 1822. Susan Magoffin, with her keen woman's eye, noticed girls " dressed in silks, satins, ginghams and lawns, embroidered crepe shawls, fine rabozos [no one ever seemed to learn how to spell this word correctly] and decked in various showy ornaments, such as huge necklaces, countless rings, combs, bows of ribbands, red and other colored handkerchiefs, and other fine fancy articles." Almost every visitor from the States commented on the fact that the women painted, and with no sparing hand. First they plastered on flour paste. Over this went the bright vermilion, on lips, in large spots on the cheeks. Perhaps we should not notice this today, but the American visitors to Santa Fe stepped straight out of a prudish age into something which, whatever else it was, certainly was not prudish. Even the Indians, who came to dance to the music of the native drums, had a flair for fancy dress, and all that went with it.

The New Mexican men, in their braided *chaquetas,* their laced *calzoneras* or trousers, their brilliant sashes, their boots of embossed leather, and with the silver of their spurs, bridles, and horse trappings, were as shamelessly lurid as their wives and sweethearts. These luxuries, like the feminine ones, really belonged to the wealthier classes. Those who had money wore a good share of it on their backs. The poorer women had to confine themselves to a blouse and flannel petticoat, and the man in the street wore a *serape,* a blanket-like garment with a hole in the centre through which he thrust his head. Mexicans wear the same garment to this day. But though the material might be plain and often tattered the colors were gaudy; and if money came one's way it went first to the luxury of dress and then to the necessities of life.

Though many were wretchedly poor no one starved. *Tortillas* were easily made by boiling corn in water with a little lime, removing the hulls, pounding the kernels to a paste, rolling the paste out thin, and baking the mess which resulted. The Mexican bean, or *frijole,* was cheap. A little higher up in the culinary scale came *chili con carne* and *tamales,* hotly seasoned but palatable to the habituated taste. The rich could afford chocolate, a fairly good native wine, the " pass brandy " from El Paso, and the wines and liquors which the traders began to bring in over the Trail. There was a little fruit — apples, peaches, apricots, and of course, grapes. Life, though showy enough, was at best exceedingly simple. But if there ever was a people undepressed by lack of worldly goods it was the inhabitants of New Mexico. They had their troubles abundantly, but they also had facility in forgetting them, or, better still, of dramatizing them. They moved through life, like " that boy Comapee . . . eternally singing."

The philosophers may argue until they are blue in the face as to whether this was happiness, or whether it was in any way preferable to the wealthier and outwardly more sedate civilization which had grown up on the other side of the great plains. The point we need to remember if we are to enter into the spirit of old Santa Fe is that the little town had a distinct way of living, which was not the Missouri way or the Massachusetts way, or even quite the Spanish or Mexican way. When the traders came whooping down the final hill, waving their hats in the air, firing off their muskets and pistols, they were not merely coming into a town though that would have been wonderful enough after eight hundred miles of wilderness. They were dipping into another world. Traders were not conspicuously men of inhibitions, but if they had any, good or bad, most of them cast them away as they charged into the old capital.

"Even the animals," to borrow again from the admirable Gregg, "seemed to participate in the humor of their riders, who grew more and more merry as they descended toward the city." The inhabitants shared the exhilaration of their visitors. They swarmed into the streets with cries of "*Los Americanos! Los carros! La entrada de la caravana!*" The girls were there, with their dark eyes and jet-black tresses; with scarves across their faces, by turns flirtatious and haughty. Light-fingered natives of a more materialistic disposition were on hand to see what they could steal. From the barracks, the soldiers came running in their nondescript uniforms, the Indians on the street-corners drew their blankets around them and watched with passionless interest, the dignified officials came forth with many bows and appraising, acquisitive eyes. So, as the caravans finally drew up before La Fonda, the two civilizations met and mingled.

Business came before pleasure, for the goods had to be unloaded and put through the ordeal of the customs-house. There was keen competition to get this painful process over with. Usually the owners of the goods rode in ahead of the wagons in order to make what arrangements they could before the caravan arrived. The " arrangement " was usually a compromise, in which, as Gregg says, " the officers are sure at least to provide for themselves." In some ports, he adds, " a custom has been said to prevail of dividing the legal duties into three equal parts — one for the officers, a second for the merchants, the other for the government." The tariff was never a simple matter because it was rarely for two consecutive years exactly the same. And one has to be cautious in accepting the figures of tariff paid to the Mexican government as representing the total exacted from the traders. Thus the government received $43,000 in 1843 out of a total trade of $450,000, $27,291 in 1842 out of a total trade of $160,000, and only $1,195 in 1841 out of a total trade of $150,000. The natural conclusion is that the officials took about what the traffic would bear, and that they sent on to Mexico as little as they conveniently could.

The treatment the traders received depended to a large extent on the whims of the governor. Manuel Armijo, who sat in the old *Palacio* from 1838 to 1841 and again until the Americans arrived in 1846, was never popular with the Gringos — and for what might mildly be called sufficient reasons. But he was in a difficult position. Though he might have been willing to stop the trade if he could it was necessary not only to the welfare of his people but to his own capacious pockets.

Armijo, incidentally, was a figure of tragi-comic relief who was as hard to ignore as to admire. According to Kendall, who had no reason to like him, he was " born of low and disreputable parents at or near Albuquerque. . . From his earliest childhood his habits were bad. He commenced his career by petty pilfering and as he advanced in years extended his operations until they grew into important larcenies." He built up an estate by stealing sheep, so the story went. He was said to have boasted to his friends that he had stolen and resold the same identical ewe to his kindly old neighbor, Francisco Chavez, fourteen times. He also added to his fortune by notorious luck at the game of monte, and doubtless supplemented it still more when he became collector of customs in 1837, the year before he was made governor. He was " a large portly man of stern countenance and

blustering manner," with a reputed habit of caning his
lesser subjects in the streets if they did not take off their
hats quickly enough as he passed by. His reputation for
ferocity was based partly on his personal appearance
and mannerisms and partly on a limp derived from
a wound received in a fight with the Indians. But Kendall says that the Indian fight was none of his choosing.
But the legends may have been lopsided; new studies
indicate that Armijo may have been more sincere and
courageous that he has heretofore been painted.

When by hook and crook the goods had been cleared
by the customs officials the trading began. The country
merchants and storekeepers commonly resorted to Santa
Fe when the caravans were due and bought largely. It
was relatively easy to sell out a stock at wholesale in
this way, but larger profits were to be had in retailing.
Sometimes the traders opened stores of their own. The
difference between the two methods was often that between a profitable venture and a losing one. When business was slow traders who had borrowed money at home,
or mortgaged their farms, as many did in the early days
of the trade, had to sell at wholesale in order to meet
their obligations.

Often, as Gregg did on at least one occasion, they took
what was left of their goods and went to the markets of
Chihuahua and even farther south. Wetmore tells of
traders who took the same mules and wagons all the way
from the Missouri River to Matamoros—a distance, as
they travelled it, of about three thousand miles. Then
they went by sea to New Orleans and up the Mississippi
and the Missouri home. There were merchants,
such as the Magoffin brothers, who had regular establishments, not only in New Mexico but in Old
Mexico. Usually, however, the traders remained in

Santa Fe for four or five weeks disposing of their goods, and then, about September 1st, started back overland.

Some stayed longer. Some fell in love with the country or with the ladies of the country and settled down there. Unless one preferred blondes it was easy to fall in love in Santa Fe. Kit Carson's wife, Maria Josefa Jaramillo, was famous for a loveliness of " the haughty, heart-breaking kind." But Garrard, who uses this phrase, adds, as his next generalization, that " though we are strangers and enemies the Mexican women were ready to greet us with a smile."

" Strangers " the Americans were up to the very end of Mexican rule. Officially they were under suspicion from the start, and this suspicion grew as the tension between the two governments increased and rumors of war, too well verified at last, became frequent. There were many quarrels. At the time of the revolution against Governor Perez in 1837 the Americans were accused of being in sympathy with the rebels and in some instances their goods were impounded. In 1839 a party of Americans went to Armijo in a body to demand action against the murderers of a man named Daly, who had been killed in the mines near Santa Fe. They received little satisfaction, and the incident caused bad feeling. It was also a little difficult to tell an American from a Texan, and the Texans were not altogether popular in New Mexico during the last years of Mexican rule. Yet, on the whole, the traders seem to have gotten on well enough with the masses of the people, and for most of them the sojourn in Santa Fe was a period of wild merry-making. For the mule-drivers and bull-whackers, who had no financial responsibilities while in town, except to spend what they could of their pay, it was four or five weeks of undiluted joy. According to their tastes they drank deeply of the wine of life.

But while they drank and danced, gambled and made love, they were in more ways than one conquerors. The Santa Fe Trail was a spearhead that stabbed the sovereignty of Mexico to the heart.

CHAPTER XII

WAR DRUMS

NOW WAS coming an event which was to beat the Trail broad and deep with the tramp of infantry, the trot of cavalry, the rolling of guncarriages and an almost endless procession of government supply trains; which was to fix upon the road to the Southwest, for many months, the eager attention of a nation; which was to make the lonely way of the prairie trader intimately known to thousands who otherwise would never have travelled it; which was to render it, in its entirety, for the first time, a national responsibility; and which, finally, was to stir the western Indians to a pitch of violence never before equalled in the history of the plains. The expansionist dreams of Wilkinson were to be realized. Where the Americans had appeared as prisoners, as suppliants, as tolerated foreigners, they were to stand at last as masters. Destiny, working in strange ways, regardless of abstract justice, would not be stayed. The Mexican War, long foreshadowed, finally, came, with marching men and the thunder of guns.

The conflict which was to make the Trail a national highway came about, curiously enough, because of the attempt of the people of Texas to open up a New Mexican trail and trade of their own, through the territory which Cabeza de Vaca had opened and Coronado had penetrated three centuries earlier. This territory had been no man's land during the greater part of the Spanish and Mexican régimes. The famous Texas Santa Fe expedition was sent to cut a path through it and probably also to add to the Republic of Texas the part of New Mexico which lay east of the Rio Grande. This region Texas had claimed since the day of its independence. It passed the claim on to the United States when it entered the Union and even made an effort to organize New Mexico as a Texas county at the conclusion of the Mexican War. The war might have come about had there been no Texas claims and no Texas expedition, but these two factors together made it inevitable.

Ostensibly the Texas Santa Fe expedition was a private enterprise, though it went forth with the knowledge and blessing of President Lamar, and was commanded by a brevet brigadier-general of the Texas army, Hugh McLeod. Whether McLeod actually contemplated subduing the New Mexicans by force has been a matter of controversy. He could hardly have hoped to do so with the three hundred men at his disposal, but there can be no doubt that he would have annexed the province if he had found a sufficient number of the inhabitants ready to support him. Reports had, in fact, come from Santa Fe that the New Mexicans, neglected by the central government of Mexico, and exploited and abused by Governor Armijo, would welcome the Texans, just as five years later many of them did welcome the Americans. Some of the Santa Fe traders apparently hoped that this would be the case.

As it set out, in June 1841, the expedition was a combination of the military and the commercial. The military part consisted of two hundred and seventy privates, officered mainly from the Texas army, and well equipped and disciplined. With the little contingent went three commissioners bearing proclamations addressed to the supposedly down-trodden inhabitants of New Mexico. George Kendall, an American journalist who wrote the history of the abortive campaign, says that the Texans never doubted that " the liberal terms offered would be at once acceded to by a population living within the limits of Texas and who had long been groaning under a misrule the most tyrannical." He insists, also, that the adventure was " commercial in its intentions, the policy of the then President of Texas, General Mirabeau B. Lamar, being to open a direct trade with Santa Fe by a route known to be much nearer than the great Missouri Trail." Gregg had, of course, passed through the northern part of Texas in 1839, in the trip which he made from the mouth of the Arkansas. So, too, had James in 1821.

With the soldiers went a number of merchants, just how many Kendall does not say. They could not have carried large stocks of goods, for the expedition had but twenty-five wagons to haul all its supplies and merchandise. Nevertheless, General Sam Houston, in a florid and indignant letter which he wrote to General Santa Anna, after the unfortunate Texans had gotten into difficulties, spoke of the caravan as " a trading company." Of course it was a good deal more, or a good deal less, than that.

The caravan organized at Austin, then the last settlement on the western frontier of Texas. Before the adventurers lay what Kendall calls " nearly a thousand miles that never had been trodden before, except by the savage " — a statement that shows how much had been forgotten since the Spanish times. The halcyon days were soon over. The route was rough, supplies gave out, wagons broke down, and the men suffered severely from hunger, thirst, and fatigue. Worse yet, Armijo had been warned that the Texans were on the way, and news had been spread among the people that they were a band of desperate cutthroats who gave no quarter. Whether Armijo really believed this is a question. Whether he had even a slight justification for doing so is another and more serious question. Subsequent events, to give him his full due, did prove, not that all Texans were blood-thirsty, but that there were some blood-thirsty characters among them. At all events the doughty governor acted promptly and energetically. Captain Dámaso Salazar, sent out to meet the invaders, captured three scouts on September 4th. The men got away but were overtaken, one man was shot because he had made a show of resistance, and the other two were later executed. Not long afterwards five more of the Texans were seized near La Cuesta, and the remainder, divided into two detachments, were captured on September 17th and October 5th. Thus ended the "invasion."

Howland, one of the three men first captured, was shot at San Miguel in the presence of his comrades. He had been terribly slashed in the face when he was taken, and his execution was attended by the most harrowing circumstances. "Thus fell," says Kendall, who was present and saw everything, "as noble, as generous, and as brave a man as ever walked the earth. He was a native of New Bedford, Massachusetts, of a good family, and by his gentlemanly and affable deportment had endeared himself to every member of the expedition. In a daring attempt to escape and reach Colonel Cooke's party in order to give important information he had been retaken after a desperate struggle and the life he could not lose in the heat of the struggle was taken from him in this base and cowardly manner." Whether Howland's

execution was justified under military law obviously depended upon whether or not Mexico and Texas could be
considered at war. If a state of war existed it may have
been technically correct to treat him as a spy. But the
inhumanity shown toward him sent a flame of anger
throughout Texas — a flame that was to be extinguished
only in blood.

When all the Texans had been made prisoners Armijo
hurried back to Santa Fe to receive a popular welcome
which, whether or not it was sincere, was at least hearty.
The wretched prisoners were then sent south. On the
way Captain Salazar, who remained in charge, behaved
with the utmost brutality. One man, McAllister, unable to keep up with the column, was shot down in cold
blood, stripped, and his body left by the roadside. Four
other men died on the way to El Paso, and, according to
Kendall, Salazar cut off their ears, strung them on a strip
of buckskin, and presented them to Colonel Elias, commandant at El Paso, in order to prove that he had let
none of his charges escape. In doing this he was well
within the instructions said to have been given him by
Armijo — " If one of them pretends to be sick or tired
on the road shoot him down and bring me his ears."
The redeeming feature of the episode was that General
Elias, who is described as " a well bred, liberal and gentlemanly officer," denounced Salazar in the severest
terms and ordered him under arrest.

The Texans were taken to the City of Mexico, where
they were held for some months and finally released on
order of General Santa Anna. One of their number,
Captain Lewis, who had lived a long time in Mexico and
spoke Spanish fluently, was later proved to have been
in the pay of the Mexicans. All the evidence shows that
the expedition was a foolhardy one, based on false in-

formation, and doomed and betrayed from the start. Nevertheless, both in its causes and in its effects, it was enormously significant. The returning captives forgot the clemency that had been showed them, and the stories they had to tell when they got home rekindled a hatred that had not died out since the massacre of the Alamo and which was to have tragic results.

Kendall, who was held prisoner with the rest, despite the fact that he was an American citizen and a non-combatant, gives many details which are of interest to our story. At San Miguel the prisoners first reached "the great Missouri Road," and we have a picture of some of the passers-by. First came a caravan " direct from St. Louis, owned by one of the Chavez family," and with it Chavez himself, riding " in a neat buggy wagon." This may have been the same Chavez who fell victim, less than two years afterwards, to what purported to be Texan revenge. Three or four days later there arrived " another caravan made up of Americans on their way to California " — tantalizingly Kendall omits to give any further facts about them — and three or four days after that Mr. Samuel Magoffin, one of the well-known Chihuahua merchants and later the husband of Susan Shelby Magoffin, passed on his way south. James Magoffin, one of Samuel's brothers and partners, will enter our narrative a little later. James had been in the Santa Fe trade as far back as 1828. With Samuel and William Magoffin he had built up an important business in New and Old Mexico. Sometimes there would be three Magoffin caravans, each in charge of one of the brothers, on the road at the same time. But none of the passing traders and teamsters could give aid to the captive Texans, though they were anxious to do so.

Kendall's book, published after his return to the

United States, could almost be called the " Uncle Tom's Cabin " of the Mexican War. Its delineation of the character of the Mexican governing classes, which was in all conscience bad enough, and its accounts of the savage treatment meted out to the prisoners, stirred up resentment far beyond the boundaries of Texas. At this distance of time it is easy to understand that the Mexicans regarded the Texans as invaders pure and simple, and it is clear that in the matter of cruelty to captured enemies there was not much to choose between the worst elements in the two republics. But hatred of the Mexicans was also fed by land hunger, which always and unavoidably existed along the border, and by the economic urge which was thrusting American enterprise farther and farther into the Southwest.

If Texas got but little credit out of the McLeod expedition she got infinitely less from the next few episodes in the struggle. Ambitious proposals for a retaliatory invasion of Mexico finally dwindled down to raids upon the Santa Fe caravans, nearly half of which at this time were manned and owned by citizens of Santa Fe. The first of these resulted in one of the most diabolical murders ever committed by white men upon the Trail. Don Antonio José Chavez, perhaps the same who rode in his neat buggy wagon past Kendall's prison at San Miguel in 1841, set out from Santa Fe on his way to Independence in February 1843. He had five servants, two wagons, fifty-five mules, a few furs, and more than $10,000 in specie and bullion. He must have been supremely confident to start at that time of year with so much wealth and so small a force. He met with bad weather, one of his wagons had to be abandoned, all but five of his mules died, and he finally limped down to the Little Arkansas, in what is now Lyons County, Kansas, on April 10th.

Meanwhile " Captain " John McDaniel, who professed to hold a commission from the Texas government,
had organized a force of fifteen desperadoes on the Missouri River and had started west with the object of holding up Mexican caravans. A certain " Colonel " Warfield, also said to be the holder of a Texas commission,
was already on the plains for the same purpose, and it was
McDaniel's purpose to join forces with him. Rumors
of what was going on reached the American military
authorities and a troop of dragoons was sent in hot haste
on McDaniel's trail. Unhappily they did not overtake
him. McDaniel's ruffians rode into Chavez's camp,
which was of course well within the boundaries of the
United States, and plundered the little caravan of all its
goods. Then they divided. Seven of the party took
their share of the loot and started back for Missouri.
The other eight took Chavez a little distance from the
Trail and shot him down in cold blood, apparently on
the principle that dead men tell no tales.

This episode was too much to stomach, even for a frontier community which did not have much affection for
Mexicans. The Chavez reputation was well known, respected, and powerful. For once border sentiment
turned against the Anglo-Saxon and demanded justice
for his victim. Eventually ten of the McDaniel party
were captured, McDaniel and his brother David were
sent to the gallows, and the other eight were fined and
imprisoned.

The same year a force of about one hundred and eighty
Texans and Texas sympathizers under Colonel Jacob
Snively assembled in northern Texas and went raiding
along the Trail. It is said that Snively at first planned
to attack Santa Fe but his forces were not quite equal
the attempt. He marched instead to the crossings of the

Arkansas, where traders could be intercepted without too much risk. Meanwhile, Colonel Warfield, with whom McDaniel and his highwaymen were to have co-operated, had been engaged in a little campaign of his own. Warfield fell upon the helpless little village of Mora — that " thriving village with its nice little cottages and court house in the center," as Susan Magoffin described it — killed five of its inhabitants and stole some horses. It is pleasant to relate that he was so hotly pursued by the vengeful Mexicans that he finally staggered into Bent's Fort minus both the captured horses and his own mounts. But he was still thirsting for blood, and with twenty men came down the Arkansas and joined Snively.

The united forces moved over to the Trail at the point where it left the river, and there, on June 19, 1843, came into conflict with one hundred Mexicans under Captain Ventura Lobato, who composed the advance guard of the escort of five hundred men which Armijo was leading to meet and protect the spring caravans. The Mexicans were outnumbered, and the conflict was short and one-sided. Eighteen of Lobato's men were killed, and all but one or two of the remainder were captured. The Texans suffered no casualties — a rather sinister comment on a " battle " in which eighteen enemy lives were lost. The New Mexican historian, Bustamente, says that Snively cut the throats of all his prisoners. This is probably untrue, but the statement is important as showing what the New Mexicans had come to expect from the Texans.

One ominous feature of the affair was that the militiamen who were slaughtered were nearly all Pueblo Indians from Taos, who had been pressed into service by Armijo much against their will. Up to this time the

Indians had not been friendly to Armijo and were consequently inclined to be tolerant of the Americans and even of the Texans. Now they turned against all " foreigners," drove several out of Taos, and committed some outrages against American property. The incident probably had more than a little to do with the bloody revolt against American domination in which these Indians played a leading part four years later. At the same time the New Mexican liberals, who also disliked and distrusted Armijo, had been outraged by the murder of Chavez. Thus, though the Texans won what might be called a victory, they greatly embittered the relations between the two races.

Armijo, as recorded on certain other occasions, behaved with discretion rather than valor. He was encamped at Cold Springs, one hundred and forty miles to the rear, when the news of the encounter reached him. With his four hundred remaining men he retreated in a panic, leaving the incoming caravans to whatever fate they might encounter.

But Snively had a more formidable foe still to deal with. The year 1843 was the third in which the caravans from the Missouri had been escorted to the Arkansas by United States troops. We have already made the acquaintance of Captain Philip St. George Cooke, who had accompanied Riley's escort in 1829 and had written so entertainingly of its adventures, and we have seen him setting out in 1843 with his two hundred dragoons and his " two hundred wagons with twelve owners, independently disposed." Snively, perhaps counting on the natural sympathy of one Nordic blond for another, ventured across the Arkansas River into American territory to visit Cooke, and was unpleasantly surprised when that energetic officer went over to the Texans' bivouac and relieved them of every weapon he could lay hands on in camp. The caravan meanwhile passed safely on its way, the Indians not being very active that year. Snively's second in command, Warfield, gathered a number of the Texans who had managed to save their guns from confiscation and gave chase. For some reason, however, he thought better of his purpose and did not attack. Perhaps there were too many sharp-shooting Missourians among the traders.

Such was the undramatic and inglorious end, for the time being, of the Texan attempts to take revenge for the fate which had befallen the Santa Fe expedition. One result, which seemed for the moment profoundly serious, was an order from President Santa Anna closing the ports of northern Mexico to commerce coming over the Santa Fe Trail. To Gregg, who wrote his book on " The Commerce of the Prairies " while this order was in force, a tragic crisis seemed to have arrived. But the mandate, issued on August 7, 1843, was rescinded on March 31, 1844, and the caravans of that year, though delayed, included two hundred men and ninety wagons, and carried $200,000 worth of merchandise.

Events were now moving with feverish haste. Both the United States and Mexico expected war, and on both sides preparations were being made. On April 24, 1846, General Arista, commanding the Mexican forces on the Rio Grande, informed General Zachary Taylor that he considered hostilities already commenced, and emphasized his point by attacking a small force of American dragoons, killing sixteen and capturing the remainder. On May 13th the American Congress, having annexed Texas, concurred in Arista's opinion and the struggle was on. With the campaigns which won glory for Zachary Taylor and Winfield Scott and gave Ulysses S.

Grant, Jefferson Davis, and Robert E. Lee their baptism of fire we have no direct concern. But the march of the Army of the West across the plains, under Kearny, Doniphan, and Price, an event to which we shall come in the next chapter, has a most important share in any story of the Trail.

The threat of war had closed the great road in 1843, the reality flung it wide open, not only to troops but to a greatly enhanced commercial traffic. The trade went on as of old to the last possible moment. The last party to traverse the route under the old conditions was one of which Dr. A. Wislizenus was a member, which left Independence early in 1846. For the last time, as Dr. Wislizenus approached the Big Blue, the prairies were, in the old primeval sense, lonely. At this spot he seemed to himself to be at the " very junction of civilization and wilderness." " Toward the East," he mused, " we perceived the blessings of civilization — fine farms with cornfields, orchards, dwelling houses and all the sweet comforts of home; toward the West the lonesome, far-reaching prairie, without houses or culture, the abode of the restless Indian, the highway of the adventurous white man."

Let us go with Wislizenus and his friend Speyer, the leader of the caravan. A troop of United States dragoons were on their track, to intercept them or turn them back, but this they either did not know or ignored. They had twenty-two wagons, each drawn by ten mules, and some smaller vehicles — perhaps " a fine buggy wagon or two." There were thirty-five men in the party. Not until they reached Cottonwood Creek, near the present town of Durham, Kansas — again that slippery climb in and out of the treacherous and unrepentant Cottonwood! — did they feel it necessary to put on a night guard. So we see that the frontier of danger had been driven back since Becknell's day. They proceeded without incident and passed the spot where Snively had ambushed the Mexicans in 1843, and which had since been known as "Battle Ground." Leaving the Arkansas they crossed the *Jornada* safely to the lower springs of the Cimarron, and there had a pow-wow with some five hundred Cheyenne Indians, who were in a reasonably amicable mood. At Wagon Mound "the usual escort" of thirty ragged Mexican soldiers met them to take them into Santa Fe. The New Mexicans already knew that war had begun, but it apparently had not entered into their heads that this fact need interfere with the regular routine of the trade with Missouri.

On the Rio Mora, near the scene of Warfield's raid of three years earlier, Wislizenus found a ranch owned and operated by "Messrs. Smith and Wells" — the beginning of permanent American penetration. These gentlemen seem to have been living in perfect peace and good will with their Mexican neighbors. From the Mora the party proceeded to Santa Fe, which struck the good doctor at first sight as "more resembling a prairie-dog village than a capital." He was, very likely, expecting at least a granite or marble dome and some Corinthian pillars. At Santa Fe they learned of the American victory at Palo Alto. Yet Governor Armijo, moving like a man in a dream or actuated by some motives still hidden, carried on as though there were no war. He inspected the wagons and for the last time imposed a duty on American products brought into New Mexico. It came to $625 a wagon.

Completing their business in Santa Fe, Wislizenus and Speyer obtained the necessary passports and went tranquilly on into Chihuahua, quite as though nothing

out of the ordinary were going on. Meanwhile, perhaps
unknown to them, the United States dragoons had pursued them as far as the frontier. There had been a report that Speyer was taking some rifles and ammunition to the Mexican troops. Other traders, starting
a little later or more susceptible to hints from the higher
authorities, were corralled at Fort Bent, as the Magoffin
train had been, while supply wagons, artillery, cavalry
and infantry, regulars and volunteers, poured across the
plains. The hour had struck. The Army of the West
was moving on.

CHAPTER XIII

PATH OF EMPIRE

EXCEPT in loving memory, the Great Missouri Road was no longer to be a Trail. It was now to rise to epic proportions, to run in broad and dusty splendor across a great page of history. Neither the Mexican War nor any war will be glorified in this book. Nevertheless, there is no denying that the Mexican War brought us New Mexico, Arizona, and California, a fact of large and growing importance in the history of America. Immigration was soon to pour westward over the Sierras and make good by process of settlement what had been won by force of arms. But the right of way for that immigration was established once and for all by troops which marched over the Trail to Santa Fe and thence across the deserts to California. Our Trail, first indicated by the unshod hoofs of horses, then marked by wheels of traders' wagons, became in due season a true Path of Empire. It brought us a few thousands of dollars in profits, incalculable wealth in the currency of romance — and three imperial states. Such was the task completed through the instrumentality of the Army of the West.

This army, under Colonel, soon to be General, Stephen W. Kearny, was organized in Missouri, and with the exception of one battalion of infantry consisted entirely of Missouri volunteers. These were as rough and undisciplined a lot of men as ever marched under the

American colors, lacking in practically all military virtues except a willingness and ability to fight. Fortunately for their success, this turned out to be all that was needed. Second in command to Kearny was Colonel Alexander W. Doniphan of Missouri, and because Doniphan led the Missourians who went from New Mexico to Old Mexico after Kearny had gone on to California, the expedition was long known as Doniphan's. Next, leading a contingent of troops which followed Kearny and Doniphan at a considerable interval, was General Sterling Price, later to distinguish himself as an officer in the Confederate Army. Finally came the famous Mormon Battalion, under the command of Captain Jefferson Hunt and later of our old friend, Captain Philip St. George Cooke. The men of this organization were destined to make a notable march and to figure collectively and individually in the history of California.

There was contrast enough between the troops and their professional commanders. Kearny, a regular army officer of the old school, was not always popular with his high-spirited volunteer soldiers. Accustomed to men to whom soldiering was a trade, he did not know quite how to deal with those to whom it was an adventure. He was the sort of officer who would order his troops to march with their coats on and buttoned in the blazing desert heat because he believed that discomfort and discipline were synonymous terms. But he was a good soldier and, which is more important for our story, he turned out to be a first-class desert freighter.

Early in June, 1846, he began sending westward, at intervals of three or four days, supply trains with orders to rendezvous at Bent's Fort. These trains, though moving more slowly than the troops, were therefore ahead of them for a considerable part of the journey across the plains. If a regiment on the march ran short of supplies, as most regiments did sooner or later, it could send word to the wagon train next ahead on the Trail to halt, and could quicken its pace to reach its dinner — a practical application of the old tradition of hanging a bundle of hay in front of a lagging horse. The result was a surprising celerity of movement.

How many hundreds of wagons went over the Trail that year cannot be more than guessed at. Writer John T. Hughes, who marched with Doniphan, says that one hundred were about a week in advance of the expedition. Kearny is said to have had three hundred for the baggage of his own command. But the wagons not only preceded the troops but new trains were continually sent out behind them, and in time the same wagons and teamsters began to make round trips between the Missouri River and New Mexico. Once begun, this army freighting grew and diminished according to the exigencies of the moment, but it never again stopped until the railroad, a generation later, made it no longer necessary.

Each of the wagon trains of the Army of the West consisted of from twenty-five to thirty vehicles, carrying bread-stuffs and flour and usually accompanied by cattle to be killed when buffalo meat could not be obtained. The wagons were driven by well-seasoned, well-armed teamsters, under the command of an officer corresponding to the old-style caravan captain. They were not escorted. Nor were they, during the summer of 1846, menaced or molested by the Indians. The redmen, surprised and dismayed at the evidence of the power wielded by the Great White Father in Washington, gave the troops a wide berth. They were especially shy in the presence of cannon, which they feared and detested. To complete the commissary department there were experienced hunters. These men went ahead of the soldiers, usually travelling all night, making their kills and bringing in their game to the spot already selected for the next camp. The buffalo, in the early summer of 1846, were scarce at many points along the Trail, but they were to be found by the hundreds of thousands and slaughtered by the thousands, in the neighborhood of Pawnee Rock. Author Hughes guessed that between five hundred thousand and eight hundred thousand were in sight at a single time from the top of the Rock. Such estimates were doubtless inflated, but it is probably true that the buffalo covered the plains as far as the eye could see. It may also be true that they were never again so numerous.

Kearny led the van of his army, leaving Fort Leavenworth on June 30th. He was entering upon an experiment heretofore untried, for no such body of troops had ever crossed the plains. Whether he could get his forces to their destination, feed them on the way, and bring them into New Mexico in fighting trim was a debatable question. His success on the Trail, marching first to Santa Fe and then to California, was perhaps more remarkable than any fighting he did. The first few days were extremely difficult, for no trail had been broken from Fort Leavenworth to the point where Kearny meant to intersect the Santa Fe Road, on the famous Narrows. In the sweating heat of Kansas the teamsters struggled in seas of mud. On the steep bluffs which were all too frequent the mules or oxen had to be unhitched, and the soldiers hauled the wagons up by hand, a hundred men pulling at a wagon. On the march the army spread out, travelling in detachments of two or three companies of one hundred and fourteen men each. On the Fourth of July — it must have seemed a lucky omen

— the advance guard " struck the great Santa Fe Road
at what is called Elm Grove."

Kearny had orders from the War Department to delay
the Santa Fe traders as little as possible, though we have
seen that he was compelled to hold them up at Bent's
Fort until the army had passed. Somewhere west of Elm
Grove he came upon the annual caravan, plodding peacefully along, four hundred and fourteen wagons " heavily
laden with dry goods for the markets of Santa Fe and
Chihuahua, lining the road for miles." Thus the two
offensives, one commercial, the other military, were seen
for a little while passing westward together.

But the greater part of Kearny's men were military
only by title of courtesy. The Army of the West was a
citizens' levy, foreshadowing those greater armies which
were to fight a war so much vaster and sadder less than
two decades later. " Every calling and profession," says
Hughes, " contributed its share. There might be seen
under arms, in the ranks, the doctor, the professor, the
student, the legislator, the farmer, the mechanic and
artisan of every description, all united as a band of brothers to defend the right and honor of their country." A
private soldier, W. P. Hill of Missouri, was elected to
Congress while with Doniphan. The news overtook
him at Santa Fe, and Doniphan, though a member of the
opposing faction, was the first to congratulate him.

The troops started out in tremendous high spirits. On
the Fourth of July, the day on which the vanguard hit
the Santa Fe Trail, they marched twenty-seven miles
under a broiling sun. But no heat could parboil the joy
out of them. " Ever and anon," Hughes says, " the en-
thusiastic shout, the loud huzza and the animating Yankee Doodle were heard in honor of Independence Day."
There was something about going west across the plains

in those times that would have cheered a man though he knew he was going to his death. For days the march was like a great jovial picnic, with the mess dishes piled high with meat of buffalo, elk, antelope, deer, and wild fowl, with fish from the Arkansas River with grapes and plums to be had for the picking. Captain Riche, sutler to the First Dragoons, organized a mail service — probably the first that ever went regularly and officially across the plains — and soldiers in camp sat down to write the folks at home what a fine time they were having. Or they went in bathing, five hundred men at a time, in the tepid waters of the Arkansas. The wide plains were safe and cheerful — and no longer lonely.

Kearny had been advised that the cut-off across the Cimarron desert — our old acquaintance, the *Jornada* — was too dangerous for an army, and he therefore marched up the Arkansas. Hughes notes that this route "diverged from the main Santa Fe road," which shows that the Cimarron cut-off was then the recognized "Trace." The weather grew warmer. The troops tramped along the banks of the river over waterworn pebbles so hot that they would blister the naked feet. Finally, about eight miles below Bent's Fort, the leading companies halted and encamped, to wait until the rear guard and supply trains had come up. The Santa Fe traders, with the exception of the evasive Speyer, waited, too. Frank S. Edwards, who went with Doniphan, estimates that Kearny had 1750 men, of whom 850 were under Doniphan's command. The figure may have been a little lower. Sixteen pieces of artillery had been trundled across the prairies.

The time in camp passed quietly enough, except for a stampede of a thousand horses, some of which ran from thirty to fifty miles before they were caught. On

August 2nd the bugles sounded and the drums beat again, and Kearny set forth for the conquest of New Mexico, heading into a gale which drove sand like sleet into the men's faces. Up they went, along the parched valley of the Timpas, where the only living things beside themselves were a few hares or antelopes scurrying along the sand ridges. The water was " scarce, muddy, bitter, filthy." The army teamsters, " when water was near, sprang from their seats and ran for it like mad men." But on August 5th the army reached the Purgatoire, and men and animals alike drank to distention of its clear, cold waters. John B. Hughes, scrambling to the top of Cimarron Peak, not far from the Purgatoire camp, and there, " surrounded by the grandest scenery the world can furnish read with double enthusiasm the first canto of Campbell's 'Pleasures of Hope.'" This conquering army was not all ferocity or drab practicality. It had its romanticists, who marched through golden clouds.

However, three days later, the rations were abbreviated to one-third of the normal allowance. The supply trains had done their best but their best was not quite good enough. They could not be sent ahead into hostile territory. From that time, practically to the end of the campaign, the soldiers rarely had enough to eat. And here and there men began to drop and die, from heat, exhaustion, under-nourishment and camp diseases. But the unwavering Kearny pushed on, over Raton Pass, down, on August 13th, to the Rio Mora and the little village which Susan Magoffin had admired and Colonel Warfield had plundered. On the 17th the army was at Pecos, facing Apache Canyon, and ready for battle.

Some doubt will always remain as to why there was no battle. General Armijo, in his breezy way, at first threatened the American forces with complete annihilation. A scouting party sent under command of Lieutenant De Courcey into the Taos valley, brought back rumors that the Utes and other tribes were combining with the Mexicans to oppose the American advance. But Kearny put on a bold as well as conciliatory front. On the last day of July, while still at Fort Bent, he had drawn up a proclamation and now he began scattering copies of it among the New Mexican villages and ranches. "The undersigned," he announced, "enters New Mexico with a large military force, for the purpose of seeking union with and ameliorating the condition of its inhabitants. This he does under instructions from his government, and with the assurance that he will be amply sustained in the accomplishment of this object. It is enjoined on the citizens of New Mexico to remain quietly at their homes and pursue their peaceful avocations. So long as they continue in such pursuits they will not be interfered with by the American army, but will be respected and protected in their rights, both civil and religious. All who take up arms against the government of the United States will be regarded as enemies and treated accordingly."

A copy of this document was given to Captain Cooke and he was sent under a flag of truce to Santa Fe, by way of Las Vegas. With him went Susan Magoffin's brother-in-law, James Magoffin, the Chihuahua trader and the "Brother James" of Susan's diary. No emissary could have been better selected. Magoffin was, as Bancroft says, "a man of wealth, with unlimited capacity for drinking wine and making friends, speaking the Spanish language, and on friendly terms with most of the leading men in New Mexico and Chihuahua." General Armijo, perhaps a bit chastened by this time, received the envoys courteously, listened to what they had to say, and sent back Cooke with the ambiguous message that he would dispatch a commissioner in return and that he would come out to meet Kearny with an army of six thousand desperate men. Taken literally this communication sounded blood-thirsty. But something of a different tenor was going on behind the scenes. Magoffin, as the bill amply proves which he subsequently rendered to the United States government, and which was in part honored, was a secret agent with the very laudable mission of inducing the New Mexicans to surrender without bloodshed. He afterwards spent many thousands of dollars in "entertaining" citizens of Santa Fe, El Paso, and Chihuahua, and the specific sum of $3,800 in bribes to procure his release when he was arrested as a spy in Chihuahua.

He did not, so far as his accounts show, pay any money to Armijo, but he does seem to have persuaded the general that the situation did not call for fighting, bleeding, and dying. To Colonel Archuleta, Armijo's second in command, he is said to have suggested that all that part of New Mexico west of the Rio Grande and not yet claimed by the Americans might very easily fall into the hands of an ambitious New Mexican general. Magoffin tarried in Santa Fe. Captain Cooke went trotting back to Kearny with the outwardly defiant message from Armijo, and he presently wrote and circulated a proclamation advising New Mexico villagers over the governor's signature calling upon the citizens of New Mexico to fight to the last ditch against "the Americans who were coming to invade their soil and destroy their property and liberties."

Then, on August 14th, the very day on which, as was subsequently discovered, Armijo had made his will and completed his preparations for a trip to Old Mexico, Kearny received from the valiant general an official communication reading as follows: "You have notified me that you intend to take possession of the country I govern. The people of the country have risen en masse in my defence. If you take the country it will be because you prove the strongest in battle. I suggest to you that you stop at the Sapello and I will march to the Vegas. We will meet and negotiate on the plains between them." An officer of lancers, with a sergeant and two privates, all rigged up in shiny new uniforms, delivered this message. Kearny's troopers, looking them over with professional eyes, arrived at the comfortable conclusion that an American dragoon could outfight three or four Mexican lancers. Kearny himself read the note without changing countenance and jogged on. On the morning of the 15th he rode into Las Vegas.

Here he was peaceably received by the alcalde and the people, made a speech from the top of a low building in which he declared that the Americans had come "as friends, not as enemies, as protectors, not as conquerors," warned the inhabitants of the dire things that would happen to them if they questioned this doctrine with arms in their hands, and ended by administering the oath of allegiance to the United States to the alcalde and other officials. Then, with colors flying and drums beating, he sallied out to look for Armijo.

But Armijo proved elusive. He was not at Tecolote. He was not at San Miguel. He was not at Pecos. Here, a record says, "the city was in a measure deserted, the inhabitants having been persuaded that we should rob and ill-treat everybody and destroy everything; sobbing and crying were heard from the houses, and it was only after a long speech from the General that they were at all pacified." Happily the general was an orator of no mean abilities.

From Pecos the Americans moved on with the expectation of an encounter in Apache Canyon, a position of great natural strength which a regiment might have held against an army. Armijo had, in fact, marched to the pass. He had then marched away again. Kearny therefore gave up his half-formed plan to turn the position by means of flanking parties sent over the adjacent mountain trails; and in fighting formation, with muskets loaded and sabres drawn, the troops approached the mouth of the defile. Not an enemy presented itself. By the middle of the afternoon the advance guard had sighted Santa Fe from the spot which had cheered the hearts of so many trail-worn traders. Before night-fall the little army was pouring into the streets of the city, and the ancient capital where for forty years Americans had been aliens became, to all intents and purposes, American soil.

This was on the 18th of August. That evening Kearny and his officers dined with the New Mexican Lieutenant-Governor, Vigil, who had stepped into Armijo's shoes, the American flag was hauled to the top of the staff above the Palace, and a sunset salute of thirteen guns was fired by the American artillery. Next morning General Kearny, again assuming the rôle of orator, addressed the populace in the plaza.

"We have come among you," he said, " to take possession of New Mexico, which we do in the name of the government of the United States. We have come with peaceable intentions and kind feelings toward you all. We come as friends to better your conditions and make you a part of the United States. We mean not to murder you or rob you of your property. Your families shall be free from molestation, your women secure from violence. My soldiers shall take nothing from you but what they pay for. . . In our government all men are equal. We esteem the most peaceable man the best man. I advise you to attend to your domestic pursuits, cultivate industry, be peaceable and obedient to the laws. Do not resort to violent means to correct abuses. . . You are no longer Mexican subjects; you are now become American citizens. . . I am your governor — henceforth look to me for protection."

In view of the existing situation and in the light of events to come, these words have an ironical ring. Nevertheless, they were accepted without protest for the time being. They had to be, for Kearny, the apostle of peace, could muster bayonets in overwhelming numbers. Moreover, many of the New Mexicans, and especially those who were engaged in the Missouri trade, were willing enough to receive the Americans. Neither in Spanish nor in Mexican times had there been intimate association with Old Mexico. New Mexico was less than a province, it was almost a separate nation. The tragedy that was soon to follow General Kearny's fair words was due to local attitudes, not loyalty to a faraway central government.

Kearny moved with all possible haste in order to resume his march to California, his ultimate goal. He received submissive delegations from the Pueblo Indians, some of whom were to sing a dreadfully different song before many months. He selected a site for a fort, and Captain Emory laid out, at Santa Fe, what was later christened Fort Marcy. He wrote to Washington that " the people of the Territory are now perfectly tranquil and can easily be kept so." He gave a grand *baile,* at which the American officers danced with the dark-

eyed daughters of Santa Fe. He marched down to Tomé
to meet a Mexican army reported to be on the way from
Chihuahua, found no enemy, and marched back again.
To Washington he again reported that " the inhabitants
of the country were found to be highly satisfied and contented with the change of government, and apparently
vied with each other to see who could show us the greatest hospitality and kindness." On the 22nd of September he organized a civil government, with Charles Bent,
one of the famous brothers of Bent's Fort, as governor,
Vigil as secretary, and another New Mexican, Antonio
José Otero, as one of the two judges of the superior court.
Three days later, well content, he set out with three
hundred dragoons on his famous march to California.

On October 9th came the first division of the Mormon
Battalion, comprising the hardier members of the expedition, and on the 12th the sick and exhausted limped
or were carried into town, five hundred men in all.
These troops had been mustered in late in July at Kanesville — or, as it was later known, Council Bluffs —
Iowa, with the understanding that they were to march
through to California, assist in the conquest of that
country, and there be discharged, to form a colony if they
wished. Their religious views and social customs had
already gotten them into trouble with their neighbors,
and it was considered good policy to help them in every
possible way on their exodus westward.

Four companies, after having been blessed by Brigham
Young, Heber Kimball, and other Mormon leaders,
started from Kanesville on July 20th. A fifth company
caught up with them a few days later, and marching
gaily to the tune of " The Girl I Left Behind Me," they
footed it to Fort Leavenworth. Here their commanding
officer, Captain James Allen of the First Dragoons, de-

tailed by the War Department to take them over the Trail, fell ill and soon afterwards died. They continued on their way, leaving Fort Leavenworth in two detachments, on August 12th and August 14th. On receiving news of Allen's death they chose their senior captain, Jefferson Hunt, in his place. They had with them twenty-seven women, most of them wives of enlisted men, carried on the rolls as laundresses, and a number of children. This was no doubt the first and last time in the history of the American army that women accompanied an invading force in that capacity.

The narratives of the march, which ultimately carried the survivors to the shores of the Pacific, are a mixture of struggles with nature and quarrels with the officers, particularly with the surgeon. The Mormons at this time believed in the possibility of miraculous cures, several of which are gravely described by their historian, Sergeant Daniel Tyler, and they were stubbornly opposed to " mineral medicines." Unhappily they were accompanied by a surgeon whose favorite dose for almost any ailment was calomel. Tyler gives us indignant pictures of Dr. Sanderson, " with horrid oaths," feeding calomel to unwilling patients out of a rusty old spoon. " It appears," so one soldier wrote gloomily in his diary, " that the colonel and surgeon are determined to kill us, first by force [sic] marches to make us sick, then by compelling us to take calomel or to walk and do duty."

It is certain that the column moved with great dispatch, calomel or no calomel. On August 31st they were at Diamond Springs, on September 2nd at Cottonwood Creek, on September 9th at Pawnee Fork. This stream they crossed with great difficulty, letting the wagons down on one side and pulling them up on the other by ropes On the 11th they reached the Arkansas, and

waded out into the stream to spear fish with their swords
and bayonets and replenish their depleted larder. It
was somewhere along the Arkansas that Parkman, returning from the journey he later described in "The
California and Oregon Trail," encountered them.
"There was," he says, "something very striking in the
half-military, half-patriarchal appearance of these
armed fanatics, thus on their way with their wives and
children to found, it might be, a Mormon empire in California. We were much more astonished than pleased at
the sight before us. . . In the morning the country
was covered with mist. We were always early risers, but
before we were ready, the voices of men driving in the
cattle sounded all around us. As we passed above their
camp we saw through the obscurity that the tents were
falling and the ranks rapidly forming; and mingled with
the cries of women and children the rolling of the Mormon drums and the clear blast of their trumpets sounded
through the mist." Parkman adds that "from that time
to the journey's end we met almost every day long trains
of government wagons, laden with stores for the troops
and crawling at a snail's pace toward Santa Fe."

Instead of following Kearny's route by way of Bent's
Fort, the Mormon Battalion took the old road from the
Arkansas across the *Jornada* to the Cimarron, spending
two days and two nights on the desert, suffering terribly
from thirst and being tantalized by mirages of lakes and
green trees. Here and there men died and were buried in
shallow graves in the sand. Not all Dr. Sanderson's
calomel could save them, nor all their faith. But on
September 20th the survivors were on Cimarron Creek.
A few days later, worrying lest Kearny disband them if
they were not in Santa Fe on October 10th, the day appointed for their arrival, the stronger pushed forward

by "force marches." Kearny was far away on the desert, but Colonel Doniphan received them with a salute of a hundred guns, fired from the roofs of the houses. No one, however little sympathetic with their religious practices, could say they had not earned it.

Behind the Mormons at the start, but beating them into Santa Fe, came Colonel Price, with thirteen hundred more Missouri volunteers, nine or ten thousand mules and oxen, and what James Madison Cutts, a contemporary historian, describes as " an immense number of wagons with stores and baggage." Among these troops were many of the Mormon's old enemies. Naturally Tyler did not think well of them. "We found them," he writes, after an encounter with a detachment on the Trail, " a profane, wicked and vulgar set of men." Parkman, who also met them, gives a better balanced but amusing description of their habits and appearance. When he saw them they were marching westward in groups of one or two companies. A delegation from a St. Louis battalion visited his camp.

" There were some ruffian faces among them," he tells us, "and some haggard with debauchery, but on the whole they were extremely good-looking men, superior beyond measure to the ordinary rank and file of an army. Except that they were booted to the knees, they wore their belts and military trappings over the ordinary dress of citizens. Besides their swords and holster pistols they carried slung from their saddles the excellent Springfield carbines, loaded at the breech." Next arrived some specimens of a company from " one of the frontier counties," who " came crowding around, pushing between our first visitors and staring at us with unabashed faces. ' Are you the captain? ' asked one fellow. ' What's your business out here? ' asked another. ' Whar do you live when you're at home?' said a third. 'I reckon you're traders,' surmised a fourth. . . A little while after, to our amazement, we saw a large cannon with four horses come lumbering up behind the crowd; and the driver, who was perched on one of the animals, stretching his neck so as to look over the rest of the men, called out: 'Whar are you from, and what's your business?' . .

"No one can deny the intrepid bravery of these men, their intelligence and the bold frankness of their character, free from all that is mean and sordid. Yet for the moment the extreme roughness of their manners half inclines one to forget their heroic qualities. Most of them seem without the least perception of delicacy or propriety, though among them individuals may be found in whose manners there is a plain courtesy, while their features bespeak a gallant spirit equal to any enterprise."

Parkman gives us another picture, this time of a caravan on the march. "At noon on the 14th of September," he relates, "a very large Santa Fe caravan came up. The plain was covered with the long files of their white-topped wagons, the close black carriages in which the traders travel and sleep, large droves of animals and men on horseback and on foot. They all stopped on the meadow near us. Our diminutive cart and handful of men made but an insignificant figure by the side of their vast and bustling camp." It is interesting to note that Parkman was struck by the contrast between "the clumsy ox-wagons" of the army supply trains and "the rakish vehicles of the Santa Fe traders." "I thought," he says of one of the army trains, "that the whole frontier might have been ransacked in vain to furnish men worse fitted to meet the dangers of the prairie. Many of

them were mere boys, fresh from the plow, and devoid
of knowledge and experience."

The Indians prowled around the camps and fired into
them, and one or two men were killed. But on the whole
the prairies were comparatively safe that summer. So
much at ease did Price's men feel, and so unmilitary
were they in the early stages of their journey, that they
sometimes slept without sentinels or pickets. Two or
three companies of the Missourians were sent by way
of Bent's Fort and Raton Pass. The others, like the
Mormon Battalion, took the Cimarron route. Price
himself, riding ahead of his troops, reached Santa Fe
on September 28th, three days after Kearny had left on
his way to California. Then the soldiery poured in until
there were 3500 armed Americans in the old provincial
city.

"The capital was now literally alive," says Hughes,
"with artillery, baggage wagons, commissary teams,
beef cattle, and a promiscuous throng of American soldiers, traders, visitors, stragglers, trappers, amateurs,
mountaineers, Mexicans, Pueblo Indians, women, and
children, numbering perhaps not less than 14,000 souls."
Every day new provision trains were rumbling in, adding
to the tumult and congestion. Traders, anxious to get
down to the rich markets of Chihuahua, champed impa-
tiently at the bit, but had to wait for Doniphan to return
from a swing through the Navajo country and march
south ahead of them.

When Doniphan did come back, after inducing the
Navajos to sign a treaty with the new lords of the land,
he marched his Missourians down the Rio Grande Valley,
suffering severely during the crossing of the *Jornada del
Muerto*, where the old trail to Chihuahua leaves the river
and cuts across a region as waterless as the other famous

Jornada of the Cimarron. His men were still very much the same undisciplined mob whom Parkman had met on the Trail, unwashed, unshaved, ragged, insubordinate, and argumentative. With them went the traders, pursuing the almighty dollar through every hardship and danger. At the Brazito, above El Paso, on Christmas Day, Doniphan met and scattered a Mexican force of seven hundred men. On the 28th he took El Paso — that is to say, the Mexican town now called Juarez — without a shot, waited there six weeks for reinforcements, and on February 8th moved forward again. On the 28th of February he met and defeated the Mexicans at Sacramento and next day occupied the city of Chihuahua. This was the final battle of his campaign, and next spring the command was sent back to the United States by way of New Orleans, having travelled, as Twitchell says, "more than six thousand miles, nearly two thousand miles more than the famous march of Xenophon and the Greeks in their retreat from Asia."

Meanwhile first Kearny and after him Cooke and the Mormon Battalion were proving that Santa Fe was, in a historic sense, but a way station on the road to California. Kearny, leaving the New Mexican capital on September 25th, made a notable march down the Rio Grande Valley, across the *Jornada del Muerto,* then westward to the Pacific Coast by way of the Mimbres Valley and the Gila. He reached San Diego in December. His encounter with the Californians in the disastrous little battle of San Pascual, his quarrel with Frémont, and his pacification of the western empire are outside the course of our narrative, though they make a story of thrilling interest. The Mormon Battalion, arriving too late to accompany Kearny, followed him un-

der the command of Captain Cooke. The Battalion
had been reduced in numbers by the withdrawal of men
who were physically unable to go on. They, with the
women and children, went north to Colorado. The
force remaining was somewhat more military in appearance and something less patriarchal than when Parkman encountered it. It left Santa Fe on October 19th,
marching by way of Tucson, and tracing over a part of
their course the route later traversed by the Southern
Pacific railway. Taking their stock and wagons with
them, marching through Mexican strongholds to beat
of drums and blast of trumpets, hewing a road where
no wagons had previously passed, they reached San Luis
Rey on January 27th and San Diego four days later.
They had marched 1400 miles in 104 days — a magnificent record through such a region for troops thus
encumbered. Some of their oxen and mules had
been driven all the way from Nauvoo to the Pacific
Coast.

Cooke, a severe but just commander, said of this
achievement that " history may be searched in vain for
an equal march of infantry." He added, in a citation
read in formal military style before the paraded battalion: " With crowbar and pick and axe in hand we have
worked our way over mountains which seemed to defy
aught save the wild goat, and hewed a passage through
a chasm of living rock more narrow than our wagons. . .
Thus, travelling half-naked and half-fed, we have discovered and made a road of great value to our country."

Price, left to command in Santa Fe, settled to guard
the country and consolidate the American position. It
was the first time that Americans in such large numbers
had tried to live for so long a time side by side with the

New Mexicans. The result was picturesque but not happy. Even regular troops in garrison in an occupied territory tend to lose their morale, and Price's troops had few of the more prosaic military virtues of the regulars.

CHAPTER XIV

AFTERMATH OF CONQUEST

AN ARMY had to be supplied. Westward across the plains rolled unceasingly the wagons of the traders and the supply trains of the army. Eastward rattled the emptier caravans. All along the borders, all across the prairies, the Indians were growing restive. Their hatred of the invading white men outran their fear. Around great fires, their shadows thrown hugely against the prairie night, they danced the wardance. . .

In Santa Fe the garrison was amusing itself, in all the good and bad ways that are open to garrisons. The officers organized a dramatic society and gave plays " in the *fandango* room in the Palace " — " Barbarossa," " Pizarro," " Bombastes Furioso," and others of similar sort. The polka was danced at one entertainment "by an American gentleman and a Spanish lady." The Virginia Minstrels gave a show at which they sang, " Get along Home, You Spanish Girl," " The Blue-Tail Fly," and " You Ain't Good-Looking and You Can't Come In."

But the Mexicans were already referring contemptuously to the Americans as Gringos, and the Americans called the Mexicans Greasers. At the same time Mexican drinks and Mexican women tempted the Missourians, as they would have tempted any army but Cromwell's. While the soldiers swaggered and the Mexican males scowled and muttered the women continued, womanlike, to smile. " They do not seem to know what virtue or industry is," said Edwards, writing of the situation in Santa Fe at this time; " and being almost the slave of the husband, who will sit day after day in the sun and smoke his cigaritos without offering to assist his hard-working wife in anything, are very fond of the attentions of strangers." And now there were plenty of strangers in town! Strangers fresh from the womanless desert and ready enough to give attention to a femininity which, if not always modelled according to the prevailing American standards, yet furnished " the most beautiful and the *boldest* walkers " that the newcomers had ever seen.

With this temptation and that, in short, the army began to deteriorate. Ruxton, who, it should be remembered, was an Englishman, not inclined to see extraordinary virtues in anything American, called the soldiers as he saw them in the streets of Santa Fe " the dirtiest, rowdiest crew I have ever seen collected together. Crowds of volunteers filled the streets, brawling and boasting but never fighting. Mexicans, wrapped in *serapes,* scowled upon them as they passed. . . Under the portales were numerous monte tables, surrounded by Mexicans and Americans. Every other house was a grocery, as they call a gin or whiskey shop, continually disgorging reeling, drunken men, and everywhere filth and dirt reigned triumphant." A Taos Indian woman, from whom Ruxton sought lodging, cried out when she learned that he was an Englishman, " Gracias a Dios! A Christian will sleep with us tonight, and not an American! " The sober truth is that for American we might substitute a volunteer soldier of any nation in such a predicament. As another and later Englishman than

Ruxton said, " Single men in barricks don't turn into plaster saints."

At all events the honeymoon period of the conquest was over. The Pueblo Indians had grown bitterly hostile to the Americans. A native party, led by the same Don Diego Archuleta whom Magoffin had bought off with golden promises, planned a general uprising against the Yankees on Christmas Eve, while the rehearsals for " Barbarossa " were going on at the Palace. The plot was discovered, and the leaders fled. But the rebellion was only delayed. On the 19th of January 1847, it broke out simultaneously in several places and with cruel violence. Governor Bent, who was at his home in Taos, relied upon the friendly relations he had always had with the New Mexicans, and paid no attention to warnings which reached him. All day on the 18th the Indians from the Pueblo flocked into the little town, and the mob spirit grew madder every hour as whiskey and oratory flowed freely. Still Bent would not take advantage of the opportunity yet open to him to make his escape. He had outlasted too many stern vigils on the plains to be frightened by a Taos mob.

On the morning of the 19th the crowd gathered in front of his house. He went to the door and tried vainly to bring them to their senses. When he turned at last to escape, it was too late. In the house were Mrs. Bent and her sister, Mrs. Kit Carson (she who had been the heartbreakingly beautiful Josefa Jaramillo) ; the Bents' two young children ; and a Mrs. Boggs, wife of the newly-appointed government mail carrier. Both Carson and Boggs were absent, Carson with Kearny in California and Boggs out on the plains with his mail. It was always believed that if Carson had been present the Indians might have spared Bent's life. But as he sprang within the doorway he was shot down, scalped while yet alive, and pierced with many wounds as he still struggled to escape. His helpless family witnessed everything. A compassionate Mexican woman sheltered them, and they and their friends escaped.

Five other persons, including Mrs. Carson's brother, himself a New Mexican, were killed in Taos. Seven were killed at Turley's Mill, near Arroyo Hondo, twelve miles from Taos. The day after Bent's murder a party of eight or nine traders on their way to the Missouri River were riding unsuspectingly into the little town of Mora — Mora, that " thriving village with its nice little cottages and court house in the center," Mora, the scene of Warfield's brutal raid in 1843. Now there was a New Mexican guerrilla leader, Manuel Cortés. Cortés seized the traders and ordered them shot. Las Vegas was saved by the presence of an American grazing detachment under Captain Hendley. Santa Fe itself was threatened.

But suppression was almost as swift and merciless as the rebellion itself. On the 24th of January, with 353 men, Price met 1500 insurgents at La Cañada de Santa Cruz and defeated them with trivial losses to himself. Five days later he beat them again at Embudo. On the 4th of February he came upon them at Taos, where they had barricaded themselves in the old church. The fury of the assault and the desperation of the defence were redoubled by the memory of Bent's murder. The Americans pounded the church with cannon, made a breach and charged through. When the smoke cleared away seven Americans and one hundred and fifty New Mexicans and Indians lay dead. The ruins of the church were left as an object lesson ; the modern tourist may still visit them.

This was the end of the insurrection, except for subsequent guerrilla warfare along the Trail in which New
Mexicans were believed to have joined with the Indians.
As late as May 1847, a mixed force of Indians and Mexicans, apparently commanded by the same Cortés who
had killed the traders up at Mora, fought a battle with
a small company of troopers under Major D. B. Ed-
mondson. The Americans lost one man killed in this
encounter and killed forty-one of the enemy. Cortés
met the Americans on one other occasion, near La
Cuesta and remained a guerrilla leader, taking refuge
in the mountains and sallying forth with his band of
Indians and New Mexicans to attack the caravans.

Meanwhile the greater part of the country was again
quiet. Lieutenant-Governor Vigil, Armijo's former second in command, became acting governor for a time as
the result of Bent's death and issued a scathing proclamation in which he denounced the slayers of his friend
and affirmed his allegiance to the American government.
Six of the conspirators were tried by civil court and condemned to death, five for murder and one, certainly with
far less justification, for treason. A number of others,
twenty-five or thirty, according to Twitchell, were tried
by court-martial and hanged. Not all of these could
have been guilty of what a civil court in a peaceful land
would have called murder. The Americans were masters. But a smouldering resentment remained and did
not soon die out. Kearny's fair words, blown down the
desert wind, had now a bitter echo. Something idyllic
in New Mexican life perhaps died out forever after that
savage revolt and its stern punishment. . .

Conditions among the American soldiers did not improve. " All is hubbub and confusion here," wrote a
correspondent of the New York *Courier and Enquirer*

on August 13th. " Discharged volunteers are leaving,
drunk, and volunteers, not discharged, are remaining,
drunk." A reporter for the St. Louis *Republican* wrote
that " nearly the whole territory has been the scene of
violence, outrage and oppression by the volunteer soldiers against all alike, without distinction." Some allowance may have to be made, in interpreting these as-
sertions, for the political passions of the day. Price had
bitter enemies at home, and in New England the war had
been violently denounced as a piece of unwarranted
aggression in the interests of the slave-holders. Yet
there can be little doubt that behind the smoke was at
least a little fire. The volunteers remained fiercely an-
tagonistic to discipline. They were idle. Their passions
had been aroused by the violent acts of some of the
rebels. They had a true frontier contempt for " the
lesser breeds without the law." If they had behaved like
Christian soldiers it would have been a miracle. The
crusading spirit, what there was of it, had exhausted
itself. All that remained was the struggle for spoils,
politician against politician, free-state men against pro-
slavery men, Texans against Missourians. It is impossible not to feel that something clean and fine, that had
been bred of the early days of the Trail, had been dragged
in the mud and blood.

Price, who had made a trip east late in 1847, came
back in December. In March 1848, he marched south
and defeated the Mexicans in a final battle at Santa
Cruz de Rosalia, in Chihuahua. He had already earned
the enmity of the Santa Fe traders by affixing duties
which, while not equal to those of the unlamented Armijo, were unjust in the eyes of men who had believed
that the conquest would relieve them of the necessity
for paying any duties at all. These amounted to six per

cent on the value of all goods, and were supposed to help pay the expenses of the civil government. Price also imposed a $4 tax on " waggons for the Arkansas and Chihuahua " and a tax of $2 each on " pleasure carriages for the above places." Free-born American citizens could not be expected to endure these taxes without complaint. Early in 1848 a protest against them was " adopted and signed by all the merchants and citizens of Santa Fe." Thus, little by little, it became evident that the conquest had not ushered in the millennium. People still had their troubles and there was still injustice in the world. Four years after the conquest John Greiner, Indian agent at Santa Fe, could still write: " There is hardly an American here that stirs abroad without being armed to the teeth, and under his pillow pistols and bowie-knife may always be found. None go to bed without these precautions."

But the factor that did most to make life tragic and exciting was the Indians, who recovered all too soon from their fear of the white soldiers and the big guns. The Navajos, with whom Doniphan had made a treaty, broke it, and peace with them was ended. The Pawnees and Comanches, perhaps at the suggestion of such men as Cortés, "committed repeated depredations on the government trains, fearlessly attacked the escorts, killed or drove off large numbers of horses, mules, and oxen belonging to the government, and in several instances overpowered and slew or captured many of our people. They openly declared that they would cut off all commerce between the United States and Mexico and kill or enslave every American who might venture to pass the plains." The Apaches did not need to boast. Their deeds spoke for them. Three weeks after Parkman reached the frontier, in the late fall of 1846, " the Paw-

nees and the Comanches began a regular series of hostilities on the Arkansas trail, killing men and driving off
horses. They attacked, without exception, every party,
large or small, that passed during the next six months."

The summer of 1847 opened with no better promise.
On the 22nd of June the Indians attacked a government
train on the Arkansas, and though they did not succeed
in killing any of the guards or drivers, drove off and
butchered eighty yoke of oxen. Four days later, em-
boldened by this exploit, they intercepted and attacked
a government convoy of thirty traders and eighty dragoons under Lieutenant Love which was carrying
$300,000 in specie with which to pay the troops at Santa
Fe. In this fight Love lost five men killed and had six
wounded, and even then extricated himself with difficulty. Never had the Indians shown such audacity or
such generalship. Lieutenant Peck, with a party which
included "Mr. McKnight from Chihuahua" and Kit
Carson himself, was waylaid by the Comanches on the
Arkansas, and though the Indians were repulsed the
party lost thirty-five horses. In the fall of the same
year Captain Mann was attacked thirty miles below the
crossing of the Arkansas, had one man killed and four
wounded, and lost all his stock.

According to Cutts, who wrote from contemporary experience and full reports, "the Indians attacked every
train that has gone or come in this year." Lieutenant-
Colonel Gilpin, who commanded at Fort Mann on the
Arkansas, estimated that during the summer of 1847
the Indians killed forty-seven Americans, destroyed 330
wagons, and ran off or butchered 6500 head of stock.
Most of these losses were suffered by the government
trains. Even at this comparatively late date there were,
on the Cimarron route, "no resting places, depots or

points of security between Council Grove and Vegas, a bleak stretch of six hundred miles." The Pawnees, Comanches and Kiowas lay in wait along the Cimarron and the Arkansas, the Apaches took their toll chiefly in the valley of the Canadian. The Apaches were thought to be negotiating with the Cheyennes and the Arapahoes for a joint war of extermination against the whites. The Indians saw their doom approaching. Gone were the days when the trappers came in little companies to hunt and barter. Gone were the days when only a few white-topped wagons came and went twice yearly across the plains. The wagons were coming thicker and thicker, like foam on the crest of a rising flood. There were too many white men. They were killing off the buffalo and driving away the other game. The redmen rose in a kind of madness.

"The Comanche and Kiowas," wrote Gilpin, in his report to the adjutant-general of the army, "dwelling on the eastern slope, issue forth and sweep at one season with destructive fury the northern states of Mexico; at another season redden with blood the frontier of Texas; and following the summer range of the buffalo murder American traders upon the Santa Fe road, and destroy their property within three hundred miles of Fort Leavenworth." Gilpin, a volunteer officer from Missouri, complained bitterly of what he called "the ignorance, the laziness and the vicious character of the [regular] officers in the frontier depots."

We seem to be looking through the dust upon a scene of wild confusion, in which motives, means, and objectives were in fierce dispute, and only the Indians knew exactly what they wanted, which was to kill, plunder, and drive back the white invaders. And so the situation was to continue for many weary years to come. General

Kearny had promised that the United States would protect the Mexicans against the Indians. To make even a
gesture toward keeping this promise was to cost the
government, between 1851 and 1863, about three million dollars a year, or fifty per cent of the total value of
New Mexican real estate after the conquest. The suggestion was seriously made that it would be profitable
for the United States to buy the whole region from its
private owners and abandon it to the Indians, the wild
animals, and the rattlesnakes. For years killings by the
Indians within the borders of New Mexico were to average between twenty and twenty-five every twelve
months. As for the Santa Fe Trail, it was more dangerous than it had been in its crystal dawn, when Becknell
first rode over it.

But the Indians could not dam back the white flood.
During the summer of 1848 Lieutenant-Colonel Gilpin,
sitting notebook in hand at his post on the Arkansas,
counted 3000 wagons, 12,000 persons and 50,000 head
of stock going past his gates. Had he stayed a little
longer he would have seen greater throngs than this, for
gold was about to be discovered in California, and the
emigrants were to try every possible way of cheating
mountains and deserts to get there.

To be sure, there were some signs of progress, viewed
through eternally hopeful western eyes. " When General
Kearny, nearly two years ago, entered Santa Fe," said
the Santa Fe *Republican* on May 15, 1848, " at that time
there was but one public house in the place and it was
so badly kept and supplied that but few paid a second
visit. Now we have several." In addition, the *Republican* rejoiced to observe, American enterprise was showing itself in the tearing down of old houses and the
building of new ones. There were only a few hundred

Americans in the whole territory but they were doing their best to make themselves felt. What they needed most was better communication with the East. In 1849 — the year of the California gold rush — this appeared in the form of a monthly stage, which left Independence in May.

There was much enthusiasm at this evidence of modernization. " The stages are gotten up in elegant style," said a writer in the Missouri *Commonwealth,* " and are each arranged to convey eight passengers. The bodies are beautifully painted and made water-tight, with a view to using them as boats in ferrying streams. The team consists of six mules to each coach. The mail is guarded by eight men, armed as follows: Each man has at his side, fastened in the stage, one of Colt's revolving rifles, in a holster below one of Colt's long revolvers, and in his belt a small Colt's revolver, besides a hunting knife, so that these eight men are ready, in case of attack, to discharge 136 shots without having to reload. This is equal to a small army armed as in ancient times, and from the look of the escort, ready as they were either for offensive or defensive warfare with the savages, we have no fear for the safety of the mails.

" The accommodating contractors have established a sort of base for refitting at Council Grove, a distance of 150 miles from this city [Independence], and have sent out a blacksmith and a number of men to cut and cure hay, with a quantity of animals, grain and provisions; and we understand they intend to make a sort of travelling station there, and commence to farm. They also, we believe, intend to make a similar settlement at Walnut Creek next season. Two of their stages will start from here the first of every month." The first steps towards taming the prairies were being taken! Stage stations were to become towns. The white man was moving out upon the plains, not to hunt, not to trade, not to camp, but to possess.

In July 1850, Waldo, Hall and Company of Independence received the contract to carry the mail once a month between that city and Santa Fe, with the understanding that they were to complete each trip within thirty days. As we shall see, the stages were soon to do much better than this. F. X. Aubry, twenty months before this contract was let, rode on horseback from Santa Fe to the Missouri River in six days—a rare exploit that showed what could be done when a traveller was in a hurry. But the wagon trains continued, then and for years afterwards, to do their fifteen or twenty miles a day and no more.

Just how much Santa Fe benefited from the gold rush to the Pacific Coast it is difficult to determine. Some gold seekers, we know, followed the old Trail to New Mexico, then went over the Spanish Trail to the Green River, over the Wasatch Mountains, down the Virgin River, and over the Tehachapi and Tejon passes to their destination. Others went by the route which Kearny had followed and which the Mormon Battalion had made passable for wagons. Between April 1848, and January 1849, no less than 8000 are said to have gone this way. But the route did not find general favor. " The emigrants by the Gila," wrote Brigadier-General Riley from California, in a report dated October 1849, " complain greatly of the thefts and hostilities committed upon them by the river Indians." " A man who has travelled the Gila route," wrote an Argonaut who managed to get through in the summer of the same year, " may throw himself on his knees and thank God for preserving him on it. The Gila route is unfit to be

travelled and suffering inevitably awaits all who under-
take it."

So we may think of Santa Fe as sitting a little apart
from the great excitement of the gold years, suffering
neglect, perhaps, because the world's attention was
momentarily drawn to greater dramas than the remote
desert city had to offer. But this relative isolation may
have had its advantages in easing the transition period,
and preserving the old Spanish province from much of
the confusion and tumult which arose in California.
Santa Fe drew within itself and continued to dream —
not the old dreams, perhaps, but dreams in which the lust
for gold was still vague and unreal.

And yet the old Trail had played its part, had made
possible those resounding events which clamored in
men's ears. Though the wagons of the emigrants rolled
far away through the northern passes of the Rocky
Mountains and down to the City of the Saints, the
southern route had been, after all, the path of empire.
It had seen the advance of Kearny's troopers, going,
though they knew it not, to open up California to the
gold diggers. It had delivered the blow without which
the long journey of the Argonauts across the plains
and mountains would have been of no avail. So it
entered into the long afternoon of its decline with a
sudden blaze of glory.

Santa Fe missed the great migration. Nevertheless,
it shook to the vibrations of those thousands of marching
men. The West was changing overnight. Multitudes
were becoming familiar with the western plains, transcontinental freight and passenger services were being
established, and the East was waking up to the wealth
and prospective importance of the newly acquired ter-
ritories. Railroads became inevitable, and once the

railroads crossed the plains it was also inevitable that sooner or later they should tap New Mexico. But development was slow. In 1850 New Mexico had a population of 61,547, not counting Indians. In 1860 the population was 80,567, certainly not a phenomenal increase. One detects in the narratives of those years a weariness, a let-down. The old civilization of New Mexico was changing, some would say deteriorating. The new showed itself all too often in its less attractive aspects.

Yet, for those who had eyes for it, the old romance survived. Lewis Garrard, then a youth of eighteen or nineteen, came over the Trail in 1847, starting from Westport with a party headed by Ceran St. Vrain. The teamsters, nineteen or twenty in number, were French-Canadians. As they lay wrapped in their blankets under the stars on fine prairie nights they sang "their beautiful and piquant songs." Sometimes it rained, but there was singing even when everyone had to lie in the mud, with only a sodden blanket to keep him warm. "They are a queer mixture, anyhow, these Canadians," commented young Lewis. "Rain or shine, hungry or satisfied, they are the same garrulous, happy fellows, generally carolling in honor of some brunette *Vide Poche* or St. Louis Creole beauty, or lauding in the words of their ancestry the soft skies and grateful winds of La Belle France." The "*Vide Poche*," it should be said, was Carondelet, the old Creole quarter of St. Louis, long surviving under the corrupted Anglo-Saxon title of "Weed Bush." Sometimes on the march a song would break out and run along the whole train. The men were omnivorous, and ate raw buffalo liver and marrow with tremendous relish. Lewis liked buffalo meat, too, though he was sufficiently affected by the effete civilization of the East to demand that it be cooked. " Talk of an emperor's table! " cried he. " Why, they could imagine nothing half so good! "

Two years after Garrard visited Bent's Fort, it was destroyed by Bent, who preferred to build a new one farther down the Arkansas River. Even this was still immeasurably picturesque. There was a runaway apprentice tailor from St. Louis, who had lived with the Cheyennes, and whose habits had induced the governor of New Mexico to put a price of $500 on his head. " The only female women there," as one old trapper expressed it, were Charlotte the cook and Rosalie, half-French, half-Indian. But they had a dance just the same, and Frenchmen from St. Louis and Canada and backwoodsmen from Missouri swayed to wild music.

An age was dying — an age heroic and epical. Trappers could still be found upon the mountain streams, but they were old and their occupation gone. Over a broad belt from the Platte to the Arkansas moved countless white-topped wagons. The buffalo were retreating and dwindling. Military posts were superseding the old trading centres. From 1850 on the federal troops in New Mexico, who were only a portion of those now permanently stationed west of the Missouri, never numbered less than 1400 men. Fort Union, off the Sapello River, northeast of Las Vegas, was a military distribing point, to which regularly came the supply trains, adding their rumbling wheels, their trampling hoofs to the growing commercial traffic from the Missouri River. More and more the old Trail was being beaten into a broad highway, on which one could not travel long without meeting or passing somebody.

An age was dying — but an age was being born.

CHAPTER XV

THE DUST THICKENS

LET us get a new picture of the Trail during these hurrying, dusty later years through the eyes of some who knew it and loved it then. There was the stout, puritanical Alexander Majors, whose lifetime from 1814 to 1893 spanned the conquest of three-fourths of a continent. Majors' pioneer father brought him from Kentucky to Missouri when the boy was five years old. Missouri was still largely wilderness then and the members of the McKnight party were languishing in Chihuahua and Durango for the crime of having attempted to open trade with Santa Fe. Majors did not go on the Trail as a youthful adventurer. He did not take up freighting until 1848, at the end of the Mexican War.

His personality comes out quaintly in the oath which he says he administered to each of his men. " While I am in the employ of Alexander Majors," it ran, " I agree not to use profane language, not to get drunk, not to treat animals cruelly, and not to do anything else that is incompatible with the character of a gentleman. And I agree if I violate any of the above conditions to accept my discharge without any pay for my services." But, according to Majors, the final clause never had to be invoked. No employee ever broke the agreement. Perhaps there were compensations. Certainly it was no hardship not to travel or do unnecessary work on Sunday, which was the rule in all of Majors' caravans, as well as in those belonging to the later and very important firm of Russell, Majors and Waddell.

Majors' first outfit left Independence on August 10, 1848, six wagons and teams. He made the round trip to Santa Fe in ninety-two days, returning, he says, with the same oxen with which he started out, and all in good condition! Oxen he found cheaper and more reliable than mules on all long trips. Often, as he drove them, they were capable of doing 2000 miles in a season. Not all freighters were so expert or so lucky. Majors prided himself on the skill of his men, who could and did yoke and hitch six pair of oxen in sixteen minutes. The caravan organization in his day was fairly simple. Each team had, of course, its driver, and the expedition was commanded by a captain and lieutenant, who corresponded to the captain and mate of a ship. No cook was carried, but the men divided themselves into messes of six or eight, and selected a chef for each mess. The man thus honored was relieved of some of his other duties. Every man was expected to stand guard for two hours out of the twenty-four. The pay was about one dollar a day and all expenses en route. As game was still plentiful, this was no great burden upon the owner of the wagons.

Majors never had serious trouble with the Indians, though they did annoy him at times. On one of his trips in 1850 they ran off his oxen at One Hundred and Ten Mile Creek. This was a little unusual, since this point is on the safe, or eastern side of Council Grove, where no difficulties with the Indians were expected. But Majors was perfectly equal to the emergency. He rode unarmed into the war-painted group and by sheer audacity and strength of character induced them to let him have back all but one of the animals. The Indians farther west were made of more steely material. During the first stage of their journey the Majors party were passed by the mail coach, trotting gaily over the prairie with ten men on board. There was an exchange of greetings, a little patronizing, no doubt, on the part of those riding the swifter vehicle. But it was Majors, after all, who came first into Santa Fe. Near Wagon Mound he came upon the burned fragments of the coach, and near by "the bones and skeletons of some of the horses that drew it, as well as the bones of the party of ten men, who were murdered by the Indians."

The tragedy was a famous one in southwestern annals. The coach, on its way from Fort Leavenworth to Santa Fe, was first attacked by the Apaches. The occupants stubbornly resisted throughout an entire day. Two wounded men were placed inside the coach, the others, perhaps sheltering themselves behind the dead horses, fought on. Perhaps they would have survived had not the Apaches been reinforced during the night by a gang of Utes. The Utes had ideas of their own as to the best way of fighting white men. At dawn they put them into execution. This time the attack was successful. There were no survivors. All that was learned of the fight was inferred from the positions in which the bodies were found, or related long afterwards by the Indians who had part in the affair. It is told of one of the victims that as he lay gasping out his life he spilled his last grains of powder in the sand and stirred them in with his foot, so that the Indians should have no use of them. Strangely enough, bows and arrows were the chief weapons used by the savages in this affair.

An even more shocking tragedy was the massacre of a small party headed by Dr. White of Santa Fe. Dr.

White was returning from Missouri in the summer of 1849 in company with one of Francois X. Aubry's wagons trains. When near enough to the settlements to feel secure he rode ahead with his wife and child, a negro servant, and three other men. They were surrounded by Apaches, who opened fire when Dr. White refused to give them presents. All except Mrs. White and the children were immediately killed. When the bearer of this dreadful news galloped into Santa Fe a company of dragoons took saddle with all possible haste and with Kit Carson as guide rode in pursuit. When the Indians were overtaken the officer in command, against Carson's advice, halted to parley. Had the dragoons charged at once, Carson always believed, the woman and child might have been rescued alive. But when the fight finally began the Indians shot Mrs. White and fled, bearing the child with them. A blinding snow-storm made further pursuit impossible. The fate of the child was never known. It disappeared forever behind the curtain of the falling snow. Kit Carson himself is authority for the statement that the Apache chief responsible for these murders appeared in Santa Fe some time later wearing a necklace made from Dr. White's teeth. It is not recorded that anything unpleasant happened to him.

Why the rapidly moving stage should have suffered while the plodding wagon trains were left alone is a problem. Perhaps it was pure luck. Certainly it was luck which the trains did not always enjoy. But Majors went often and safely to New Mexico and made large profits. Once he crossed the plains with ten wagons and a hundred and thirty oxen, carrying goods on consignment. For this he received $13,000 in Mexican money, or about half that sum in American currency. In 1853 he made two trips, one from Kansas City to Santa Fe,

and one from Kansas City to Fort Union. The following year, 1854, witnessed an epidemic of cholera, and the
plains were full of panic and rumors of death. Trade
languished. Men were glad enough to escape with their
lives. But 1855 and 1856 were fat ones for Majors and
his new partners, Russell and Waddell. They had 350
wagons, a good many of them in the New Mexican trade,
and they cleared in the two years about $300,000 — a
neat little pile for men who had formerly walked in the
dust beside the oxen. Majors took his trains across
the arid *Jornada,* which he called the "Hornather."
Whether or not it was because his piety attracted the
attention of an approving Providence he prospered exceedingly. In 1858 his firm had 3500 wagons, between
4000 and 5000 men, 40,000 oxen and 1000 mules on the
plains, and carried 16,000,000 pounds. Most of this, to
be sure, went not to Santa Fe but to the troops which
were then engaged in overawing the Mormons in Salt
Lake City.

Another old-timer whose experiences spanned a vast
deal of western history was Richens Wootton, who came
to be known to thousands of stage-coach passengers in
the later days as "Uncle Dick." Wootton first went
west with one of the Bent and St. Vrain trains to Bent's
Fort in 1836. He soon became, according to his own
account and probably in reality, one of the best frontiersmen in the West. In 1838 and 1839, in company with
nineteen other trappers and hunters, he made a most
remarkable journey. The party followed the Arkansas
to its source, pushed on through Utah, Wyoming, and
Montana to the Yellowstone, hankered for more travel,
traced the Snake and Salmon Rivers to the Columbia,
visited Vancouver, went down the coast to Southern
California, and returned through Arizona and Utah to

Bent's Fort — a jaunt of 5000 miles. Five of the party
were killed by savages. Uncle Dick — a very young
Uncle Dick at the time — came through in perfect health
and spirits. He was not only a good shot and a good
trailer but a horseman of renown. In 1851 he rode from
Raton to Kansas City in seven days.

Once, just after the Mexican War, he was on his way
east with a caravan from Santa Fe. He had with him a
few Americans, some of them discharged soldiers who
had paid $30 apiece to go as passengers. These men were
allowed to ride in the wagons and were given their food.
Their only duties were to take their turn in standing
guard. With the caravan were also about thirty Mexicans, who greatly outnumbered the American passengers
and drivers. Angered at a real or imagined insult to one
of their number the Mexicans one day rushed Wootton,
shooting as they came. Thirteen bullets, he says, pierced
his clothing, and some twenty other shots went wild.
He stood his ground and escaped without a scratch.
Apparently the drivers had shot off all their ammunition, for they did not reload and the caravan resumed its
peaceful march. But Uncle Dick's suspicions were
aroused. "This encounter," he gravely states, "had
convinced me that my life was in constant peril." He
kept close watch for the rest of the journey and came in
safe and sound.

Some wagon captains had worse luck. There was a
piracy of the plains as well as of the high seas. The
freighters often carried between one and two hundred
thousand dollars' worth of goods, for which they were
responsible for all losses or damages not caused by Indians or by " acts of God." The temptation to mutiny
was very strong, and there had to be a correspondingly
rigid discipline. " It was as absolutely necessary," says

Wootton, "that a crew of teamsters should obey promptly and implicitly the orders of one man as it is that a crew of sailors shall obey the commands of their captain. We were governed by practically the same laws that govern men at sea and dealt with a mutinous or unruly band of teamsters in pretty much the same way that a mutinous crew of sailors is generally dealt with." But sometimes the mutineers got the upper hand. One train was seized by its drivers, near Fort Kearny, the captain killed and the wagons driven into Oregon. So far as Wootton knew the criminals were never captured. The Trail, it will be seen, was growing civilized. It was no longer white men against unfriendly nature and hostile Indians, it was also white men against white men, lawlessness against the law.

But the wagons went rolling on. In 1856 Wootton took from Fort Union to Kansas City what he calls a "typical train." It consisted of thirty-six wagons, each with five yoke of oxen, and a crew of forty men. When the train was in line and ready to start it was nearly a mile long. Usually the start was made early in the morning, without breakfast, and a mid-day halt was made from about ten in the morning until as late as two or three o'clock in the afternoon, giving men and animals time to drink, eat, and rest. The day's journey was from fifteen to twenty miles, with an average of about sixteen miles. Wootton took about four months to go from Kansas City to Fort Union and back, or about a month longer than the time reported by Majors.

The big loads and the big profits were now on the west-bound trip. As we have seen in an earlier chapter, the usual load ranged from three to seven thousand pounds to a wagon, and the average was about five thousand pounds. But Wootton loaded his vehicles with six, eight, or even ten thousand pounds each. His thirty-six wagons could carry at least two hundred thousand pounds. The rate from Kansas City to Fort Union in the fifties was $8 a hundred. Consequently the gross profit on a single west-bound trip, with such a load, was $16,000. Teamsters were then receiving a little less than Majors paid, or about $20 a month and expenses. The total of these could not have come to more than four or five thousand dollars. The rest was nearly all net profit. Coming back, however, the wagons were usually not more than half loaded. A few furs were still being carried, but the east-bound traffic was not remunerative. Silver and mules had been New Mexico's best exports. The silver was now being mined in Colorado, and before long was to be mined in Nevada, and it had been found that mules could be successfully nurtured in Missouri.

The Trail was still a long and weary one. It had not shrunk with the years; indeed, because most of the caravans now went by the mountain division, it had grown from 780 to 825 miles, 300 miles of which, as Wootton said, were "certainly a rough and rugged road." One reason for following the longer route through southern Colorado was that there began to be settlements there, and settlements meant additional freight. "Crossing the plains and keeping clear of mud holes," Wootton tells us, "was the most difficult feature of the first five hundred miles' travel. The mud holes we could fill with hay cut on the surrounding plains and the roads were not hard to make. It was different, though, going through the mountains. There the trail had to be hewn out of the steep hillsides, the oxen had to be used to clear the trees and logs out of the canyons, and when the roadmakers had done their best travel was difficult and dangerous. In the winter the snow would frequently drift into the canyons, and keep piling up until it obliterated every trace of the trail, and breaking a road through these deep snows was no easy matter."

But it was not all hard work and no play. It seems difficult to believe that men with lively sporting instincts would bet on ox races, but they did, and just as readily, says Wootton, " as on a mile dash of Kentucky thoroughbreds or native bronchos." One can imagine the wild excitement as two rival trains approached the end of a five-hundred-mile sprint, conducted at an average speed of a mile and a half or two miles an hour. But these races were of serious importance to the trains' captains. A captain who brought his caravan in ahead of time earned a prestige which he could turn into dollars.

Wootton later became famous as the builder and keeper of the toll road over Raton Pass, but that picturesque incident in the history of the Trail comes a little later in our story. He was a life-long friend of Kit Carson's, owned a rifle presented to him by Carson, and had almost as great a reputation among mountain men and plainsmen as Kit himself.

We have a vivid glimpse or two of conditions on the Trail at the end of the administration of James S. Calhoun, governor of New Mexico from 1851 to 1852. Calhoun fell ill of scurvy — surely a sign that the flesh-pots of New Mexico were not yielding all they might have! — and started for home in June 1852. At first he seemed to improve, as so many persons did when they set out over the plains in either direction. Then he grew ill and died. In preparation for this emergency he had carried his coffin with him all the way from Santa Fe, and it was in the coffin that he arrived at Kansas City. His successor, William Carr Lane, left St. Louis on

July 31, 1852, went by steamer to Independence, where he arrived on August 4th, and started across the plains with the mail stage. He reached Fort Atkinson, at the crossing of the Arkansas, on August 14th. There a military escort awaited him and he was conducted with due ceremony the rest of the way into Santa Fe. Already the wilder life of the prairies was in its decadence. Lane saw at a single moment, he estimated, between one and two hundred thousand buffalo. But west of the Arkansas they had nearly disappeared, and their "roads and wallows were all growing up in grass."

Lane held office for about a year, then started for home again in September 1853. This time he slighted the Trail. He went first to Albuquerque, then down the old caravan road to El Paso, then across country to San Antonio, then by a steamer from the port of Lavaca to New Orleans, then up the river to St. Louis. He does not say in his letters, which were later published, why he chose this route. He may have wanted to see the country. It certainly took longer than the stage-coach run to St. Louis.

In this same year, 1853, W. W. H. Davis, newly-appointed attorney-general and later secretary and acting governor of New Mexico, found himself bound westward by the still slow and infrequent stage. This was a rich man's way of travelling — the extra-fare, all-compartment-car train of its day. Men who had their fortunes still to seek usually earned their passage by chaperoning the patient ox or prodding the unenthusiastic mule. Nevertheless, stage travel over the Trail in 1853, though it cost the traveller the tidy sum of $150, was not the height of luxury. Davis left Independence on November 1st. Let us ride with him. Council Grove, once so lovely, he finds fallen into a wretched

half-way state between primitive charm and village comfort. A " filthy old cabin, windowless and doorless,"
has been nicknamed by " some of the boys " the Astor
House. There is a blacksmith, however, and a Mr.
Withington, agent for the mail contractors. The stage
is hauled by mules, and reasonably fast mules they are.

On November 9th, eight days out, the travellers are at
the Little Arkansas. On the 13th they are at the middle
crossing of the Arkansas, that is to say at the one which
leaves the river near Cimarron. They are thus about
three days slower than Lane had been the year before.
They cross the *Jornada,* sixty waterless miles, in fifteen
hours of driving, punctuated by a dry camp. But when
one is carrying enough water and has no fear of being
lost a night on the *Jornada* is not unpleasant. Here is a
kind of peace that the safe regions of the world never
know. The velvet darkness sinks gently into one's soul.

On November 16th they reach the Cimarron. Now,
as they go up the river toward Round Mound, the
mules have to stretch their legs and they make fifty miles
in a single day. At Rock Creek, on November 29th,
they come upon a party of one hundred and fifty Mexicans, with five hundred animals and fifty carts, out on
their annual buffalo hunt. Perhaps this helps to explain
why, as Lane noted, buffalo were growing scarcer west
of the Arkansas. At Wagon Mound, two days later,
Davis is reminded of the tragedy of the mail party three
years before, though the bones have long since been
deeply and decently buried.

The stage rolls into Fort Union, in the Mora Valley,
one hundred and ten miles from Santa Fe, on the 23rd.
No one in the party has had anything to eat, beyond
one scanty meal, during the preceding forty-eight hours
— which is money saved for the stage company, bound

by contract to feed and lodge its passengers. Fort Union
has little of the look of a fortification. Its houses are of
pine, arranged in streets, and it has neither breastworks
nor stockades. Barclay's Post, a little further along in
the same day's journey, had been established as a private
trading venture during the war with Mexico. Its stout
loop-holed walls and battlements frown upon all and
sundry who may have designs upon its stores. Next day
the stage rolls into Las Vegas, now a " dirty mud town
of some seven hundred inhabitants." American occupation does not seem to have done it much good, for many
of its houses are in ruins and " most of the others wear
an exceedingly uncomfortable appearance." " A few
Americans are living there, who seem to control the
trade of the place." At Tecolote abide an American
store-keeper and a Methodist missionary, catering to the
bodily and spiritual needs of the inhabitants, more or
less successfully. On the 26th of November, twenty-
five days after leaving Independence, Davis finds himself
at last in Santa Fe. If the stage upon which he travelled
had been supplied with sufficient relays of horses and
gone forward by night as well as day, as the stages were
soon to do, the time might easily have been cut in two.

Four years after Davis's journey Hockaday and Hall
took over the mail route and inserted the following ad-
vertisement in the Santa Fe and eastern newspapers:
" Santa Fe Traders and those desirous of crossing the
Plains to New Mexico are informed that the undersigned will carry the United States Mail from Independence to Santa Fe for four years, commencing on the
first day of July 1857, in stages drawn by six mules. The
Stages will leave Independence and Santa Fe on the first
and fifteenth of each month. They will be entirely new
and comfortable for passengers, well guarded, and run-

ning through each way in from twenty to twenty-five days. Travellers to and from New Mexico will doubtless find this the safest and most expeditious and comfortable, as well as the cheapest mode of crossing the plains. . . Provisions, arms and ammunition furnished by the proprietors.

"Packages and extra baggage will be transported when possible to do so, at the rate of 35 cents per pound in summer and 50 cents in winter, but no package will be charged less than one dollar. The proprietors will not be responsible for any package worth more than fifty dollars, unless contents given and specially contracted for, and all baggage at all times at the risk of the owner thereof. In all cases the passage money must be paid in advance and passengers must stipulate to conform to the rules which may be established by the undersigned for the government of their line of stages and those travelling with them on the plains. No passenger allowed more than forty pounds of baggage in addition to the necessary bedding."

The fare, which had been at one time as high as $250, was put at $125 between May and November and $150 between November and May — the same as Davis had paid. But fares fluctuated considerably, rising again to about $200 during the Civil War. By the early sixties stages were going through from Kansas City to Santa Fe in thirteen days and six hours. The unfortunate travellers slept in the coach or stayed awake, just as they chose, and subsisted principally upon salt pork and hardtack. The modern rush and whirl were beginning. Gone were the days when anyone who could avoid it would pause to taste the infinite leisure of the prairies. That was left for the freighters. It was said that one became accustomed to night-and-day stage travel after a few days and did not mind it much.

Even at a relatively high fare the stage companies did not find it easy to make their business pay. In 1854 the government appropriated $10,990 to have the mails carried between Independence and Santa Fe. The company lost heavily and secured an increase to $25,000. Even then it did not make money. But the stage was a necessity, and speed, in the new order of things, also seemed essential. Little by little the running time between Santa Fe and Kansas City was whittled down until the trip could be made in eleven days—or five days longer than Aubry's famous ride. Stage companies might fail, but the mail went through. Waldo, Hall and Company; Hockaday and Hall; Barnum, Vail and Vickery; Barlow and Sanderson — all had their days, and every day the letter-bags grew heavier. Butterfield got his short-lived contract for the southern overland mail in 1857 — from St. Louis and Memphis, through Fort Smith, Preston, El Paso, Santa Fe, and on through Yuma to California. But the southern route never prospered. The old Trail, Trail of the buffalo, Trail of the Indian, Trail of the Spaniard and Mexican, Trail of the hunter and the freighter, had a magic that would not be denied. It was as though the pattern of it had been ordained before anything human ever traversed it. Not until the railroads came did any route into New Mexico seriously threaten its supremacy, and even then, and to this day, rail and Trail ran for many long miles literally side by side.

Gold was found in Colorado ten years after it had been discovered in California. There were two routes into Colorado after 1841, one leaving the Oregon Trail at Julesburg, the other following the Mountain Division of the Santa Fe Trail on to Pueblo and beyond. Later there was a third, the so-called Smoky Hill route, going up the Smoky Hill fork of the Kansas. Some of the emigrants of the California gold rush of 1849 rushed no further than Colorado. Pueblo, settled first by a few trappers some years before the Mexican War, inhabited for a time during the war by a party of Mormons, grew into a town. So, little by little, a nucleus of population began to form in this region, and in large part this nucleus had to be supplied over the Santa Fe Trail, or that part of it lying east of the present city of La Junta. The discovery of gold in 1858 and the gold rush of 1859 sent many hundreds over the Arkansas route. Uncle Dick Wootton, with his customary energy, took a load of goods through to Denver, and is said to have opened the third store there, though he did not long remain. Pueblo and Colorado City, both established as booming American communities by the end of the fifties, might have rivalled Denver and drawn thousands instead of hundreds along the old Trail up the Arkansas had not the Civil War made the southern routes too dangerous. But though the Smoky Hill and the South Platte became the favorite roads to Colorado, the importance of the Santa Fe Trail increased.

Meanwhile, what of Santa Fe itself? What changes had the American occupation made? How much of old Santa Fe remained? Attorney-General Davis, whose westward journey we followed a few pages back, noted some Americanisms as early at 1853. There had been no sawmills or flour mills before the Gringo's conquest. Now the region had both. Santa Fe itself, toward which the old plainsmen had looked with such longing eyes, was not yet beautiful to the more hard-boiled outsiders. " If," said Davis, " it were not for the circumstances under which the traveller first enters Santa Fe he would be tempted to leave again in disgust ere the sound of his footfall had died away in the streets." But always, it seems, Santa Fe was best seen through a veil of illusions — illusions, nevertheless, which were as real in their way as the 'dobe walls and the muddy streets. One had to come to it with a childlike willingness to accept it for the thing it inwardly was. If one carried to it memories of New England villages it turned miserable and tawdry.

New Mexico had long been isolated and contented in its isolation. But no American could for a moment accept such a destiny. Davis loved to let his mind wander from the lackadaisical present to the bustling future. "New Mexico being set in the middle of the continent," he pointed out, "has communication with both seaboards, the Atlantic and the Pacific — with the former by regular monthly mails and private trains. The communication with the Pacific is less frequent and more dangerous; the distance, though not so great, is more difficult to travel and the trip is only occasionally made. Now and then a party of returned Californians come home the overland route and take Santa Fe on the way." On Christmas Day, 1853, a party of Americans headed by Kit Carson and Lucien Maxwell, the latter the future proprietor of the famous Maxwell ranch at Cimarron, came in from California. They had driven ten or twelve thousand sheep from New Mexico past Pueblo to the Oregon Trail, and then to the Humboldt and the Sacramento. In California the sheep were worth $5.50 apiece, and the venture was profitable. Returning they had journeyed by way of Los Angeles, the Colorado and Gila rivers, Fort Webster and Fort Conrad. On the way home, they said, they passed more than one hundred thousand sheep being driven from New Mexico to California.

Meanwhile the Santa Fe trade was increasing steadily but not phenomenally. In 1843, the last year reported by Gregg, the total had been $450,000. In 1846, on the eve of the Mexican War, 414 wagons had gone out, carrying $1,752,250 worth of goods. In 1850 Kansas City alone sent 500 wagon loads. In 1855 the total trade was estimated at $5,000,000. The estimates are often provokingly at variance and hard to compare. In 1860 a total of 16,439,000 pounds is said to have been carried, 9084 men were employed, and 6147 mules, 27,920 oxen and 3033 wagons were used. If these wagons carried freight at the rates given by Wootton for the fifties the charge for that alone would have been $1,300,000. Of course this sum would not be enough to make Santa Fe freighting a major industry, even in the United States of 1860. But no more in this later stage of the Trail than in the earlier ones can its real significance be measured by counting dollars, pounds, or noses. The lumbering, white-topped wagons, the hurrying stages, the little army of men on horseback and afoot were preparing the way for the great forward lunge of trade and settlement which was to come with the railroads. The West had to be made familiar, even commonplace, before it could be conquered. The old romance had to be rolled flat, trampled into the dust, blown away by the prairie winds to the back of nowhere, before the new romance could be born. By the sixties the morning mists had lifted forever. We moderns can now begin to visualize the vast scene, with its moving dots of brown and white, with cinematographic vividness.

But now comes the Civil War, which is to disrupt so many things, north and south, east and west, and which is to usher in the last, yet not the least dramatic and stirring phase of the old Trail's history.

CHAPTER XVI

THE GREAT DIVIDE

IT WAS New Mexico's hard luck, within fourteen years of her conquest by General Kearny, to be dragged into another war in which the majority of her people had no direct concern. Remote though she was she could not remain aloof. Too many currents, political as well as commercial, met and opposed one another within her boundaries. The Americans who had opened up her commerce with the United States were from the slave-holding state of Missouri, but their wagon trains crossed the whole width of the free state of Kansas. The Texans, who had by no means forgotten their earlier claims to the valley of the Rio Grande, shared in ambitious projects of the Confederacy to push the slave republic through to the Pacific Coast. In California and in Colorado it was not at first certain whether Unionists or Confederates would get the upper hand.

Even in New Mexico there smouldered more than a little Secessionist, or at least anti-Yankee, sentiment. The survivors of the generation of Indians and Spanish-Americans who had risen in such wild rebellion in 1847 were not all reconciled. To them the breaking-up of the Union offered a possible independence. On the other side of the scale the Southern cause was weakened by being personified by an invading Texas army. Since the days of the Texas Santa Fe Expedition Texans had not been unduly popular in New Mexico. Not only was

there a blood feud, but there was also more than a suspicion among the darker-skinned Spanish-Americans
that the Texans regarded them, largely on account of
their complexions, as an inferior race.

When the war broke out New Mexico was garrisoned
by regular troops in which many officers of southern
sympathies held commands. A regular army major, H.
H. Sibley, who had been stationed at a New Mexican
post, was made a brigadier-general by the Confederates
and sent back with an invading army. Even before he
arrived the Texans had seized Fort Bliss and La Mesilla,
near El Paso, and had captured nearly one-half of the
twelve hundred loyal regulars in the territory. Colonel
E. R. S. Canby, the ranking federal commander, re-
cruited his depleted companies with militia and volunteers, and met Sibley at Valverde, not far from the
northern end of the present Elephant Butte reservoir.
This was in February 1862. After a desperate struggle
Canby was defeated with heavy loss and driven within
the walls of Fort Craig. Sibley went on up the Rio
Grande and captured Albuquerque and Santa Fe. Fort
Union alone held out.

Meanwhile Governor Gilpin of Colorado, a strong
Union sympathizer — he was the same Gilpin, by the
way, who commanded Fort Mann in 1848 and counted
the thousands of men, wagons, and cattle as they went
by — had organized and drilled a small force of infantry
and a troop of cavalry. These stalwart volunteers, leaving Denver at the end of February, crossed the Raton
Mountains in deep snow. In a single day they marched,
horse and foot, the incredible distance of sixty-seven
miles, and on March 11th they arrived safely at Fort
Union. From this base a detachment set out in an
effort to recapture Santa Fe and ran into Confederate

troops under Major Pyron in Apache canyon. For two days, on March 27th and 28th, the battle was waged with varying fortunes in the canyon and at Pigeon's Ranch. Then the Confederates, defeated, their supply train destroyed, retired first to Santa Fe, then back down the valley of the Rio Grande. Colonel Kit Carson played a creditable part in this campaign, though fortune did not allow him to play a brilliant one. After these battles the Confederates were never again a serious menace in New Mexico. Sibley made good his retreat down the river nearly to the Texas border, and the invasion from the east and northeast which would have cut the Santa Fe Trail never took place. In August the California Column, 2350 strong, under command of General James H. Carleton, emerged from the western desert, looking for trouble. The Confederates now withdrew completely from New Mexico and were driven out of northwestern Texas.

The Trail was thus made secure against conquest, but not against constant and ferocious interruption. For greater safety from Confederate raiders its eastern terminals were moved northward from Kansas City to Fort Leavenworth, Atchison, and Nebraska City. The connecting routes from these points naturally hit the main Trail at different places, but in general the old line to the Arkansas continued to be followed. After 1861 and until the close of the war the Cimarron cutoff was practically abandoned, principally because of Indian activities. One unfortunate, a Santa Fe merchant named Wilson, ventured over it, accompanied by his wife and child, in 1863. It was an act of folly. Near Cedar Springs, not far from McNees' Creek, the Wilsons were overtaken by Indians and all three were butchered. But most of the traffic during those troubled years went

over the Raton Pass. William Bent had abandoned
and destroyed his old fort in 1849 and had built a new
one, forty miles farther down the river. This was taken
over by the government in 1859 and rechristened Fort
Lyon. Later a new Fort Lyon was built, nine miles east
of Las Animas, but the old one continued to be an important station on the stage route.

To the discredit of the white civilization the danger
on the Trail during the Civil War was not all on the
Cimarron nor were the Indians the only blood-thirsty
humans who infested it. The old belt of safety just west
of the Missouri was safe no more. Guerrillas came riding over the prairie, riff-raff of the border, insanely cruel,
representing no honest cause. In 1863, according to
one traveller who passed that way in that year, "the
country was dotted with bare chimneys and blackened
ruins from a few miles west of Westport to Council
Grove." Diamond Springs — "Diamond of the
Plains " — was not spared. The guerrillas descended
upon it, killed its unoffending civilian inhabitants, and
burned the houses.

But though the Indians were no more savage than
the border ruffians, there were more of them and, quanti-
tatively speaking, they raised more hell. When there
seemed even a remote possibility that their energies
might flag, the old deadly circle of atrocity and retalia-
tion was renewed by such episodes as the massacre of
defenceless Indians, including women and children, by
Major Chivington's troops at Sand Creek, north of old
Fort Lyon, in 1864. But the Indians did not need much
encouragement. In January 1863, they killed all but
one of a party of nine freighters whom they caught on the
way east, at Nine-Mile Ridge, about seventy-five miles
west of Fort Larned. Next year they attacked a caravan

near Fort Dodge and killed Andrew Blanchard of Leavenworth, one of the leaders. All along the line they were energetic and vicious not only during the war but for some years after the war.

The Trail was now punctuated by forts, toward which the freighters in their hours of peril turned longing eyes. From Kansas City to Fort Larned, the long first division, the distance was about three hundred miles, from Leavenworth perhaps a little more. Fort Larned, established in 1859, had during the war a garrison of about one thousand men. From Larned to new Fort Lyons, near Las Animas, was two hundred and forty miles. This was the most dangerous part of the journey, for at first it had no stations. William H. Ryus, an old stage driver who published his recollections some years ago, covered this stretch sixty-five times in four years, " driving one set of mules the whole distance, camping out and sleeping on the ground." Fort Dodge, established in 1864, not far from the present Dodge City, broke this terrible journey. Fort Zarah, near Great Bend, was also established in 1864. The stage route used to leave the river at this point and cut across the dry lands, a distance of one hundred and ten miles, to Fort Dodge. This part of the road took over the name of " The Long Route," which had formerly been applied to the run from Larned to Lyon. There was no water, and severe suffering from heat and thirst was a common experience. " The Long Route " was commonly made in two days' travel, with a " dry camp " to rest the animals. From Fort Lyon to Fort Union was one hundred and eighty miles, and another journey of the same length brought the traveller into Santa Fe.

During the early sixties, when Ryus was driving, the stages were making from fifty to sixty miles a day, though as the number of relay stations grew the pace was increased. When the stage lines were in their glory horses were changed every fifteen, twenty, or twenty-five miles, according to the nature of the country. Ryus, in his more primitive times, had a schedule of two meals a day, a long drive before breakfast, another long drive until the supper halt at four in the afternoon, and a third drive until long after nightfall. The stages crossed the Arkansas at the new Fort Lyon, and then followed the " Picketwire " for a considerable distance, crossing and recrossing the stream twenty-six times. A dangerous point in the Raton Pass, above Trinidad, was " The Devil's Gate," where an overhanging rock forced the stages to the very edge of the precipice. A little careless driving here and neither stage, mules, nor passengers were likely to be of much use thereafter.

Near Springer, New Mexico, the road entered the famous Maxwell grant. This lordly tract of 1,700,000 acres had been granted by Governor Armijo in 1841 to Guadalupe Miranda and Charles Beaubien — or, to give the latter the full title which he had brought with him from his native Canada, Charles Hipollyte Trotier, Sieur de Beaubien. Beaubien bought out Miranda's share, then Lucien Maxwell, marrying Beaubien's daughter, first managed and then inherited the great ranch. Here, for a time, lived Maxwell's friend, Kit Carson, going east at least once with Maxwell's wagon train. Men held their lands then by their own strength and courage, for this was Ute and Comanche country.

But danger and splendor went together. In 1864 Maxwell was said to be the largest land-holder in the United States. For forty-five miles the Trail was never out of sight of his great herds of cattle, sheep, and horses, and at the " Manor House " a feudal welcome awaited every passer-by. "This house," says Twitchell, "was as much of a palace as the times and the country could afford. Many men famous in those days were [Maxwell's] guests. His table service was for the most part of sterling silver. Covers were laid daily for more than two dozen persons. Maxwell invariably kept a large amount of money — gold and silver coin — on hand. This money was the proceeds of the sale of his sheep, cattle, and grain, principally to the United States government, at enormous figures." But destiny had in store for Maxwell an old age almost as dreary as that of his famous prototype, Sutter of California. He sold the vast property in 1871, it is said for $750,000, dabbled unsuccessfully in banking and railroading, and died in 1875 in anything but affluence. But he left behind a tradition long cherished and still fondly remembered.

Beyond the Maxwell ranch the route was well travelled and comparatively safe and easy. The tourist was whirled serenely along, perhaps stopping to replenish his larder at one of Moore, Mitchel and Company's "sutler's stores" at Fort Union or Tecolote, and went over the well-worn old road into Santa Fe. When he saw the roofs of that strange city he sometimes forgot the terrible cold of "The Long Route," if it were winter, or the terrible heat, if it were summer, and the ever-present danger from Indians which had made that part of the trip a nightmare.

Uncle Dick Wootton, inspecting the road over Raton Pass with his shrewd eyes, thought that something might be done about the Devil's Rock and other obstructions. Shortly after the Civil War he got charters from the legislatures of Colorado and New Mexico and built his famous toll road — twenty-seven writhing miles of it. He blasted away the Devil's Rock, straightened out the kinks so that a stage-coach could go through without breaking in the middle, and sat down to wait for customers. He also built a store, where with his partner, George C. McBride, he soon had plenty to do. He had, as he says in his memoirs, five varieties of trade. First there was the stage company, with which he had an agreement. Then there were the soldiers, who marched and freighted over the pass. Then there were the Americans, with their great white-topped wagons. Next came the Mexicans, peaceably enough inclined but always surprised to have to pay toll over any kind of road. Finally arrived the Indians. Wootton never asked any Indians to pay toll. He was glad enough to raise the bars and let them go by, as far and as fast as they liked, free of charge.

The venture paid well, and Wootton tossed his silver coin as he collected it into an empty whiskey keg. When the keg was full he drove down to Trinidad to put the money in the bank. He kept no books, but during one of his absences the more methodical McBride did. These accounts, fortunately preserved, show that during a period of fifteen months the partners took in $9,193.64. This included not only tolls but sales from the store, for Wootton and McBride disposed of their meat, bread, sugar, whiskey, corn, and oats to needful travellers at profitable rates. Wagons paid a toll of $1.50, while lighter vehicles got off with $1. Horsemen could pass the gates for twenty-five cents, and five cents was charged for each head of stock. Meals at the hotel were seventy-five cents, and a lodging for the night could be had for fifty cents. In a single year, in late freighting days, at least a thousand vehicles went over the pass and paid toll. An occasional gold rush was always good for business. When pay dirt was reported in the

Moreno valley in New Mexico in 1867 thousands of
Coloradans swarmed over the pass, and Uncle Dick was
in clover. Sometimes the road agents, modernized imi-
tators of the plundering Indian, took toll on the road,
too, but never, so far as history relates, from Uncle Dick.

In 1866, at about the time that Uncle Dick was getting
his road under way, Colonel J. F. Meline made a tour
of the plains to New Mexico and back with a troop of
cavalry. His narrative shows what certain portions of
the Trail were like — for he did not traverse all of it —
just after the Civil War. Meline " jumped off," as the
frontier phrase had it, from Leavenworth, which had
then attained the considerable size of from twenty to
twenty-five thousand inhabitants. The freighters were
still using this point as their eastern headquarters. " Returning from town," Meline says, " I passed numbers
of the ox teams used in freighting to New Mexico. They
are remarkable, each wagon team consisting of ten yokes
of fine oxen, selected and arranged not only for drawing
but for pictorial effect, in sets of twenty, either all black,
all white, all spotted or otherwise marked uniformly."
Obviously the Trail was already undergoing a process of
refinement. It was becoming conscious of its own
quaintness. Civilization was approaching. The motion
picture camera was still far, far in the future but it was
foreshadowed.

Meline pursued his westward journey by a northerly
route which did not bring him back to the Trail until he
reached Raton Pass. Somewhere in this neighborhood
he came upon a new ranch — " the joint stock concern
of a Canadian and a Massachusetts man." Evidently
this was one of the ancestors of the modern road-house.
It did not dispense hospitality freely to all comers, as
Maxwell did. Milk could be had at twenty-five cents

a quart, perhaps not a high price compared with present-day metropolitan prices, and butter at $1.25 a pound. A little farther on, at a ranch on the Ocate, Meline and his comrades were able to "likker up," though claret cost $2 a bottle and whiskey was $15 a gallon. Thus civilization had spread her blessings into the wilderness. But the wilderness was no longer quite a wilderness. Even cheese could be had if one were willing to pay a dollar a pound for it.

At Mora was living Lieutenant-Colonel Ceran St. Vrain, the veteran trader and soldier, looking back in hale old age upon a West which had once been as strange and mysterious as Homer's Greece, but was so no longer. Las Vegas was already becoming an American town, with signs in two languages. At Tecolote the old days were recalled by "one valid and one invalid fiddle, aggravated by a husky guitar," which paraded the streets to announce *bailes*. At Koslowski's ranch Meline found a Pole who had served in the first regiment of United States dragoons and had retired to this peaceful spot to end his days. But he had smelled powder again, for not far away, in March 1862, the Union and Confederate troops had fought over the possession of Apache Canyon and Pigeon's ranch.

American customs and costumes were affecting the old native simplicity. The picturesque *rebozo,* with which the women used to do such remarkable things, had almost disappeared. "Hoop-skirts appeared to find ready sale at the mercantile emporiums of Isaac, Jacob and Abraham." The *serape* was rarely seen. The best of these had come from Old Mexico, and there was now little trade with that country. But one relic of the good old days survived — the morals of the country, among natives and newcomers alike, were still spectacularly free and easy. The Americans " made no secret of leav-

ing their strict notions of morality behind them " when
they came to New Mexico. Morality's loss was perhaps
romance's gain. Who can say? The old *fandango* had
lost caste and disappeared. Every kind of dance was
now a *baile*. The American spirit had conquered.
Democracy was rampant.

Meline had some instructive comments to make on the
Santa Fe trade. " In 1845," he says, " the total number
of wagons crossing the plains from the United States to
Mexico and representing the sum total of its commerce
was just two hundred." This is true, but hardly a fair
comparison, for the total was more than twice that a
year later. But Meline continues: " In 1865 there came
into New Mexico from the States three thousand wagons
belonging to traders alone, exclusive of government
transportation. This year [1866] there will be from
five to six thousand wagons, two hundred and fifty of
which are now between Fort Union and Santa Fe, coming in. Most of the large trains return empty. Some
of them occasionally get a freight of copper or other
mineral, and a still greater number take in wool. The
exports of both these articles should and will be indefi-
nitely increased. The yield of wool could be made enormous and in proportion to extent of territory not even
California is richer in mineral wealth. But one condition is needed for all this, which stands for prosperity
and civilization. It is a condition precedent — get rid of
the Indian! " Thus was the former lord of the prairies
and the mountains brought low. No longer did he hold
this vast empire in the hollow of his hand. He was now
merely an annoyance to the pushing Anglo.

Meline and his companions returned by way of the
old Cimarron crossing, the *Jornada,* a hundred miles
shorter than the Raton route. " A nearly direct line
drawn on the map from Fort Union to Fort Dodge," he

explains, " will approximate the route we follow." The
Cimarron road, after five years of disuse, had regained
a little of its former glory. On the banks of the sandy
river Meline met " large trains going to New Mexico;
long ropes on both sides of the wagon festooned with
strips of meat told the story of buffalo, which the teamsters announced as being thick on the Arkansas." At
the Arkansas crossing the soldiers did indeed kill buffalo.
But Meline saw that the animal was growing scarcer
and predicted that men then living would " see the last
of him." The prediction came true, so far as wandering
herds of wild bison were concerned, sooner than even
Meline could have foreseen. At Waumega, thirty miles
east of Fort Riley, Kansas, Meline came upon the thing
which was to do most to exterminate the wild game and
ultimately put an end to the old Trail. He reined in his
horse, grey with mud and dust which had never felt the
plow, and saw a brand-new railhead — " depot, eating-
houses, trains of cars, and other appliances of railway
civilization."

In forty-five years from Becknell's first trip to Santa
Fe it had come to this — that the long-dammed-up civilization of the East was sweeping westward like a prairie
fire. From days too remote to be remembered the life
of the western plains had been determined by the migrations of the buffalo. Then this slender thread of a Trail,
so tenuous as to be snapped by a blizzard or an Indian
raid, had been unrolled across the billowing prairie.
Still, save for oases of safety and cultivation, the land had
lain primeval. Now approached a new conqueror, with
a great striding clangor.

With war and the restless energies released by war
the life of the Trail had come to its Great Divide.

CHAPTER XVII

TRAILS OF STEEL

LONG AGO the stage-coach, the emigrants' cart and the white-topped freight wagon had been driven from the main highways east of the Mississippi. Sectional quarrels, an uncertain Indian policy and doubts as to the value of the western country for purposes of settlement had halted the railroads for a time at the Missouri River. The Civil War settled the sectional issue, the Indians were crowded off lands which white men wanted, and the released tides of settlement flowed over the plains, into the mountains, to the Pacific Coast. It was seen that if there were to be an inter-oceanic Union there would have to be inter-oceanic railways. As early as 1861 work was begun, though not vigorously pushed, on the Central Pacific from the California end; work on the Union Pacific, west from Omaha, was started in 1865. Four years later the two lines met at Promontory Point, Utah, and the historic last spike was driven.

The trails of mud and dust and sand could not hold their own against the trail of steel. The Union Pacific was too far north to be a substitute for the old road to Santa Fe. But the Kansas Pacific, later to become a part of the Union Pacific system, was a more direct menace. It began at Wyandotte, opposite Kansas City. There, in 1863, its first rails gleamed. Then, very slowly at first, it pushed westward. The Indians fought the construction gangs, wrecked the trains, killed the crews. The new railway did not halt for such trivialities. It had, for positive incentive, gifts from Congress of $16,000 worth of bonds and 12,800 acres of land for every mile of track laid down. It had behind it the westward thrust of new populations, the eager energy of a nation which was bursting its old boundaries and outgrowing its old ambitions.

The Kansas Pacific headed for Denver. By 1865 it had reached Lawrence, Kansas. By 1866 it had got to Topeka and Junction City. Next year the clatter of rails and merry clang of hammers on spikes were heard at the new town of Hays City, under the protecting wing of Fort Hays. And now the old Trail began to bend like a vine toward this stouter trunk, and to wither at the roots. The established route east of Cottonwood Creek — the Narrows, Council Grove, Diamond Springs, many a spot familiar to thousands of traders and travellers — was suddenly no more followed. The Trail ran now by Ellsworth and back to the old line at Fort Larned. " A few years ago," said the Junction City *Union* in August 1867, " the freight wagons and oxen passing through Council Grove were counted by thousands, the value of merchandise by millions. But the shriek of the iron horse has silenced the lowing of the panting ox and the old Trail looks desolate. The track of the commerce of the plains has changed and with the change is [sic] destined to come other changes better and more blessed."

Blessed or not, changes were coming like the beating of hurrying wings. Destiny swooped upon the prairies. Cattle ranches were springing up in the old wilderness of the Texas Panhandle, where cowboys, successors to the hunters, trappers, and freighters, were riding fenceless ranges. In 1867 37,400 head of Texas longhorns were driven north and shipped over the Kansas Pacific. The railhead towns, as a guidebook of the early seventies described them, were " full of business and iniquity." The western bad man and the exuberant range rider galloped along streets of flimsy wooden shacks, yelling and shooting, drank themselves into blind staggers in the numerous saloons, gambled, quarrelled — and desecrated, beyond the power of any incense or any prayers to resanctify, the serene, primeval virginity of the plains. . . Railhead reached Sheridan in 1869. In twelve months thirty or forty healthy men in the prime of life were shot or hanged and tucked away in the little graveyard. Then this peripatetic hell moved on to the famous little city of Kit Carson, Colorado.

The railroad's traffic grew as it extended itself. In 1870 it carried 131,360 cattle, in 1871, 161,320. No longer was it necessary to drive steers eastward across the Kansas plains. The Santa Fe Trail was shrinking fast. It had lost Kansas altogether. The successors of the caravans which once had set out from Franklin, Independence, and Westport now had their easternmost terminal at Kit Carson. Pullman cars were already being run to Oakland, California, over a route where men still in hale middle age had risked death by thirst, starvation, heat, cold, and hostile Indians. Even at Fort Hays, in 1871, one had only to go back three years to come to a time when the Indians were so aggressive that it was unsafe to venture half a mile outside of town. The old and the new were jumbled in amazing fashion, the nineteenth century and the middle ages now encountered each other daily on the prairie and in the mountains. The Connecticut Yankee, in sober fact, walked into King Arthur's court. A westbound traveller came as

far as Kit Carson by rail in 1871. Then he stepped
from his Pullman car into a " two-seated affair drawn by
four mules," which carried him to Trinidad. At Trinidad he changed again, this time to a "big Concord
coach with six horses and a shot-gun messenger on the
box with the driver." He stopped for the night at Dick
Wootton's, and Uncle Dick spun long yarns of adventures in the mountains and on the plains. So much had
happened! To talk with Uncle Dick was like inter-
viewing a sailor from the *Pinta* or one of Cortez's men.
He represented many centuries rolled into a few decades.

The Kansas Pacific shot an iron tentacle southward
and in 1873 reached West Las Animas, near the site of
Bent's Fort. But now we have to double back on our
story in order to follow the westward course of another
railroad which was to bear the name of the Santa Fe
Trail and more than any other to follow its route. The
Atchison, Topeka, and Santa Fe was the child of the
dreams of Cyrus K. Holliday, a Pennsylvania lawyer
who went to Kansas in its early days and helped found
Topeka. "Here," says Bradley, in his "Story of the
Santa Fe," " was a great river, plenty of water and, above
all, the two great trails of the continent, Fort Leavenworth and Saint Joe to Santa Fe and Independence to
California, crossed at this point." No locomotive had
touched the soil of Kansas until 1860, and one intro-
duced during that year was withdrawn as the Civil War
came on. But in February 1859, Holliday secured the
first charter of the "Atchison and Topeka Railroad
Company," with a capital stock which reached the tremendous figure of $52,000. Four years later President
Lincoln signed an " act for a grant of lands to the State
of Kansas in alternate sections to aid in the construction
of certain railroads and telegraphs in the said State."

This agreement was ratified by the Kansas legislature the following year. Under it the new railroad was to receive three million acres of Kansas land — a modest grant compared with the twenty-six million or more given by the government to the Union Pacific. The Santa Fe never received any government bonds.

Ground was broken at Topeka in November 1868. The Central and Union Pacific were already drawing close to Promontory Point. The Kansas Pacific was beyond Hays City. But when Holliday, delivering a fervid speech as the first sod was turned, declared that men then living would see the Atchison and Topeka completed to Santa Fe he was laughed at. However, the rails began to stretch their new and shining way westward. In June 1869, the new road positively had to issue a time-table, for its trains were already running from Topeka to Carbondale, seventeen miles away. In August 1870, it reached Emporia, and in July 1871, it got to Newton.

This was well enough, for 137 miles of rails had been laid. But the land grant act of 1863 had stipulated that the line must be completed to the Colorado boundary by 1873, and Colorado was still 332 miles away. The directors voted to raise funds to accomplish the task within the stipulated time. Pushing out from Newton, in May, 1872, the rails flashed westward with a speed almost rivalling that of the Union Pacific's builders. James Criley, " a profane but exceedingly proficient Irishman," was the general construction boss. On June 17th Criley had his men hammering rails through Hutchinson; on August 5th he was at Great Bend, near old Fort Zarah; he plunged ahead over the once-deadly " Long Route," got to Larned on August 12th, got to Dodge on September 19th.

Dodge City, founded a few weeks before the railroad arrived, was five miles away from the fort. It was long to be famous as one of the roughest of the western cattle towns; its graveyard on the hill above the tracks was to be well filled with violent men who had died with their boots on. Thither came the Texas cattlemen, abandoning their old terminals at the once great cattle towns of Abilene, Salina and Ellsworth. Thither, too, came the diminishing band of Santa Fe traders and other plains freighters. Soldiers from the fort mingled with the crowds on streets and in saloons and other places of public entertainment. Buffalo hunters sometimes made a hundred dollars a day and came into Dodge to spend it. Drunken men were thrown into a fifteen-foot well and left there until they had cooled off. Fourteen men were shot dead within the first year of the town's existence. Vigilantes were organized, and presently there were more bad men than good among them. The shooting, yelling, and carousing went on day and night. The respectable people lived north of the tracks, but stray shots often came in their direction.

Having deposited this evidence of advanced civilization the railroad moved on. On December 28, 1872, well within the ten years of grace, it crossed the Colorado state line. Next year it reached Granada, and this town became a competing point with Las Animas, the Kansas Pacific terminal. The ruts of the old Santa Fe Trail could still be seen leading across Kansas, but no caravans traversed them any more. The people of Quivira did not eat out of golden dishes or lull themselves to sleep with the tinkle of golden bells, as Coronado had imagined them, but they had now become accustomed to going about on steel rails, which was probably more surprising.

What was left of the Trail probably owed its prolonged lease on life to the hard times of 1873, which caused an abrupt slowing-down in railroad building. But in 1875 both the Kansas Pacific and the Santa Fe reached La Junta, the one by a branch line, the other over its main line. In the same year the Santa Fe obtained access to Kansas City, so that it now followed substantially the line of the old Trail from the Missouri River to the Colorado Mountains. That same year it was estimated that 6000 tourists visited Colorado. . . In March 1876, the Santa Fe extended a line to Pueblo, where it came into contact with a narrow-gauge line which the Denver and Rio Grande had built down from Denver. The subsequent fight between the two railroads for the Grand Canyon of the Arkansas, dramatic though it was, touched our vanishing Trail only indirectly. But it did make the Denver and Rio Grande and the Santa Fe sworn enemies and when each at the same time turned toward the unexploited wealth of the Southwest the sparks began to fly.

Civilization lay in narrow strips along the railroads. Wild life still held the spaces between. Early in the seventies travellers had been able to shoot buffalo from the car windows. Antelope were not an uncommon sight. Men were making modest incomes by collecting and selling wagon-loads of buffalo bones. The Santa Fe trade was shrinking; in 1876 it was said to have a value of $2,000,000 — less than half the estimate for 1855. To one who loved the old days all this was sad and bewildering. What was the world coming to?

But still the wagons rolled to and fro, over the ever-diminishing Trail. " If we stop at a little station called La Junta," wrote one traveller, in 1876, " about twenty-one miles west of the old cattle-trading place of Las

Animas, we shall strike what is left of the old Santa Fe Trail and business, and see the Ship of the Plains in dock, loading for a southern voyage. Here are large storehouses which feed these unwieldy transports with merchandise for New Mexico and Arizona. When loaded they roll leisurely out across the country, drawn invariably by oxen and driven by the equally bovine Greasers. And the last that is seen of them are the canvas sails as they disappear slowly over the undulating country. It will take them from two weeks to two months to make the voyage, and then they will reload with wool, hides and ore and set upon their return trip."

One of the last of the great Santa Fe traders was Don Miguel Otero, member of a family distinguished both before and since his time. Otero's eastern headquarters, as A. A. Hayes says, made "seven jumps in eleven years." In 1868 they were at Hays City, Kansas; then, with the advancing rails, they were moved to Sheridan, Kit Carson, Granada, La Junta, El Moro, Otero, and Las Vegas. Las Vegas was the last stand. When that station was abandoned by the freighters there was no other to take its place. But Otero was no hidebound conservative, sorrowing for an irrevocable past. He had lived through and profited by the old times; he welcomed the new ones. In 1878 he went down to Santa Fe with General Manager William B. Strong, later to be president of the Santa Fe Railroad, to lobby for bills to encourage the railroad builders. Not all the New Mexicans welcomed what they called "The Yankee Mission." "We don't want you damned Yankees in the country," said one of them. "We can't compete with you; you will drive us all out and we shall have no homes left. We won't have you here." But the majority sentiment in New Mexico was favorable enough to induce Strong to direct his chief engineer, A. A. Robinson, to proceed to Raton Pass, seize it, hold it, and survey a line through it. There was need for haste. The Denver and Rio Grande was driving hard for the same pass.

Chief Engineer Robinson of the Santa Fe and Chief Engineer McMurtrie of the Denver and Rio Grande rode over from Pueblo to El Moro, then the terminus of the Denver and Rio Grande, on the same train. McMurtrie, tired by his journey, went to bed. Robinson went on to Uncle Dick Wootton's, where he arrived about eleven o'clock at night. There he learned that the rival road had organized a grading crew which was even then approaching the pass from the direction of Trinidad. Robinson, still sleepless, hurried to Trinidad, got together a crew of his own, and reached the entrance of the pass before five o'clock in the morning. Uncle Dick, who was a friend of the railroad, even though he knew it would render his toll road and himself obsolete, was with him, spitting on his hands and plying pick and shovel lustily as the cold February morning dawned. He had known the region when it was well-nigh as lonesome as the mountains of the moon; now, thinking, perhaps, of the days when he had roamed for thousands of miles without encountering a fence or a white man's house, he dug a path for the Pullman car and the lolling tourist.

When the work was well under way the Denver and Rio Grande grading crew arrived, too late. The diggers stood up and reached for whatever weapons were handy. But the tension dissipated itself in a flood of profanity. The rival graders withdrew, tried to find a route up Chicken Creek, gave it up in disgust, and retired. The Denver and Rio Grande had the Grand Canyon of the

Arkansas, but the Santa Fe had the road to New Mexico and the Southwest.

The Santa Fe drove ahead with renewed energy. In January 1879, it reached the southern slope of the Raton, taking its locomotives over the pass at first by means of a switchback, zig-zagging up and up to those rocky ridges over which the early freighters had travelled with such infinite difficulty. On the Fourth of July, 1879, it ran its first train into Las Vegas. Ten days later the Raton tunnel was pierced to daylight on the southern side, and on September 7th was opened to traffic. No more white-topped wagons jogging over Uncle Dick's road; the Santa Fe Trail was shrinking like a wet raw-hide drying in the sun. The Santa Fe trade, as Hays said, had " now passed completely out of the realm of the romantic and into that of the commonplace." The wonderful journey of eight hundred miles or more had dwindled to a hundred. The only remaining source of excitement for the freighters or the stage-coach passengers, whom the Southern Overland Mail Company carried from Las Vegas to Santa Fe, was the road agents. Once these gentry held up and robbed a government detective who was riding one of the coaches in an effort to get evidence against them. Sometimes the law laid them by the heels and sometimes the vigilantes hung them to convenient trees. But usually wagons and coaches went safely through, over the last hill, down to La Fonda — then as ever the end of the Trail.

The Santa Fe Railroad, with many interruptions and complications which are no part of this story, continued westward, the main line passing by Santa Fe because the little city lay too high in the hills. The railroad shot out a branch line to El Paso and eventually reached the Pacific at Guaymas, Mexico. For a time it used the tracks of the Southern Pacific west of Deming, New Mexico, running trains into Los Angeles by this route as early as 1885. Finally it took over the Atlantic and Pacific and, in May 1888, reached San Francisco Bay.

Meanwhile a branch line was run up from Lamy to Santa Fe. On February 9, 1880, the first train entered the city. After sixty-one years of growth and glory and decline, the Santa Fe Trail was dead. The last of the great oxen chewed their cuds, the stage horses stamped in the stables for lack of work to do. Perhaps, in some far Valhalla, Lieutenant Pike and the McKnight brothers and Captain Becknell and many another valiant man who had known the Trail in its rosy dawn fell silent around their smouldering campfires . . . remembering, and wondering. And there were living ghosts who had seen all and remembered all. Sixty-one years! The audience had scarcely settled themselves in their seats, the actors seemed but to have spoken their opening lines — and now the play was over, another and mightier drama demanded a theatre.

CHAPTER XVIII

RECESSIONAL

IN APRIL the trees along the watercourses west of Topeka are already beginning to leaf out, the grass is springing up in the wrinkles and dimples of this old-young land. Warm winds come out of the still-mysterious west, great clouds pile up into thunderheads, the rain comes, the sky clears, automobiles slip along the glistening wet surfaces of roads beside the railway track. There are no longer any buffalo to block the way, no calves running beside their mothers, no bulls with great shaggy heads and little, mean red eyes. There are no antelope. No Indians come riding over the rises, leaving us uncertain whether to pick up our guns or get out our beads and bacon — or if they ride it is in motor cars. Oil derricks, like hurrying giants, stride across the landscape. Night comes, the great velvet night of the plains, pierced through with stars, and far off to the north glows a beacon that lights the way for the transcontinental airplanes, which swoop from coast to coast more quickly than the traders on the old Trail could make their burning way across the *Jornada.* . .

In Dodge City not a saddle horse is to be seen. The one livery stable is boarded up. If there are saloons they are not for the casual passer-by. There are stores with neat plate-glass fronts, rows of neat bungalows, churches, schools, people dressed no differently from those in Boston, New York, Chicago, and San Francisco.

The trains stop in the drowsy, hot afternoons, or the cool nights, and the modern followers of the Trail descend to stretch, to walk up and down, to eat abundantly at the station restaurant. . .

The Arkansas River in western Kansas is a small stream, even in early April, wandering around a great bed of sand. It is bordered still with dunes. But people sink wells and get abundant water for irrigating fertile fields. The low hills on the south, leading toward the *Jornada,* are overgrown with buffalo grass. . . We pass single freight trains carrying more goods than the old Trail saw in its best years. Here and there we can still distinguish the old wagon tracks. . . For passengers on the night limiteds the Raton is a rumbling, heard vaguely as they lie half-asleep in their berths. . .

Across a canyon, beneath a majestic circle of mountains, on a slope which affords views for many miles in three directions, lie the ruins of the old church and pueblo of Pecos, Coronado's Cicuyé. . . The pass where Armijo stood fast, then thought better of his resolution and fled, narrows before us. Here, to the left turns off the old road that went over the hills to Santa Fe. Here went the mules, their little legs bending under heavy loads, following the leader's bell; here strained the oxen, while the great white tops rolled like ships at sea; here the stages creaked, while the hold-up men behind the rocks adjusted their bandannas and looked to their revolvers. . . A bus, that modern jazz-minded daughter of the stage-coach, rolls up to Santa Fe over the new road from Lamy to a new La Fonda. The trees in the plaza have grown tall, there are benches and a monument to Kearny, sometimes the band plays there. The old *Palacio,* shorn of its outer buildings, stretches its arcades along the northern side; there is a street called

Palace Avenue. There are a federal court-house, an Elks' lodge, a Presbyterian church, a new capitol. Pueblo Indians come into the hotels and loiter along the streets, selling curios. . . In the early fall there is a *fiesta*, and De Vargas rides again into the reconquered city. . . Half the population speaks the melodious Spanish of generations ago, not too much modified. There will be a dance on Saturday night. They do not call it a *fandango* now. The crowd in the motion-picture theatre's lobby waits as patiently as it can for the first performance to end and the second to begin. . .

For the casual stranger there is not very much to do but dream. The traders and freighters of old would be lost if they could come again, to the squeak of dry axles, to the cracking of whips. Their haunts are closed, perhaps torn down long ago; the girls who welcomed them are dead. . . A radio broadcasts the latest Broadway song. . . One captures and loses, captures and loses again, the image of that older, less beautiful, perhaps more alluring Santa Fe, toward which men plodded through six weeks of heat and rain and cold, and entered as joyfully as the crusaders rode into Jerusalem — city of mud houses, city of brick-kilns, city of dirt and beggars, city which often inspired the neat and cold-blooded with disgust, city of romance all the same.

After midnight it is dark and still, and the ghosts come; the Indians with their dark hair down their backs; the Spaniards in their hats of steel, sandal-shod padres clad in black; Frenchmen singing their songs of the *Vide Poche*, of the northern rivers, of a half-forgotten France; Pike and his limping, ragged company; that gay rascal, Baptiste La Lande, cheating his employer and dying rich amid the tears of a numerous and adoring family. Here are the McKnight party, being led into the Palace to face Governor Manrique, with nine years of Mexican prisons ahead of them; David Meriwether, appearing first in the role of ragged prisoner, then returning as American governor; Captain Becknell, father of the Trail, tying up his Spanish dollars in rawhide packages and loading them on mules in front of the old Fonda; disgruntled Thomas James, robbed by the Texas Indians, irritated by the city and everything in it. Here strides Cooper, his face still haggard from his terrible experience on the *Jornada;* and with him Storrs, Marmaduke, and Gregg, cool Anglo-Saxons looking with observant and critical eyes at the customs of this strange country. Their hats sweep the ground at sight of Susan Magoffin, nineteen, romantic, beautiful, so much in love with her weather-beaten husband, so innocently willing to be admired by other men as well, and no less for Dona Tules, eyes flashing, retaining to the last some remnants of her youthful loveliness. Here limp the tattered, blood-stained survivors of the Texas Expedition, and here come Kit Carson, slight of stature, eagle-eyed; Armijo, laying about him with his stick when his ragamuffin subjects do not uncover to him; the eloquent Kearny with his Missourians; Price, not yet clad in Confederate grey; Cooke marshalling his footsore Mormons, with their trumpets and their drums. We see march past troops of North and South engaged in this remote corner of the States in a conflict strangely meaningless here; and a countless host of men who loved, feared, hated the Trail as sailors do the sea, who lived by it and could not abandon it, though they would; Mexicans, Spaniards, Frenchmen, Missourians, New Englanders, all drawn by the same magnet, all with that free swing and swagger that comes from outfacing danger and hardship.

Never did the Trail to Santa Fe approach in popu-
lousness those northern routes that went to Oregon and
California. Never did it carry such wealth in goods as
went west to Salt Lake City and over the Sierras. In its
wealthiest years its total traffic, counted though it might
be in bags of silver dollars, was but small change in the
growing wealth of the United States. Yet from the very
beginning it captivated men's imaginations, it capti-
vates one's imagination today as no other trail does.
To try to explain why is to pursue so elusive a thing as
the substance of men's dreams. Something there was
in the days when the great central plains were no man's
land and the mountains were dim with mystery that
drew multitudes westward; something additional drew
them south from the bend of the Arkansas, across the
Jornada or over the Raton, into the colorful, the fantastic region above the Rio Grande, into that little city
where the streets were so muddy, the men so lazy, and
where the women walked so proudly.

Men who went west were glad to come back with bags
of silver. But the shrewd could make money at home.
While the Santa Fe trade was developing, the empty
spaces back of the Missouri and the Mississippi were
filling up, the cities were growing, the nation hummed
with profitable activity, one had only to sit down where
two rivers met and riches would be brought to him. The
men who went to Santa Fe turned their backs on this
comparative certainty to gamble, not only with their
savings but with their lives. Those who had no savings
to invest went west for wages, and not generous wages
even according to the standards of those times. Men
had their goods confiscated by the Mexican governors,
were robbed of them by Indians, yet returned again and
again to the scenes of their disasters. Land hunger

played a part, yet the traders went forth when they knew that there was no land to be had, or at least no land that they could cultivate. Not for them the black furrow, the fields of wheat and corn, the rude homestead sprouting first a cabin, then a house. Something of the Indian had gotten into them, as it did before their time into the trappers. They were not content to look very long on the same horizon, nor to build their fires too many times in the same place. They were a breed for which the settled and smug civilizations of their day had no occupation. To find their place in the scheme of things they had to leave the nineteenth century behind.

They had to pass, as the buffalo passed, because the world in which they lived was already out of date and was preserved for a few additional decades only by a historical accident. They spent their vigorous youth in an environment less civilized than that of Charlemagne or the Phœnicians; centuries whirled by them like hours, and men who had wandered over the West when it was as boundless as the sky lived to see it subjugated, plowed, mined, and chained with steel rails. There is in all history no transformation that can surpass this one for swiftness, completeness, and permanence. All that lusty life has gone for ever behind the curtains of the years.

What then remains except a narrative, told imperfectly and stumblingly either by men who were too busy to write it or by others who were born too late to live through it? Much, perhaps, if we try to understand the America that exists by understanding a little of the America that has been. The Santa Fe was the first of the great transcontinental trails, for two decades it was the most travelled, in the dramatic contrasts that arose because it linked together two opposing civilizations it never had an equal. The other trails went either to an almost virgin territory, as was the case in Oregon, or to a region where the existing culture was quickly submerged, as was the case in California. But the Americans penetrated and influenced New Mexico gradually, over a long period of years, and in so doing were themselves altered. It was thus in New Mexico that they had their longest and most fruitful contact with the transplanted traditions of old Spain. Spain, indirectly and after an interval of generations, had a deep and pervasive influence upon the customs and ways of the American Southwest.

The Trail was but a single thread in that vast roaring loom on which was woven the fabric of modern America. Yet there it still shines, if we bend to look, like a pattern of untarnishable gold.

A SELECTED BIBLIOGRAPHY

Bancroft, Hubert Howe. *Works*. Vol. 12. Arizona and New Mexico. San Francisco, 1890.

Becknell, Captain William. *Journal*. (In Missouri Historical Society. Vol. 2, No. 6, p. 56.)

Benton, Senator Thomas H. *Thirty Years' View*. Vol. 1. New York, 1854.

Bieber, Ralph P. *Some Aspects of the Santa Fé Trade*, 1848–80. (In Missouri Historical Review. Vol. 18, No. 2, p. 158 ff.)

Bolton, Herbert E., and Marshall, Thomas M. *The Colonization of North America, 1492–1783*. New York, 1920.

Bradley, Glenn Danford. *Winning the Southwest*. Chicago, 1912.

——, *The Story of the Santa Fé*. Boston, 1920.

Channing, Edward. *The Jeffersonian System*. (In the American Nation, a History. Vol. 12.)

Chittenden, Horace. *The American Fur Trade in the Far West*. Vol. 2.

Clum, John P. *Santa Fé in the 'Seventies*. (In New Mexican Historical Review. Vol. 2.)

Coan, Charles F. *A History of New Mexico*. 3 vols. Chicago and New York. 1925.

Conard, Howard Louis. *"Uncle Dick" Wootton*. Chicago, 1890.

Cooper, Major Stephen. *Narrative*. (In History of Howard and Cooper Counties, Missouri, 1883.)

Cutts, James Madison. *The Conquest of California and New Mexico*. Philadelphia, 1847.

Darton, N. H., and others. *Guide-book of the Western United States*. Part C. The Santa Fé Route. Washington, Government Printing Office. 1915.

Davis, W. W. H. *El Gringo, or New Mexico and Her People*. New York, 1857.

Dellenbaugh, F. S. *Breaking the Wilderness*. New York, 1905.

Dunbar, Seymour. *History of Travel in America*. Vol. 4. Indianapolis, 1915.

Edwards, Frank S. *A Campaign in New Mexico with Colonel Doniphan*. London, 1848.

Emory, William H. *Notes of a Military Reconnaissance from Ft. Leavenworth in Missouri to San Diego in California*. (With Report of Lt.

J. W. Abert of the Examination of New Mexico in the Years 1846–47;
Report of Lt.-Col. P. St. George Cooke of His March from Santa Fé,
New Mexico, to San Diego, Upper California; and Journal of Capt.
A. R. Johnston.) Washington, 1848.

Farnham, Thomas Jefferson. *Travels in the Great Western Prairies. See*
Thwaites.

Fowler, Jacob. *Journal, 1821–22.* Edited with notes by Elliott Coues.
New York, 1898.

Garrard, Lewis H. *Wah-to-Yah, or The Taos Trail.* Cincinnati, 1850.

Gilpin, Lt. Col. W. *Letter to Adjutant-General Jones.* (In House Ex.
Doct. No. 1, 30th Cong., Session 2.)

Greene, Jeremiah Evarts. *The Santa Fé Trade: Its Route and Character.*
(Part of the Report of the Council of the American Antiquarian Society,
April 26, 1893.)

Gregg, Josiah. *Commerce of the Prairies.* (The classical account of the
early history of the Santa Fé Trail.) Eight editions in English and one
in German between 1845 and 1857. Reprinted in Thwaites, q. v.

Greiner, John. (Galloway, T. Ed.) *Private Letters of a Government
Official in the Southwest.* (In Journal of the American Historical Association. Vol. 3, p. 541 ff.)

Hayes, A. A. *New Colorado and the Santa Fé Trail.* New York, 1880.

Hulbert, Archer Butler, ed. Crown Collection of American Maps,
Series 4, Vol. 5.

Higgins, Charles A. *To California and Back.* Chicago, 1900.

Houck, Louis. *A History of Missouri from the Earliest Explorations and
Settlements until the Admission of the State into the Union.* Vol. 3,
Chicago, 1908.

Hughes, Colonel John T. *Doniphan's Expedition and the Conquest of
New Mexico and California.* Cincinnati, 1847. (Reprinted in Con-
nolly, William Elsey: *War with Mexico,* 1846–7. Topeka, 1907.)

Inman, Henry. *The Old Santa Fé Trail: The Story of a Great Highway.*
(Picturesque and atmospheric but inaccurate.) New York, 1897.

James, Thomas. *Three Years among the Indians and Mexicans.* 1846.
(Reprinted with notes and biographical sketches by Walter B. Douglas.
St. Louis. Missouri Historical Society, 1916.)

Kendall, George Wilkins. *Narrative of the Texan Santa Fé Expedition.*
Two volumes. New York, 1844, 1846, 1847, 1856. London, 1845,
1846.

Ladd, Horace O. *The Story of New Mexico.* Boston, 1891.

Lane, Governor William Carr. *Letters.* (In New Mexican Historical
Review. Vol. 3.)

Long, S. H. *Expeditions.* (*See* Thwaites.)

Magoffin, Susan Shelby. (Ed. Stella Drum.) *Down to Santa Fé and into*

BIBLIOGRAPHY 277

Mexico: The Diary of Susan Shelby Magoffin, 1846–1847. St. Louis. Missouri Historical Society, 1926.

Majors, Alexander. *Seventy Years on the Frontier.* Denver, 1893.

Marmaduke, M. M. *Journal.* (In Missouri Historical Review, October, 1911, p. 1 ff.)

McKinnon, Bess. *The Toll Road over Raton Pass.* (In New Mexican Historical Review. Vol. 2, 1927.)

Meline, Colonel James F. *Two Thousand Miles on Horseback. Santa Fé and Back. A Summer Tour through Kansas, Nebraska, Colorado and New Mexico in the year* 1866. New York, 1867. London, 1868.

Pattie, James O. *The Personal Narrative of James Ohio Pattie of Kentucky during an Expedition from St. Louis through the Vast Regions between that Place and the Pacific and Back through the City of Mexico.* Ed. T. Flint. Cincinnati, 1831. (Also see Thwaites.)

Paxson, Frederick Logan. *The Last American Frontier.* Chapter IV. Boston, 1910.

Perrine, Fred S. *Military Escorts on the Santa Fé Trail.* New Mexican Historical Society, 1927.

Pike, Zebulon Montgomery. *Expeditions.* Ed. Elliott Coues. Vol. 2.

Pino, Pedro Bautista. *Noticias Historicas y Estadisticas de la Antigua Provincia del Nuevo-México.* Mexico, 1849.

Rister, Carl Coke. *The Southwestern Frontier, 1865–81.* Cleveland, 1928.

Root, Frank A., and Connelley, W.E. *Overland Stage to California.* Topeka, 1901.

Ruxton, George Frederick Augustus. *Life in the Far West.* (Also published as *In the Old West.*) New York, 1859. New York, 1915.

Ryus, William H. *The Second William Penn.* Kansas City, 1913.

Sibley, George C. *Route to Santa Fe.* (In Western Journal, Vol. 5.)

Smithsonian Institution. *Report,* 1883. Pp. 59–61.

Stephens, F. F. *Missouri and the Santa Fé Trail.* (In Missouri Historical Review. Vol. 10.)

Storrs, Augustus. *Letter to Senator Benton,* 1824. ("Answers . . . to certain queries upon the origin, present state and future prospects of trade and intercourse between Missouri and the internal provinces of Mexico, propounded by the Hon. Mr. Benton.") (In 18th Cong., 2nd Sess., Senate Report 7. Washington, 1825.)

Thwaites, Reuben Gold. *Early Western Travels, 1748–1846.* See index for narratives of Farnham, Pattie, Long and others. Cleveland, 1904–7.

Twitchell, Ralph Emerson. *Leading Facts of New Mexican History.* (Not always minutely accurate but the best and most complete history of New Mexico.) 2 vols. Cedar Rapids, Iowa, 1911.

Tyler, Sergeant Daniel. *A Concise History of the Mormon Battalion in the Mexican War*, 1846–7. Salt Lake City, 1881.

Weston, W., Ed. *Weston's Guide to the Kansas Pacific Railway.* Kansas City, 1872.

Wetmore, Alphonso. *Letter to John Scott, M. C.*, August 9th, 1824. (Including Diary.) (In Missouri Historical Review, July, 1914.)

Williams, Ezekial. *Letter.* (In Missouri Historical Society. Vol. 2.)

Wislizenus, Adolphus. *Memoir of a Tour to Northern Mexico, Connected with Col. Doniphan's Expedition in* 1846 *and* 1847. Washington, 1848. (Also a German edition, 1850.)

INDEX

A

Adams, President J. Q., appoints Storrs and Pilcher, 90
Alarcón, Hernando de, 9
Alarí, Jean de, 22
Alencaster, Governor, 46 *f*
Allande, Pedro Maria de, 62
Allen, James, 204 *f*
Appropriation Bill, signed, 89
Armijo, Manuel, 174 *f*, 181, 187, 198 *f*
Atchison, Topeka & Santa Fe Railroad, 260 *f*
Aubrey, F. X., 224-231
Austria, war declared on Prussia, 25

B

Baca, Alonso, 17
Baird, James, 60, 79 *f*
Barceló, Dona Gertrudes, 167 *f*
Baudouin, Louis, 55
Becknell, William, 67 *f*, 76 *f*
Beltrán, Bernadino, 14
Bent, massacred, 215 *f*
Bent's Fort, 95; original name, 150
Benton, Thomas Hart, 85 *f*
Bienville, Governor, 22 *f*
Blanco, Emanuel, 56
Bolton, Herbert E., 51
Bonilla, Leyva de, 14 *f*
Brown, Joseph C., 89 *f*; describes trail, 96 *f*
Bull fighting, 168

C

Cabeza de Vaca, 6 *f*
Calhoun, James S., death, 236

Campo, Andrés del, 13
Canby, E. R. S., 245 *ff*
Carleton, James H., 247
Carson, Kit, works for McKnight, 60; quoted on massacre of Dr. White, 231; 243, 247
Castañeda de Naçera, Pedro de, 9 *f*
Cattle, shipments in 1867, 259
Cavalry, United States organizes, 118
Central Pacific Railroad, 257 *f*
Chapuis, Jean, 24
Chavez, Antonio José, 184 *f*
Chihuahua, 49
Cholera, 232
Chouteau, Pierre, 56, 61
Christianity, among Indians, 16
Civil War, dangers on trail during, 248
Comanches, 127 *f*; early name, 36; insurrection after New Mexico conquest, 219
Cooke, Philip St. George, 124, 187; praises Mormon Battalion, 211
Cooper, Benjamin, 76
Cooper, Braxton, 83
Cooper, Stephen, 80 *f*
Coronado, 7 *ff*; strangles El Turco, 12; sets out for Quivira, 10 *f*
Cortés, Manuel, 216 *f*
Cosmetics, New Mexican use, 171
Council Grove, origin of name, 89
Criley, James, 261

D

Dancing, 168 *f*; *see also* Social customs

279